TEN MEN WON THE LEAGUE

STEPHEN MURRAY

To Mum, Dad, Susanne and Michael - the best team ever.

And to the members of the Govan South West Celtic supporters' club, (Donnelly's bar 1947-1980), who ensured that Celtic never walked alone.

Contents

FOREWORD by Davie Provan 4
INTRODUCTION 7
CHAPTER 1 • SUMMER 1978 - ABDICATION 9
CHAPTER 2 • THE BEST OF STARTS 19
CHAPTER 3 • CONSOLIDATION 47
CHAPTER 4 • THE MOMENTUM ENDS 74
CHAPTER 5 • A WINTER OF DISCONTENT BEGINS ... 92
CHAPTER 6 • FESTIVE DESPAIR 109
CHAPTER 7 • THE BIG FREEZE 127
CHAPTER 8 • FRUSTRATION CONTINUES 140
CHAPTER 9 • THE CAPTAIN RETURNS 151
CHAPTER 10 • THE CELTS CLICKS INTO GEAR 173
CHAPTER 11 • EXPECTATION GROWS 194
CHAPTER 12 • THE SHOWDOWN 217
CHAPTER 13 • THE AFTERMATH 235
CHAPTER 14 • RECOLLECTIONS 251
EPILOGUE 276
THE LAST WORD 286
APPENDIX 288
ACKNOWLEDGEMENTS 293

FOREWORD by Davie Provan

On the eighteenth of September 1978 I found myself driving through Glasgow's east end to sign for Celtic. After rejecting two transfer requests, my club Kilmarnock had finally agreed to sell me and as I turned the car into Kerrydale Street I was nervous as a kitten. I'd never met Billy McNeill before and the thought of becoming the new Celtic manager's first signing was daunting.

Celtic had agreed a fee of £120,000, beating the record transfer between two Scottish clubs. No pressure then. With the formalities completed Billy talked of the season ahead and what he expected of me. He explained he was rebuilding the squad he'd inherited from Jock Stein but still thought we could win the title from champions Rangers. What neither of us knew at the time was that season 1978-79 would produce a script so dramatic it could have been written by Hitchcock.

Eight months after we'd sat in Billy's office it all boiled down to this. Celtic versus Rangers at Celtic Park on the last day of the season for the title. Winner takes all. That the game is still known simply as "The 4-2 game" says it all. Winning any Old Firm game is special. But beating Rangers with ten men from a goal down to win the league is the stuff of fantasy. Described on the night by Celtic chairman Desmond White as, "the club's finest hour since Lisbon", the game produced a storyline to stretch credibility.

But as the author Stephen Murray meticulously recalls, this was no ordinary season. It was a campaign ravaged by a Scottish winter that saw Celtic go more than two months without a league game and left us playing three games a week during the run in. Remember, this was long before sports science had been invented.

Not that fitness was ever a problem for that squad. When the country was snowbound as it was throughout that winter, Billy and his assistant John Clark would always find somewhere to train us. If the training pitch at Barrowfield was frozen, they'd run us on the concourses under the main stand at Celtic Park. The beach at Seamill was another venue and we even headed for a winter break in Portugal where the squad bonded over a few beers.

By that time there were signs Billy had the squad mix just right. Myself, Murdo MacLeod, Tommy Burns, Mike Conroy, Roy Aitken and George McCluskey provided the young blood. Older heads included Andy Lynch, Johnny Doyle, Danny McGrain, Peter Latchford, Alfie Conn, Tom McAdam, Vic Davidson and the remarkable Bobby Lennox. In the years ahead I'd be part of more talented Celtic teams but when it came to grit and spirit, the class of 1979 was in a league of its own.

Not that the season went smoothly. After a heavy defeat at Aberdeen, Billy read the riot act when discovering a few of the boys had gone for a few beers when returning to Glasgow. Caesar was big on discipline and expected defeat to be taken personally by every one of us. He also gave us a public caning after we'd lost to a poor Hearts side at Tynecastle. He usually got the reaction he was looking for.

The trip to Portugal allowed us to top fitness levels up again and by the time the weather relented at the beginning of March we were straining at the leash. An Alfie Conn goal was enough to beat Aberdeen at home, a crucial win given we were third bottom of the league at the time.

Still, it would have taken a brave man or a fool to back us for the title at that stage. There were still setbacks to be faced along the way, but we knew we were building up a head of steam. That momentum eventually led us to the ultimate confrontation with Rangers and a game that shredded the nerves of all who saw it.

For Celtic supporters of all ages this book recalls every step of that remarkable season. It retraces every twist of a campaign that culminated in one of the greatest games of Celtic's long history-The Four-Two Game.

Davie Provan
October 2014

INTRODUCTION

This book details the events of one of the most incredible seasons in the history of Celtic Football Club, the 1978-79 Premier Division campaign. During the summer of 1978, Celtic appointed their fifth manager, Lisbon Lion captain, Billy McNeill. The winter of 1978-79 brought extreme arctic conditions, which prevented the team from playing a league game for ten long weeks. No one was to realise it at the time, but the enforced winter break would be a major factor in Celtic's quest to win the Scottish Premier Division title.

It was a season where the league title was decided in the final game, when Celtic faced their oldest and greatest rivals, Rangers. In a classic winner takes all scenario, the drama unfolded. A victory for either team would have given them the League Championship and these two great clubs have seldom met in such dramatic fashion.

On Monday 21st May 1979, the two teams met to decide the title. Against all the odds, with Celtic reduced to ten men, 0-1 down, and only twenty five minutes remaining, they stormed back to win 4-2. This victory gave Celtic the league title, in a game which will never be forgotten. Tales of that legendary game have been proudly passed from father to son, and it is reckoned by many to be the most incredible Old Firm game ever played.

One observer was moved to describe it as, *'the closest I ever came to a religious experience',* but frustratingly, a strike by television cameramen ensured that no quality footage was recorded for posterity. All that remains is some grainy old black and white film, produced by the amateur volunteers of the Celtic Film Club, and Celtic fans remain ever grateful for their efforts.

In addition to that pivotal match, this book also covers the other dramatic events of the season.

- The controversial departure of the legendary manager Jock Stein
- The infamous riot in Burnley in the ill fated Anglo Scottish Cup campaign
- Davie Provan's record breaking transfer from Kilmarnock
- A highly controversial Old Firm League Cup semi-final defeat
- And, the most welcome return to the fold of Celtic's inspirational captain, Danny McGrain, after a long absence through injury.

In those more carefree and liberal times, football supporters could smoke and drink alcohol freely on the terraces. Celtic were better referred to as, 'The Celts' rather than the increasingly common term, 'The Hoops', the fans referred to their team as the 'Tim Malloys', and not 'The Bhoys', and the media referred to the club's ground as Parkhead and not Celtic Park. For the princely sum of £1 the supporters could stand on the terraces cheering on their team, whilst the more privileged paid £2 for a seat in the main stand. A blind eye was turned to boys under sixteen being given free entry into the ground, and they were physically lifted over turnstiles by adults. *'Geez a lift in big man?',* they would ask. Hawkers still wandered the terraces with their wares in cardboard boxes, *'Ezra macaroon 'n spearmint chewing gum!'*

For the generation of Celtic followers who just missed out on the 1967 European Cup triumph, this was their own unforgettable moment, a game to be remembered and cherished in the memory for all time.

The stories of the Celtic players and fans who battled through that long, arduous and ultimately memorable season, when 'Ten Men Won the League', will now be told.

CHAPTER 1 • SUMMER 1978 - ABDICATION

The legendary Jock Stein's long, glorious reign as Celtic manager officially came to an end on 29th May 1978. The great man brought Celtic and their supporters a level of success they could not possibly have dreamed of when he took over the helm at Celtic Park in 1965. Before Stein's arrival, the club had suffered a long period of underachievement and mismanagement. His tenure brought home the coveted European Cup, ten Scottish league titles, eight Scottish Cups and six League Cups, assuring him a special place in the annals of football history. His achievements were not in silverware alone. His personal, moral and social values helped to shape the club and its ethos.

As much as Stein's domestic domination was to be admired, it was his consistent success in Europe that set his Celtic team apart. Their success not only made them European Champions, but Stein also created an attacking football style that won widespread admiration across the continent. Journalist Ian Archer well describes Celtic's reputation abroad whilst Stein was at the peak of his managerial prowess.

'Those of us who have tugged at their shirt tails for so long and felt proud to be with them when the plane touched down at some foreign capital, to find that their fame had preceded them… this last decade has established Celtic as one of the great clubs in the world. Not as lastingly famous as the unique Real Madrid, not as individually talented or explosive as Ajax of Amsterdam. But friendlier and better loved than Inter, more attractive than any English club since the last revival of Tottenham Hotspur. They trod more new paths than any Scotsman since David Livingstone left Blantyre'.

By 1978 that glorious era had long passed and Stein left behind a Celtic squad who were desperately low in confidence after his final campaign. The '*Annus Horribilis*' of 1977-78 saw Celtic finish fifth in the Premier Division, which resulted in them failing to qualify for European competition for the first time since 1962. That season also saw Celtic lose to Kilmarnock, (who were then a league below them), in a Scottish Cup replay. They also lost in their thirteenth successive League Cup final to a Rangers team who subsequently went on to clinch the Scottish domestic treble.

On the night of the Scottish Cup defeat at Rugby Park, the thousands of Celtic supporters who attended the match returned home across the Fenwick Moors, in a sombre mood that was said to be akin to *'Napoleon's retreat from Moscow.'* Added to that was an ignominious European Cup defeat to the Austrian champions, SSW Innsbruck, despite the Austrians being required to play their home game in the neutral (sic) venue of Salzburg. The season proved a harrowing experience for players and supporters alike, an absolute catalogue of disasters from beginning to end.

The depths that Celtic sank to during that season had to be seen to be believed. To put matters into context, St Mirren and Clydebank were newly promoted clubs. Over the course of the league campaign, the 'Buddies' accumulated an incredible seven league points from a possible eight against the hapless Celts, whilst the 'Bankies' earned a credible three. Possibly the nadir was at relegated Clydebank's tight little Kilbowie Park in April, when Celtic surrendered a 2-1 lead to lose 3-2. It was no great surprise when a defeat at Love Street, in a must win final league match, resulted in Celtic failing to qualify for European football for the first time in sixteen years.

Despite the poor results against lower ranked opposition, the team performed fairly well in the matches against Rangers. However, the Ibrox side gained a major, psychological advantage after winning the first Glasgow derby game in September, in dramatic circumstances. Celtic, influenced by a young Tommy Burns, had been in control at half-time, after two Johannes 'Shuggie' Edvaldsson headers gave them a comfortable 2-0 lead. On the open Ibrox terracing Celtic fans sang loudly throughout the half-time interval, in anticipation of a decisive victory to come. They could only look on in horror as Rangers, inspired by their new signing Gordon Smith, roared back in the second-half to deservedly win 3-2. The contrast from half-time was stark and it was now the turn of the Rangers fans to make all the noise.

There had certainly been some mitigating circumstances for such desperately poor form. In early August of 1977, Kenny Dalglish departed to European champions Liverpool, for a British record transfer fee of £444,000. At that time, Dalglish was peerless within the British game, and it was a near impossible task to replace him, as Stein himself lamented on Dalglish's departure. However, what infuriated the Celtic support was the fact that the management made no serious attempt to bring any players of proven quality to the club after Dalglish had gone south. In 1977 Celtic could only realistically afford to buy players from the Scottish market. The days of bringing quality players from foreign shores were still a long way off. The club was rumoured to be interested in promising young talent such as Arthur Graham (Aberdeen), Frank McGarvey (St Mirren), Paul Sturrock (Dundee United) and Mark McGhee (Morton), but no significant signings had materialised.

Before his departure Jock Stein had made some signings. However, Roy Kay, Ian McWilliams, John Dowie, Tom McAdam, Frank Munro and Joe Filippi failed to make any real impression during the course of Stein's final season. It does have to be said that injuries also played a major part in proceedings. Danny McGrain, a magnificent player and widely regarded as the best attacking full-back in the world, was badly injured against Hibs on the first day of October 1977. He was destined to miss the rest of the season. This was a huge blow to Celtic, as McGrain had been appointed captain after Dalglish's departure. His influence and leadership were badly missed, not only by Celtic, but by Ally MacLeod's Scotland team, who were on their journey to qualifying for the 1978 World Cup finals. Had McGrain's settling presence been available during that fateful summer tournament, then the history of Scottish football may have taken another course altogether.

The vastly experienced duo of Pat Stanton and Alfie Conn had been excellent acquisitions during 1976-77. On the opening day of the new season the league flag was unfurled by Jock Stein's wife, Jean. Celtic were hosting Dundee United and it was a huge disappointment when Stanton and Conn were both injured during the game. Stanton was to miss the entire season, and Conn was to play only intermittently for the rest of that campaign. All these issues combined to determine that Celtic would endure a torrid season. It wouldn't be so much a football season, but more a test of endurance.

Danny McGrain's autobiography, 'Celtic My Team', was published in the autumn of 1978. He was scathing in his criticism of Celtic's more experienced players, who he felt had let Stein and the Celtic supporters down badly. In a forthright serialisation in the Evening Times he made the following observations:

'I sat in the stand and marvelled at the fans. They turned out in their thousands to roar the team on and to be brutally frank it didn't deserve that kind of support. Never can so many have suffered because of so few. I exonerate kids such as Tommy Burns, Roy Aitken and Roddy MacDonald from blame. They are youngsters who should have been given help in a crisis season. Instead they found themselves carrying experienced players many of whom had been bought for big transfer fees. It would be easy to point to injuries to myself, Pat Stanton and Alfie Conn as reasons for the flop but it wouldn't be right.'

Behind the scenes, Jock Stein had decided that the time was right for him to step down from his Celtic throne. The general feeling amongst the support was that he had never fully recovered from the physical and mental trauma of a serious car crash in July 1975, when he had been lucky to survive. Many Celtic players and officials have testified to the fact that he was a different man when he returned to the club in the summer of

1976. Minutes from Celtic's board meetings at the time indicate that he had discussed his position with the directors. It was subsequently agreed, by mutual consent, that he would depart his position as Celtic manager at the end of the season. Celtic was seen as a very stable club at this time, and this period of upheaval at managerial level was a most unusual experience. The new manager would be only the club's fifth, in their illustrious ninety year history. Times were changing, and the managerial role was no longer the long term position it once was, at any football club.

It had been an open secret for some time that Celtic were casting admiring glances towards their ex-captain Billy McNeill, who had already achieved a fine record with Aberdeen. It is believed that Celtic informally interviewed McNeill, but also spoke with Partick Thistle manager Bertie Auld and former Manchester United assistant manager Pat Crerand, in an effort to find the right candidate for the new post. Both Auld and Crerand had excellent Celtic pedigrees, having been great players for the club, which was certainly a necessary requirement for the post at that time. McNeill's stature, reputation and leadership qualities as Stein's renowned captain, made him first choice for the board and fans alike. Shortly after Aberdeen permitted him to speak to the Celtic board, *Caesar* was appointed as Celtic manager, and his appointment met with great approval.

'It is Billy McNeill's responsibility to follow in these (Stein's) giant footsteps and I can think of no higher compliment to Billy to say there is nobody more qualified.' – John Fairgrieve, Sunday Mail, 4th June 1978.

Although the news of McNeill's appointment was welcomed by Celtic fans, there was ultimately a sense of disappointment. Jock Stein was dearly loved by the Celtic supporters and to this day there remains resentment that a suitable role was not found for him at Celtic Park. There is an infamous photograph from the time which shows new manager Billy McNeill and chairman Desmond White shaking hands, with Stein standing between them looking rather pensive. This picture was painful viewing and for the fans from that era, the foot soldiers who faithfully followed their manager as Celtic blazed a trail across Europe, it was a time of reflection.

This image may have been accepted by the viewing public, but the truth is the photo was slightly misleading. There are several others taken at the same time which show Stein and McNeill much more at ease with each other, although these are rarely seen.

It was reported that there were likely to have been two main options open to Stein at Celtic.

Firstly, he could have been appointed General Manager, in a similar role to that which Willie Waddell held at Rangers.

Billy McNeill shakes hands with Desmond White, after being appointed new Celtic manager, as Jock Stein looks on.

Secondly, he could join the board of directors and become the first non Catholic director in Celtic's history, which in itself would have been a most newsworthy story at that time.

On 1st June 1978 it was officially reported by the club that Jock Stein had indeed been invited to join the board, and that he was to be awarded a testimonial match against European champions, Liverpool. It was also announced that faithful servant Sean Fallon and assistant manager Davie McParland had both left the club, *'with substantial golden handshakes'*, as a wind of change swept through Celtic Park. Chairman Desmond White informed the public of the club's plans but was notably short on detail.

'After his testimonial he (Stein) will join the board. His name can open many doors and attract many ideas from many directions. We will be delighted to have him on the board.' Daily Record, 1st June 1978.

As it turned out, the Celtic board did offer Stein a post, but it was a position on the periphery of the club, managing the Celtic Development Pools organisation. This job was referred to by the newspapers as that of 'a mere ticket salesman.' In fairness to the Celtic board, it should be noted that in 1978 the Celtic Pools provided a great deal of revenue for the club, and perhaps the directors hoped to use Stein's influence in order to increase commercial income from that source. Jimmy Farrell, a Celtic director of the period, recalled that:

'He (Stein) had always been interested in the commercial side of the club and was very interested in ideas about raising finance. We felt that this was a job he could do very well, and without too much stress - but it was presented in the press as 'selling tickets' which was completely wrong.'

Even in view of Farrell's observations, it must have been devastating to Stein that the club he had led to unparallelled success no longer wanted him to contribute on the playing side, the part of the game he loved most. The feeling was, that the board offered Stein this position, safe in the knowledge that he would not accept it. He would therefore have to move on, which would no doubt suit some board members, who were envious of Stein's huge stature and popularity amongst the club's supporters.

Gerry Woolard, a close confidante of Stein's, recalled the sense of disappointment he had to endure by leaving his beloved Celtic Park:

'It was a terrible blow to him when he left Celtic, you know. He did not expect that kind of treatment from them even though he had been disappointed by the board's attitude on other matters. After the board told him they wanted him to sell pools tickets for the club he came to me for advice. I will never forget him that day. I've never seen him so badly affected by anything. He was shattered, totally and absolutely devastated. Celtic did nothing wrong legally, they could offer him any job they wanted to. But the morality of the whole business left a lot to be desired. If Sir Robert Kelly had been alive then this would never have happened.'

Stein had enjoyed a special rapport with Sir Robert Kelly, who was Celtic chairman until his sad passing in 1971. It was common knowledge around Glasgow that Stein, and new chairman, Desmond White, did not enjoy the same positive working relationship. During Stein's great years he had shown Celtic tremendous loyalty, particularly when he had declined Manchester United's advances to replace Sir Matt Busby as manager at Old Trafford. Stein had not been particularly well rewarded financially during his tenure as Celtic manager, and the feeling held by the general public was that the Celtic board had totally betrayed the loyalty he had shown them.

Celtic's vice captain at that time, Andy Lynch, recalls the mood from the players' perspective. *'There were rumours that possibly something would happen at the end of the season, and when it eventually did happen it was a big shock and a big cloud hung over Celtic Park when it was announced that Jock was leaving.*

When he eventually left I certainly couldn't think of anyone who else who could lift the club again other than Billy McNeill.'

Scottish football was already reeling from the news that Jock Wallace had unexpectedly resigned as Rangers manager, after winning the Scottish domestic treble. Wallace was replaced by Billy McNeill's old adversary from his playing days, the legendary Rangers captain John Greig, who had just captained his side to that very treble success. To this day, it is not entirely certain why Wallace left Rangers in such a hurry for the modest setting of Leicester City, (then in the second tier of the English league). However, the Rangers' directors were said to be keen to encourage a sense of continuity by appointing Greig from within the club.

The Scottish football media has seldom had to cope with such hectic news activity than that which occurred in the summer of 1978. The Scottish national side were given more prominence then, and were participating in the 1978 World Cup finals in Argentina. Ally MacLeod's squad became the focus of world media exposure and humiliation after their insipid performances, which saw them lose to Peru and draw with Iran, countries well below Scotland's ranking. The results had been bad enough, but the sight of class players like Dalglish, Buchan, Jordan and Rioch performing so poorly left the nation frustrated and angry. As if this wasn't bad enough, Willie Johnston was sent home in disgrace for failing a drugs test. Further stories of ill-discipline and unrest in the Scotland camp also filtered back home, and several Scotland players received lifetime bans from playing for their country, following a variety of misdemeanours.

It's interesting to note that in a recent Ally MacLeod biography, his family claim that following Jock Wallace's resignation, Willie Waddell contacted MacLeod to offer him the position as Rangers manager. This was only a few weeks before Scotland departed for Argentina. MacLeod was said to be flattered but rebuffed Waddell, although this was not common knowledge in 1978.

Around this time, St Mirren sensationally sacked their ambitious young manager, Alex Ferguson. He had only been out of work for a matter of days when the call came from Pittodrie for him to replace Billy McNeill at Aberdeen. With all these events happening in such a short space of time the Scottish football media was close to combustion. But, there could be no doubting that the two biggest stories involved the two big Glasgow clubs, and their new managerial appointments.

Celtic and Rangers were to be led by men who had recently captained their sides. McNeill and Greig, at the ages of thirty eight and thirty five respectively, were still relatively young men and they had the biggest jobs in Scottish football. Both men had careers with almost parallel success. They were club legends, long serving captains who had led their clubs to success in the European arena. They had both represented and captained their country with great distinction, and had both gone out at the top, lifting the Scottish Cup after memorable victories at Hampden Park. As the dust began to settle in the late summer of 1978, the scene was set for a fascinating season, for Celtic and for Scottish football in general.

CHAPTER 2 • THE BEST OF STARTS

On his return to Parkhead, Billy McNeill brought with him his trusted assistant manager from Aberdeen, John Clark. The two men had been Celtic's defensive rock during the glory days of the Lisbon era, where they had developed a tremendous understanding on the field of play as a distinguished centre-back partnership. The new manager was keen to explain the importance of having a capable assistant.

'I think it is good to have someone you can work with, someone you can rely on and make his own contribution. Believe me John has his own ideas and sometimes they don't coincide with mine but I respect that. From a temperamental viewpoint he is more on the level whereas I tend to be high or low. We work well as a team.' Sunday Mail, 16th July 1978.

McNeill was a modern, track suited manager and went to work immediately, casting his eye over his new squad of players. He had inherited the following group:

Goalkeepers: Peter Latchford, Roy Baines.

Full backs: Danny McGrain, Andy Lynch, Alan Sneddon, Joe Filippi.

Centre backs: Roddy MacDonald, Johannes Edvaldsson, Pat Stanton.

Midfielders: Roy Aitken, Ronnie Glavin, Tommy Burns, Mike Conroy, Jim Casey, John Dowie, Peter Mackie.

Forwards: George McCluskey, Joe Craig, Tom McAdam, Johnny Doyle, Paul Wilson, Alfie Conn.

After building a fine side at Aberdeen, McNeill was initially underwhelmed by the team he acquired on his return to

Parkhead, and in later years he confided: *'The Celtic Park I had left in 1975 was a place crammed with quality players but when I came back the good players had gone. Dalglish was away, McGrain and Stanton were injured and the quality men seemed to have disappeared.'*

In retrospect, a quick glance at that list will show that there was still a decent standard of player available for the new manager to work with. On the down side there was no date set for the return of the influential McGrain. However, the ageing Stanton and injury prone Conn were now said to be fit and raring to go. McNeill was to take time to assess his new squad and would not be quick to enter the transfer market. Nevertheless transfer rumours abounded and Celtic were linked in the media with Anglo Scots Gerry Gow (Bristol City), Tommy Craig (Aston Villa), John Duncan (Spurs), Mark McGhee (Newcastle) and a possible return for the ex-Celtic favourite, David Hay who was then at Chelsea. Ultimately, none of these players were to find their way to Celtic Park, at least not in the short term, and the first team remained unchanged for some time.

Much to the dismay of the Celtic support, most of the Dalglish transfer fee remained unspent. McNeill had already shown a great eye for talent at Aberdeen and his signings, Gordon Strachan, Steve Archibald and Ian Scanlon had all made a great impression at Pittodrie. Celtic fans now hoped that McNeill would be able to identify players of a similar calibre and bring them to Parkhead.

The one early signing made by the manager was the experienced midfielder, Jim Lumsden, from Clydebank. However McNeill made it clear that Lumsden would play mainly for the reserve team, and also assist with the development of the younger players. It was intended that he would have a future coaching role at the club.

On a more positive note McNeill inherited some fine upcoming talent. Tommy Burns, Roy Aitken and George McCluskey were all first team players with huge potential, and were rated amongst the best young players in Scotland. It was said that they had learned greatly from the previous traumatic season. They had matured and would be mentally stronger as a result of that experience. Mike Conroy and Alan Sneddon were brought directly into the Celtic first team from the lower reaches of junior football, which was an enormous jump. Both coped admirably during difficult circumstances and the manager had high hopes for his young charges.

In a sign of solidarity, McNeill moved quickly to announce that Danny McGrain would remain as the first team captain, even whilst absent through injury. This was a confidence boost for him as he was known to still be some distance from a return to the first team. The experienced Andy Lynch continued to deputise for McGrain in his absence. They say that hope springs eternal, and as the start of the new season approached, the Celtic faithful had high hopes for a turnaround following such a dispiriting season.

Andy Lynch recalled the mood of the new manager just after his appointment - *'When Billy took over he called me into the manager's office and he spelled out very clearly that things had to change and that he needed to hit the ground running. He wanted everyone behind him and he was full of enthusiasm and that was passed on to the players. I was to continue being team captain in Danny's absence as Billy said that I'd been through it all before and he wanted the younger guys to know what the Celtic way was.'*

Peter Latchford recalled a more light hearted moment - *'I remember Billy's first meeting at training when he took over as manager. He said, 'I know there are a few of you who I played with and I knew you socially. This has to stop now and I want to be known as boss or gaffer.' The whole squad was standing there very solemn and silent and he then asked Danny McGrain, as captain, if there was anything he'd like to say. Danny replied 'Naw Billy', and everybody fell apart laughing. Billy had to walk away to keep a straight face.'*

McNeill worked his players hard in pre-season training, but arranged only one pre-season game. He opted to play Montrose in the modest surroundings of their homely Links Park ground, having declined the opportunity of travelling further afield to play games in England or Ireland.

Against Montrose, on the final Saturday in July, the new manager sprang a few surprises with his first ever team selection. Youngster Alan Sneddon was in the right-back position, with Tommy Burns dropping back to play in an unfamiliar left-back role. The small band of Celtic fans in the 2,300 crowd were delighted to see the morale boosting return of inspirational duo Stanton and Conn. Andy Lynch and Paul Wilson were suspended for the beginning of the season, with Joe Craig the only absentee through injury.

For the first twenty minutes Montrose were the better side against a disorganised Celtic, and they took a deserving lead, before Roy Aitken quickly equalised. The Celts then regrouped and eventually won well in the end, by 3-1, therefore sparing any blushes. Their fitness and sharpness needed work but young striker George McCluskey looked especially keen to impress, scoring two goals in terrific fashion, giving the supporters a glimpse of what was to come.

The season was now upon them, and the Celtic support hoped that McNeill could replicate just a fraction of the success that he had enjoyed with the club as captain during Celtic's golden era. The supporters still had fresh memories of the many successes of the past decade, and McNeill was well aware of the expectations placed upon him.

Billy McNeill is in the dugout as Celtic manager for the first time at Links Park, July 1978, with Neilly Mochan and Bob Rooney.

3 August 1978: Anglo-Scottish Cup, first leg tie

Celtic   2-1   Clyde
Conn 60   Ward 4
Burns 87

Attendance: 10,000

Depressingly for the club, Celtic had no European football available to them. Instead they entered the Anglo Scottish Cup, a competition between Scottish and English clubs who had been unable to qualify for European competition. In order to qualify to play against English opposition, Celtic were required to face Clyde in a two legged preliminary round. McNeill was happy to participate as part of his preparation for the league campaign.

Just four years previously, Celtic had competed in the semi-final of the European Cup against Atletico Madrid. Now, the famed Glasgow Celtic were taking part in a competition which was perceived as being beneath a club of their standing. It was a sharp reminder of how far Celtic's stock had fallen.

Clyde at that time were actually a capable first division side, with future Scotland manager Craig Brown having been appointed as their new manager. The newspapers pointed out that McNeill and Brown knew each other well from a long way back, having been team mates for Scotland schoolboys when Scotland defeated England 3-0 at Celtic Park in 1957.

As a measure of the Anglo-Scottish Cup's importance, only 10,000 fans bothered to turn up at Parkhead to watch Billy McNeill's first competitive game as Celtic manager. After only four minutes Clyde took the lead, and the fans could not be blamed for believing that nothing much had changed since the previous season. Clyde's Brian Ahern took a quick free-kick straight through the centre of the Celtic defence, and their promising young striker, Joe Ward, raced through to score with comparative ease. If McNeill needed any reminding of the task facing him, then that this was a fair reminder.

Celtic fought back and Clyde's veteran goalkeeper, John Arrol, held them at bay until the 54th minute, when a fine move by Glavin and Burns allowed Alfie Conn to score with a close range volley for the equaliser. Celtic mustered a rousing finish, and with minutes remaining Tommy Burns scored the winning goal with a firm shot, after substitute Peter Mackie provided the opening.

Celtic supporters left the ground that night feeling rather underwhelmed by the overall performance, but satisfied that there was at least some spirit in the team and that they had actually fought to the end.

Celtic: Latchford Sneddon Aitken (Mackie) Edvaldsson MacDonald Burns Conn Lumsden McAdam Glavin McCluskey Sub: Lynch

Clyde: Arrol Anderson Boyd Clougherty Kinnear Ahern Brogan O'Neill Marshall McCabe (Hood) Ward Sub: Martin

5 August 1978: Anglo-Scottish Cup, second leg tie

Clyde	**1-6**	**Celtic (Aggregate 2-8)**
O'Neill 68		Conn 48, 65
		McAdam 55, 80
		Glavin 75, 86

Attendance: 12,000

At half-time in this second leg tie, Clyde could have been forgiven for feeling rather content in holding Celtic to a goalless score line. In the second half McNeill's men struck some kind of form, and went through the gears, rather than through the motions. They proceeded to rattle six goals past a hapless Clyde defence in the process.

There were many plus points in the second half for the new manager. Tom McAdam scored two excellent goals, the first a bullet of a shot and the second a delightful lob. He looked an excellent prospect at centre-forward. Alfie Conn showed great touches and vision. The hope was that he could give the team some much needed flair, style and a sense of the unexpected, which had been missing for so long. Ronnie Glavin gave a glimpse of the old form that had once made him the best attacking midfielder in the country. All three had scored impressive doubles as the forward line found their collective form.

McNeill could be satisfied that his new charges had gone through comfortably by 8-2 on aggregate. When the draw for the next round was made, Celtic were given a two legged tie against English second division side Burnley, which was to be played in September.

The new league campaign was fast approaching when Celtic would face much stronger opposition. McNeill knew it would be vital to begin well: *'With all due respect to the Anglo-Scottish Cup competition, the Premier League is the big kick off, and I can only hope we get off to the right start.'*

Clyde: Arrol Anderson Boyd (Martin) Clougherty Kinnear Ahern Hood (McNaughton) O'Neill Marshall McCabe (Hood) Ward

Celtic: Latchford Sneddon Lynch Aitken MacDonald Edvaldsson Conn Glavin McAdam Burns McCluskey (Wilson) Sub: Lumsden

Twenty four hours after the Shawfield match, the Sunday newspapers reported the shock news that Pat Stanton had announced his retirement from football. This was an enormous blow to everyone at the club because Stanton was such a talented, respected and influential player. He was easily the most experienced player in the Celtic squad. McNeill was disappointed but said he understood Stanton's decision. Stanton, despite his own deep disappointment, sounded pragmatic.

'One or two things had happened in the Montrose game that worried me. I feel if you have set yourself standards and cannot maintain them then you have to give up. I suppose I could have played on. My knee is okay and my fitness has improved since we started training but it wasn't good enough for me. To quit at the start of the season is strange but I had to do it.'

Pat Stanton was a footballer of the highest calibre and would be a difficult player to replace. He would be best remembered for his notable career at Easter Road, but also for his superb displays in a Celtic jersey.

Billy McNeill then looked forward to a glamour friendly with English giants Arsenal. In the press interviews leading up to the midweek fixture he reiterated his intention to bring in new players, and indicated that he had signing targets in mind.

There was some good news for the Celtic manager when Icelandic international defender, Johannes Edvaldsson, withdrew his transfer request from the previous season. Edvaldsson had been very unhappy with the direction in which Celtic had been heading, but was so impressed by his new manager, that he no longer had any desire to leave Parkhead. McNeill welcomed the Icelander's change of heart. He would have been relieved to retain such an experienced player, as the retirement of Stanton left him with only Edvaldsson and Roddy MacDonald as recognised centre-halves. Roy Aitken could certainly deputise in an emergency, but it was felt that Aitken was at his best in the forceful midfield role, in which he performed so well. It was therefore vital in the short term that Celtic kept 'Big Shuggie', and having withdrawn his transfer request it was hoped he would return to his best form.

Newspaper reports also linked Bobby Lennox with a return to Scotland. Ayr United had tried to take him from Celtic previously, but Bobby had opted for an American adventure in the popular, but unchallenging North American Soccer League. He signed for the Houston Hurricanes club who were based in Texas.

The Ayrshire duo of Kilmarnock and Ayr were said to be trying to entice the Saltcoats man back to Scotland. It was also reported that Billy McNeill wished to persuade his old team mate to return to Celtic. Lennox was due to travel back from the States for Jock Stein's testimonial game against Liverpool, and was certain to be in demand on his return to home soil.

8 August 1978: Challenge Match

Celtic   0-3   Arsenal
Lynch (og) 29
MacDonald (og) 76
Stapleton 83

Attendance: 24,000

At first glance at this score line you couldn't be blamed for thinking that Celtic had suffered a comprehensive defeat, and yet this was nothing of the sort. It was a night of misfortune for Andy Lynch and Roddy MacDonald as they scored own goals past a helpless Peter Latchford, much to the dismay of the Celtic fans standing in the summer rain.

Celtic had actually played well and created chances. Roy Aitken broke through the Arsenal offside trap but then shot tamely at the experienced Gunners' keeper, Pat Jennings. Northern Ireland internationalist Jennings had played against Celtic for Tottenham Hotspur as far back as their North American tour in 1966, and gave a faultless display of goalkeeping on the night. He was given a great reception by the appreciative Celtic support. Jennings made a great save from George McCluskey after Alfie Conn sent him through on goal. When the Irish goalkeeper saved with his feet, the young Celtic striker sent the rebound into the side netting.

The own goals were truly unfortunate affairs. In twenty nine minutes a Sammy Nelson cross was headed on by Stapleton. Andy Lynch, running back towards goal, unwittingly sent a knee high effort into his own net. Then, in seventy six minutes, Roddy MacDonald inadvertently turned the ball into his own goal, as he tried to intercept a Nelson cross to John Kosmina.

Although Celtic made all the running on the night, Arsenal looked happy to defend in depth and hit Celtic on the break. In eighty three minutes the London side found the net with their first real attack of the evening. Frank Stapleton scored with a rebound, after Alan Sneddon cleared a Kosmina shot off the line.

The local press felt Arsenal were something of a disappointment. Neither the much vaunted Liam Brady or Malcolm MacDonald, Arsenal's two biggest assets, had shown much on the night. Their defensive system of play did not endear them to the rain soaked Parkhead crowd. There was concern for Celtic when Johannes Edvaldsson was taken off with a knee injury and replaced by young Jim Casey. It was hoped that this was a precaution and that the big defender would be available for the important opening league game at Cappielow. The Arsenal manager Terry Neill had some encouraging words for the home fans.

'Celtic are a young team, they've got promise all right. But they need someone to put the ball in the net and they need an old head in midfield. But I know Billy McNeill and he is the man to sort it all out'.

The 24,000 crowd could not have agreed more.

Celtic – Latchford Sneddon Lynch Aitken MacDonald Edvaldsson Conn Glavin McAdam Burns McCluskey

Arsenal – Jennings Rice Nelson Price O'Leary Young Brady Sunderland MacDonald (Kosmina) Stapleton Rix

As his testimonial game approached, Jock Stein may no longer have been Celtic boss, but he still had Celtic very much in his thoughts. In a searching interview with the Evening Times he explained why Celtic meant so much to him.

'It hasn't been money that has kept me at Celtic Park. I've done what I've done out of a kind of passion. See, Celtic have been wonderful to me. You've heard of people being brought back from the dead? Well it was Celtic that brought me back from the dead.'

He went on to explain how Celtic had brought him back to Scotland from the relative obscurity of Llanelli, South Wales, in 1951, and how his career had then fallen into place.

Interestingly, he then discussed a job he was offered as a consultant to the national side of Kuwait. He told of how he met a Kuwaiti representative in London and had been his guest for lunch, where he had been treated to a traditional dish of sheeps' eyes cooked in rice.

'I could have earned more in one year there than in a lifetime here but they wanted me to leave within three days and it just felt wrong at the time.'

Stein's refusal was not a surprise to those who knew him well as he was a renowned home bird. Other British managerial names such as Don Revie, Dave Mackay, Frank O'Farrell and Jimmy Hill had all conceded to the lure of Arabian riches, but it was obvious that Jock Stein was different. On a possible departure from Celtic he remarked:

'When I leave I don't think I'll be completely severed from the club. Its 20 years of your life isn't it?'

Jock wasn't entirely looking forward to his testimonial game against Liverpool:

'The worst moment will be walking out to the middle of the field on Monday night....I don't mean to sound reluctant because the fact that Liverpool, the European champions, are coming to play here is the biggest compliment I could have got out of the game. It will be an emotional occasion. All of my family will be there including my two sisters from Burnbank. But one way or another it will be an ordeal, I can tell you.'

He did touch upon managing elsewhere in Britain. In what would be a somewhat prophetic statement Stein said, *'If I went to England, it would only be for the money.'*

12 August 1978: Premier Division

Morton   **1-2**   **Celtic**
Ritchie 75   Glavin 32
                          MacDonald 70

Attendance: 12,000

The season then started for real, with Celtic's opening league game ending in a narrow but deserved victory at Cappielow. Newly promoted to the Premier Division, Morton were keen to make an impression. Their manager Benny Rooney and his assistant, Mike Jackson, were both ex-Celts and close personal friends of Billy McNeill, which only served to add to the occasion.

Ronnie Glavin had given Celtic a deserved half-time lead when he scored at the back post from a low cross from Johnny Doyle. Morton had ex-Celts Denis Connaghan and Andy Ritchie in their line up, and both men had fine matches, although Morton rarely threatened during the first half. In seventy minutes Roddy MacDonald scored Celtic's second from an Alan Sneddon cross from the left, after he accepted a short corner from Alfie Conn.

At this point, Morton threw caution to the wind, as Celtic relaxed with their two goal advantage. Rooney threw defender Neil Orr into midfield and went man for man at the back. These changes gave Morton new energy, and in seventy five minutes Andy Ritchie scored a fine opportunist goal, after taking a cross on his chest with his back to goal.

Celtic became nervous and were reeling in the closing stages. With just minutes remaining, Peter Latchford made a magnificent, diving save from a powerful Neil Orr shot to deny Morton a share of the points, which would have been a travesty for Celtic.

'Celtic had an inspired and intelligent keeper in Peter Latchford who is proving a worthy successor to Ronnie Simpson, the last man to hold that position with true distinction.' Daily Express, 14th August 1978.

On a sour note, there had been fighting in the covered enclosure at half-time. This had caused youngsters to spill on to the field to escape flying cans and bottles. This only ceased when Police moved into the area and arrests were made.

There were two pieces of good news for Celtic after the final whistle. Firstly, a huge roar had gone up from Celtic fans when it was announced that St Mirren had beaten Rangers at Ibrox by 1-0. Rangers had unfurled their league flag in celebratory fashion prior to the game, but in the last minute Saints' substitute Bobby Torrance had scored the only goal of the game, spoiling the mood of the Ibrox party.

Later that afternoon, it was announced that Danny McGrain had surprisingly returned to action at Parkhead, as a second half substitute in a reserve game against Morton, following his ten month absence through injury. Things had gone well and it was reported that he would play some part in Stein's testimonial match against Liverpool. As he continued to improve his fitness for the season ahead, McGrain would have been desperately keen to play in this game as tribute to his old mentor.
All in all, it had been an excellent day for Celtic.

Celtic – Latchford Filippi Sneddon Aitken MacDonald Edvaldsson Doyle Glavin McAdam Burns Conn Subs: Casey Lumsden

Morton – Connaghan Hayes Holmes Evans Orr Rooney Russell Miller Scott Rae Ritchie Subs: Hutchison McLean

14 August 1978: Jock Stein Testimonial Match

Celtic   **2-3**   **Liverpool**
Glavin 21   Dalglish 40, 55
McAdam 44   A. Kennedy 32

Attendance: 62,600

Seldom has the old Celtic Park main stand hosted the number of celebrities and personalities than on this dull August evening. From the political world there was former Scottish Secretary of State Willie Ross, Scottish Secretary of State Bruce Millan, and a good number of other Scottish politicians. From the show business world there was Billy Connolly, and the former James Bond, Sean Connery. From the footballing fraternity there were Stein's contemporaries, Southampton manager Lawrie McMenemy, and the legendary ex-Liverpool manager, Bill Shankly. In a nice touch, Leicester City manager Jock Wallace, Stein's old adversary from their Old Firm days, was also present, as well as a host of other names from within the Scottish game.

However the highlight of the night came before kick-off, when the magnificent Lisbon Lions side took to the field to salute their old boss. As the persistent rain which had lashed Glasgow all day relented, the deafening roars of approval from over 62,000 throats pierced the night air with emotion. Stein held court in the centre circle, surrounded by the elite squad of players who had made their mark under his guidance, as the fans roared out their names in approval, one by one.

The noise continued when the teams took to the field. Liverpool, reigning European Champions, boasted the ex- Celtic captain, Kenny Dalglish. He was said to be keen to revisit his old football home. Dalglish was made honorary captain for the Anfield side to mark the occasion. They also fielded their new £300,000 signing from Newcastle United, left-back Alan Kennedy. His signing had been rushed through with the FA only hours before, in order to play him at Parkhead.

For their part, Celtic were led on to the field by Danny McGrain, who was set to make his long awaited come back from injury. Although listed as a substitute, Danny was permitted to lead the Celts out as captain, alongside his great friend, and Scotland colleague, Kenny Dalglish. McGrain stayed for the tossing of the coin then made his way to the Celtic bench.

The game was a fitting tribute to Jock Stein as both teams went for victory and entertained the massive crowd crammed into the old ground. Celtic started well, looking to impress their new manager and their English rivals. In three minutes Tommy Burns scored with a diving header, but referee Brian McGinlay adjudged that Tom McAdam had fouled the Liverpool goalkeeper, Ray Clemence.

In twenty one minutes Celtic took the lead. Burns beat three Liverpool players before being hauled down by Graeme Souness just outside the area. From the free kick Ronnie Glavin sent a thundering low shot past the Liverpool wall and into the net. It was a tremendous shot, and one which Lisbon veteran Tommy Gemmell would have been proud of at his peak.

Liverpool's pride was clearly hurt, and they fought back almost immediately when they equalised through their bearded debutant Alan Kennedy. In a simple move, Ray Kennedy headed the ball to Souness who then sent Alan Kennedy clear on goal. He calmly side stepped Peter Latchford before scoring neatly from a narrow angle.

Seven minutes later and Liverpool had taken the lead. Ray Kennedy sent Steve Heighway racing down the inside left channel and when Latchford parried his shot, Kenny Dalglish reacted first to head into the net. Celtic then roared back with the goal of the game before half-time. Alan Sneddon crossed from the right and Andy Lynch performed a great dummy to allow Tom McAdam to hook home a fantastic shot on the volley.

Dalglish was clearly on form on his old stamping ground, and he settled matters in the second half when he scored with a typical, clinical twenty yard shot. Clemence made a superb save from Tom McAdam late on. Danny McGrain was given a magnificent ovation when he came on for the last ten minutes, in an unusual midfield role, when he replaced Ronnie Glavin. In the end Liverpool were worthy winners and took home the 'Jock Stein Cup', awarded by his testimonial committee. Stein himself made the presentation of the trophy to his old captain, Dalglish, who showed his trade mark gleaming smile as he received it.

Dalglish had been jeered and roundly barracked by a section of the Celtic crowd all night, particularly by the younger element in the 'Jungle' who used to worship him. This hurt him deeply and angered the majority of Celtic fans who still admired him greatly. It was remarked afterwards that, 'The Pope would have got a better reception at Ibrox'. Some Celtic fans were still angered by his departure and had obvious difficulty dealing with the mercenary attitudes of 1970's footballers. For days afterwards the newspapers' letters pages were full of complaints from enraged Celtic fans. They were angered by the ignorant minority in their midst, and their attitude towards an all-time Celtic great who deserved better, given his tremendous service over many seasons. Many fans were also of the opinion that Kenny had carried the team in his latter years at the club.

This game proved to be a great draw for the public, and the 62,600 official attendance was the biggest crowd seen at Celtic Park for a number of years. Stein earned an £85,000 bonanza on the night. It is well documented that he was not a high earner in his Parkhead years and the fans rallied to the cause, handing him what was then a small fortune, which he thoroughly merited and deserved. In Ken Gallagher's excellent biography of Stein, members of his family are quoted as saying that he had never really been financially independent until then, but the testimonial cheque he received made him comfortable for the rest of his days. And, fittingly, it came from the Celtic supporters who worshipped him.

Dalglish was magnanimous after the match despite his difficult reception and stated that it was a pleasure to play in the game. Liverpool and England captain Emlyn Hughes said, *'I was most impressed with Celtic. We all know they had a bad season last year but I thought they were a useful side against us tonight.'*

We can only wonder what went through Jock Stein's mind, on that wonderfully emotional night, as he faced up to a new challenge as a Celtic director.

However, it was to be a position he would not take up.

Celtic: Latchford Sneddon Lynch Aitken MacDonald Edvaldsson Conn Glavin (McGrain) McAdam Burns Wilson Subs: Baines Filippi Doyle Casey

Liverpool: Clemence Neal A Kennedy Thompson R Kennedy Hughes Dalglish Case Heighway McDermott Souness Subs: Fairclough Hansen Jones

16 August 1978: League Cup, first leg tie

Celtic	**3-1**	**Dundee**
McAdam 52, 84		Sinclair 64
Glavin 73		

Attendance: 12,000

On the day before this game, Jock Stein's celebrations continued with a testimonial dinner in the Grand Banqueting Hall in Glasgow City Chambers. Hundreds were in attendance and a telegram message from Nottingham Forest manager Brian Clough, was read out, proudly stating that, *'Jock Stein is the manager of the century.'* In his speech, the Lord Provost David Hodge described Jock as, *'the greatest manager of all time.'*

Sean Connery took a break from filming in Gleneagles to attend and he brought further testimonials from the illustrious England cricket captain Colin Cowdrey, heavyweight boxing champion Henry Cooper, comedian Jimmy Tarbuck and football personality and great friend of Stein's, Jimmy Hill.

In his reply an emotional Jock Stein declared that: *'The real fans of this club are the salt of the earth and no words of mine can fully express my feelings and reaction to the game with Liverpool and this testimonial dinner. I hope that the next thirteen years for Celtic are as successful as the last thirteen have been.'*

Stein once commented that, *'Unlike many other Celts, I cannot say that Celtic were my first love... but I can say that they will be my last love.'* His affection for the club and its supporters was absolute and he regarded the fans as family. That feeling was reciprocated by the supporters and Stein remains the most important and revered figure in the club's history

As we can all attest, after every good party there is always a hangover, and the media were discussing Stein's benefit game for days afterwards. Liverpool had made a tremendous impression with the quality of their football and Celtic had also shown that they were still capable of competing with the best on their day.

Forty eight hours later, Celtic faced ex-Celt Tommy Gemmell's Dundee side in the League Cup. The ever proud Gemmell was still smarting from a 7-1 thrashing his side had received at Parkhead in the Scottish Cup the previous February. He was determined the Dens Park men would not collapse again in a similar fashion.

Dundee defended dourly and resolutely for fifty two minutes, with Celtic looking lethargic after their exertions against Liverpool. McAdam gave them the lead, after Edvaldsson had forced his way through the Dundee defence. This goal forced Dundee out of their shell, and they equalised soon after when

Sinclair headed in a fine cross by Redford. This rocked Celtic and Peter Latchford twice made great saves from Alex McGhee to keep the score level.

The encouraging thing was that Celtic did not buckle. They seized the initiative and forced Dundee back. Glavin grabbed the goal of the game when he scored after playing a fine one-two with Joe Filippi. Glavin was on form, and from his cross Tom McAdam grabbed Celtic's third, with six minutes remaining.

This had been an encouraging win and gave Celtic a two goal lead to take to Dundee for the second leg.

Celtic – Latchford Filippi Lynch Aitken MacDonald Edvaldsson Doyle Glavin McAdam Burns Conn Subs: Lumsden Casey

Dundee: Donaldson Barr Watson McDougall Glennie McPhail Lamb McKinnon Sinclair McGhee Redford Subs: Williamson Shirra

19 August 1978: Premier Division

Celtic   4-0   Hearts
McAdam 8
Burns 18
Conn 75, 77

Attendance: 24,000

The popular Alfie Conn had experienced injury problems since he joined Celtic in March 1977, but no one could question his ability and he used this game as a showcase to display his talents to the full.

'Alfie, confident again, sharp and a picture of class as he weaved nimbly past defenders, his hair waving like a cavalier's

in the breeze, got the goal which made it 4-0, with flair and distinction.' Evening Times, 21st August 1978.

The goal referred to was a glorious, curling twenty yard free-kick into the top corner, past Hearts' keeper Ray Dunlop. Billy McNeill commented after the game that had the goal been scored by a foreigner, the press would have been raving about it. To be fair, the media were full of praise for this entertaining Celtic performance. There were plaudits for Burns, McAdam and Edvaldsson who all had splendid games. But, Alfie Conn on this form was exceptional, and we can only wonder what he could have achieved without the recurring injuries that hampered his time at Celtic.

Media reports indicated that Leeds United had approached Jock Stein to be their new manager, after the Elland Road club sacked Jimmy Armfield. Stein travelled to Highbury to watch Leeds and Arsenal play out an entertaining 2-2 draw. Stein was said to be greatly tempted by Leeds' £30,000 per annum offer, which was a considerable increase on his more modest Celtic salary. Leeds were still a prominent side within the English game in 1978. They were desperately seeking a powerful personality to lead the club in the way Don Revie did, before he left to manage the England national team in 1974. Stein returned to Glasgow to discuss matters with Chairman Desmond White. It was then common knowledge that Stein would prefer to remain in the game in a managerial capacity, than accept Celtic's offer of a place on the board, with responsibility for the Celtic Development Pools.

Leeds chairman Manny Cussins excitedly told the English press that it was his intention to bring Stein to Elland Road, as he was the best in the business. This would be seen as a major coup for Leeds, as Stein had declined several big money offers from English clubs through the years. For his part, Stein stated that he wished to consider his family before making any decision. After a few days of negotiation and consideration, Jock Stein was paraded at Elland Road as Leeds United's new manager.

After thirteen wonderful seasons and twenty five major trophies, Jock said his farewell to Parkhead and departed for Yorkshire. He was only fifty four years old at the time, and the feeling of the vast majority of Celtic fans was that he still had many good years left in him.

In later years it was suggested that part of the reason behind Stein's decision to go to Leeds was to give Billy McNeill his own space. Manchester United managers had long complained about the presence of Matt Busby hovering over them, and this was said to be one of the main reasons Stein declined United's offer to manage them in 1971.

Shortly after McNeill became Celtic manager, he was in an office within Celtic Park when the phone rang. Jim Kennedy answered it, shouting, 'It's for you, boss.' McNeill moved to answer it and noticed that Jimmy McGrory and Jock Stein, who were both in the room, moved to answer it too. As ex-Celtic managers, they were used to being called 'Boss' around the ground as a mark of the respect in which they were held. Stein even continued to refer to McGrory by this title after he himself became manager. He would no doubt have been conscious of being in McNeill's way, and would not have wished to impose on his former captain.

Jock Stein set off for his new career in Yorkshire but there was little doubt that he left Celtic Park with a very heavy heart.

Celtic: Latchford Fillippi Lynch Aitken MacDonald Edvaldsson Doyle Glavin McAdam Burns (Casey) Conn (Wilson)

Hearts: Dunlop Kidd Fraser McNicholl Jefferies Liddell Robertson (Park) Bannon Gibson Shaw (Tierney) Prentice

23 August 1978: League Cup

Dundee 0-3 Celtic (Aggregate 1-6)
Doyle 23, 31
Conn 67

Attendance: 12,698

Celtic held a 3-1 advantage from the home leg and for Dundee to have any chance of causing an upset they really needed to score the first goal.

The opening goal came in twenty three minutes, but it was Celtic who scored and it was regarded as controversial. Ronnie Glavin played a long through ball to Alfie Conn, who looked yards offside. The referee and linesman allowed play to go on as Conn ran on, squaring the ball to John Doyle to score easily, as the Dundee players protested to the officials.

Doyle scored his second in thirty one minutes. Conn fired over a fierce cross from a free-kick for Doyle to divert into the net with his head. In the second half Conn then rounded off the scoring with an exquisite goal, when he robbed Ian Philip of possession, ran forward and cracked a shot past keeper Donaldson from twenty five yards.

Since the start of the season, Conn had found his best form, much to the delight of the Celtic support, and those who had travelled to Dens on this late summer's night chanted his name loudly. The media reported Celtic's performance with admiration:

'Although there may have been a doubt about the first goal, the sad fact for Dundee was that they were never really in with a chance against a Celtic team, zipping along with zest, all their former buoyancy, will to win the ball first and eagerness to back each other restored.' Evening Times, 24th August 1978.

Dundee: Donaldson Barr Watson Lamb Glennie Philip McGhee Shirra Pirie Sinclair Redford Subs: Scott Williamson

Celtic: Latchford Filippi Lynch Aitken MacDonald Edvaldsson Doyle (Casey) Glavin McAdam Burns Conn Sub: Wilson

26 August 1978: Premier Division

Motherwell	**1-5**	**Celtic**
Edvaldsson (og) 41		Conn 25, 78
		Aitken 50, 86
		McAdam 53

Attendance: 19,710

Such was the interest in this game, that the start of the match was delayed by over five minutes to allow the crowd queuing outside to enter the ground. In the end, almost 20,000 crammed in to the tight Fir Park stadium, the vast majority of the fans wearing green and white colours. Their team did not disappoint them with a performance which was in keeping with the fine weather.

The press interest before the game focussed on the Latchford brothers, who were in opposition against each other in Scotland for the first time. Peter Latchford had been Celtic's goalkeeper for a number of seasons, and Motherwell had signed Dave Latchford, who was also a goalkeeper. Football was clearly in the Latchford blood because a third brother, Bob, was a renowned England and Everton centre forward, and perhaps the most famous and successful of all three, following his record breaking £300,000 transfer to Goodison Park in 1974.

Peter Latchford was happy to see his brother come north, if only to continue their sibling rivalry. *'Dave signed for Motherwell because he knew the 'Well manager, Roger Hynd, from his days at Birmingham. I called him up the night before to warn him to get plenty of sleep as we were going to give them a beating and as it turned out we won 5-1. I wound him up as much as I could because as boys, if we weren't winding each other up we were scrapping, so it came naturally.'*

Celtic took the lead in twenty five minutes when Ronnie Glavin fired in a long range shot which Dave Latchford couldn't hold, and the ever alert Alfie Conn reacted first to score. Just before half-time the Celts were dealt a blow when Peter Marinello's shot was turned into his own net by the unfortunate Johannes Edvaldsson. Marinello was now plying his trade at Fir Park, after his heady days at Arsenal in the early years of the decade. He was transferred from Hibs to Arsenal for an enormous fee and the English press hyped him up to be a southern equivalent of George Best. Sadly, his big move did not work out, and he found himself back in Scotland, following an uneventful period at Portsmouth.

In the second half, Celtic grabbed the initiative, as Motherwell failed to cope with their movement and sharpness. In fifty minutes Roy Aitken gave Celtic the lead, when he scored with a powerful shot after Conn set him up. Celtic were in full flow, and the third goal came three minutes later when Conn crossed for Tom McAdam to score with an excellent header. This resulted in fans spilling on to park from the crammed terracing behind the goal. The spectators were then moved along the track by police and stewards to the east terracing, which looked slightly less over crowded.

Celtic smelled blood and rammed home their superiority. Aitken sent Conn clean through to score, and Conn then reciprocated for Aitken to score the fifth. So far McNeill had made no new signings and relied on the players he had inherited. This had not gone unnoticed: *'Players who struggled to maintain a dull mediocrity last season have become tigers, fighting for every ball and winning most of them.'* Glasgow Herald, 28th August 1978.

When asked what the difference was McNeill was suitably modest: *'I am not in a position to judge last season's happenings...I was at Aberdeen.'*

A good day was rounded off when it was announced that Partick Thistle had held Rangers to a scoreless draw at Ibrox. After only three league games Celtic sat on top of the table and were already four points ahead of Rangers, who had not yet managed to win a game.

Motherwell - Latchford Millar Wark Boyd Mackin Stevens Marinello Pettigrew Larnach McLaren Lindsay Subs - McLeod Sommerville

Celtic - Latchford Fillipi Lynch Aitken McDonald Edvaldsson Doyle Glavin McAdam Burns Conn Subs - Wilson, Lumsden

30 August 1978: League Cup

Dundee United	**2-3**	**Celtic**
Fleming 42		Lynch 32
Sturrock 68		MacDonald 58
		Conroy 67

Attendance: 12,648

This was a wonderfully entertaining cup tie on the tight Tannadice pitch, and the result could have gone either way right until the very end. Both sides employed a policy of all out attack from the start.

United started brightly, and Latchford made a superb one handed save to deny Fleming when he was in the clear. Stewart and Fleming both came close to scoring shortly afterwards.

Alfie Conn was again in fine form, and Celtic took the lead when he teed up Andy Lynch from a free-kick. Lynch's twenty five yard low shot grazed a United defender on its way past

McAlpine. Lynch then went from hero to villain when he conceded a penalty kick, after handling a Holt cross. Latchford then redeemed his team mate by making an excellent save from Sturrock's penalty, with Fleming slicing the rebound wide. Fleming's luck improved in forty two minutes when he touched home a Payne cross to give United a deserved equaliser. Celtic finally took the initiative in the second half and scored twice within a ten minute period. Firstly, Roddy MacDonald took advantage of confusion in the United defence, prodding the ball home to give his side the lead. Celtic then scored the goal of the night. Latchford's long clearance was headed down by McAdam to the on rushing Mike Conroy, who fairly blasted his twenty yard shot into the net. Conroy had earlier appeared as a replacement for the injured Glavin and was obviously intent on taking his opportunity to impress.

Within a minute United had reduced Celtic's lead, when Latchford could only parry Holt's shot, and Sturrock scored with the rebound. United then threw everything at the Celtic goal, and with time against them, Sturrock missed two chances to equalise. His first effort was cleared off the line by Edvaldsson, and he then missed the target at the back post. Celtic weathered the storm to take a 3-2 lead back to Parkhead for the second leg.

United's manager Jim McLean was a notoriously hard man to please, though he waxed lyrical about the entertainment on show at Tannadice. *'Some game wasn't it?.....if anyone left here tonight complaining that they didn't get value for money then I just don't know what could be done to satisfy them.'* He added, *'This tie is not over, not by a long way'* and everyone looked forward greatly to the second leg.

Dundee Utd: McAlpine Stewart Kopel Fleming Hegarty Narey Sturrock Addison Frye (Kirkwood) Holt Payne Sub: Stark

Celtic: Latchford Filippi Lynch Aitken MacDonald Edvaldsson Doyle Conroy McAdam Burns Conn (Wilson) Sub: Lumsden

Mike Conroy and Joe Filippi combine to stop Dundee United's Paul Sturrock.

League table at the end of August 1978

	P	W	D	L	F	A	Pts
Celtic	3	3	0	0	11	2	6
Aberdeen	3	2	1	0	8	3	5
St Mirren	3	2	0	1	4	2	4
Partick Thistle	3	1	2	0	2	1	4
Dundee Utd	3	0	3	0	2	1	3
Hibernian	3	0	3	0	1	1	3
Motherwell	3	1	0	2	2	6	2
Rangers	3	0	2	1	0	1	2
Hearts	3	0	1	2	2	9	1
Morton	3	0	0	3	3	8	0

CHAPTER 3 • CONSOLIDATION

2 September 1978: League Cup 2nd leg tie

Celtic   **1-0**   **Dundee United (Aggregate 4-2)**
Glavin pen 83

Attendance 30,000

Sadly, this game was a dull anticlimax after the excitement of the first leg. United's early tough tackling did not endear them to the Parkhead crowd, with Tommy Burns in particular being the focus of attention. It took some resolute defending by United to stop Celtic breaking through.

Roddy MacDonald received a nasty knock after half an hour, and eventually had to be substituted, with Roy Aitken moving back into defence, and Ronnie Glavin coming on as his midfield replacement. This seemed to knock Celtic out of their stride and United began to dictate the play without actually creating any real chances.

At the start of the second half, Celtic's frustration grew when Doyle missed a fine chance. In fifty nine minutes United were reduced to ten men when Fleming, who had previously been booked, was ordered off for a foul on McAdam. The game then sadly descended into a physical encounter, with Aitken booked for a violent charge on Hegarty, and John Holt shown a yellow card for fouling Aitken.

Celtic badly missed the subtlety of the injured Conn, but with seven minutes remaining, they were awarded a disputed penalty when Tommy Burns went down in the area in full flight. David Narey was booked for his protests. Ronnie Glavin made no mistake from the spot, as he blasted the ball past McAlpine to give Celtic a 4-2 win on aggregate.

Paul Wilson played in this game, and this was to be the last appearance in a Celtic jersey for a player who had been a fine servant for more than ten years.

Although the game was disappointing, the departing Celtic fans left in the knowledge that their team was not the easy touch they had been in the previous season. *'Celtic, without Conn, did not look as effective as they have been in recent matches, but they have got into the habit of winning and that is important for any side which has an eye on the honours.'* Glasgow Herald, 4th September 1978.

The authorities had decided to take a stance regarding the escalating bad behaviour and 'vile' chants from the terraces. Chanting at football matches at that time was vastly different from the modern day, and often related to the political situation of the time. Celtic fans were generally regarded as pro Irish Republican. Some of the chants were deemed as being particularly offensive and the club, after receiving complaints from some supporters, decided to assist the authorities in making a stand.

During the game, the police made sixty five arrests for various misdemeanours, with the full backing of the club, as the Celtic management sought to make the match day experience more pleasant for the vast majority of fans.

Celtic then looked forward to the next fixture, the derby game against Rangers. This would provide a real measure of the team's progress.

Celtic: Latchford Filippi Lynch Aitken MacDonald (Glavin) Edvaldsson Doyle Conroy McAdam Burns Wilson (McCluskey)

Dundee Utd: McAlpine Stewart Kopel Fleming Hegarty Narey Sturrock Addison Frye (Kirkwood) Holt Payne Sub: Stark

9 September 1978: Premier Division

Celtic   **3-1**   **Rangers**
McAdam 2, 76   Parlane 49
McCluskey 14

Attendance 60,000

The first Old Firm fixture of the season was always a highly anticipated affair, but this one was even more keenly awaited than usual. As both clubs had appointed new managers in old adversaries Billy McNeill and John Greig, this ensured it was to be a fascinating confrontation between the two sides who were expected to fight it out for the league title.

Celtic went into the game in fine fettle, following a nine match winning streak in which they had been scoring freely. In comparison, Rangers had yet to win a league game, and looked to be a shadow of the successful side which swept the boards domestically the previous season.

Derek Johnstone, the Rangers star striker who scored forty goals during their treble win, had a disappointing summer. He was unaccountably left out of Scotland's three games during the 1978 World Cup finals, despite being the country's most in form striker. This seemed to have an adverse affect on Johnstone, and on his return to Ibrox he demanded a transfer, only relenting when his wish to play in his preferred position of centre-half had been granted.

Many observers found this a strange move on the part of the new Rangers manager. By giving in to Johnstone's demands, Greig, who had been such an uncompromising player, could be perceived as displaying a sense of weakness, which his predecessor Jock Wallace would never have shown. As it was, Johnstone was fielded at centre-half as he requested. He was also given the Ibrox captaincy as a sweetener for staying at Rangers and declining the advances of several English clubs.

Greig had made two fairly insignificant signings since taking over at Ibrox. Billy Urquhart had joined from the Highland League club, Inverness Caledonian, for a nominal fee. Greig also signed the experienced Scottish international, Alex Forsyth, on loan from Manchester United, to fill the left-back position which Greig himself had vacated.

Rangers had impressed in pre-season by winning the Tennent Caledonian cup tournament, thrashing English first division side Southampton 4-1. Greig encouraged his side to play a more patient, fluent style of football, with Johnstone at centre-half and the capable Derek Parlane in the forward line. However, they then went on to draw two and lose one of their first three league games. Although they were known to be notoriously slow starters, the problem was a lack of goals, with Johnstone's absence in attack considered to be the main problem.

John Greig could be forgiven for being somewhat distracted as the Celtic game approached. As Scottish champions, Rangers had been drawn against Juventus in the European Cup. Italy had fielded as many as ten 'Juve' players at the World Cup finals, and not many observers gave Rangers much of a chance against the Italian champions. Greig would have had the first leg, which was due to be played on the Wednesday after the Parkhead match, firmly on his mind.

The European tie was a mouth watering prospect for Rangers. The Rangers supporters keenly anticipated watching such world class players as Dino Zoff, Gaetano Scirea, Claudio Gentile, Franco Causio and Roberto Bettega. Tickets for the home tie, at a 44,000 reduced capacity at Ibrox, were sold out well in advance. The newspapers reported that Juventus manager, Giovanni Trappatoni, had flown to Glasgow to observe the match with Celtic, during a spying mission of his Scottish opponents.

On the day of the match Celtic were hit with two huge blows, when the experienced duo of Roddy MacDonald and Alfie Conn failed fitness tests. The capable Johannes Edvaldsson would cover for MacDonald at centre-half and young George McCluskey was drafted in to replace Conn in attack. By comparison Rangers were at full strength. Greig fielded Derek Johnstone at number ten, as a dual spearhead strike force with Derek Parlane, in a concerted effort to boost Rangers' fire power.

The game was a one o'clock kick off, as the authorities made an effort to curb the intake of alcohol before the match. This was intended to cut down potential for the hooliganism and violence which tended to mar this fixture. Heavy drizzle fell in Glasgow that morning and this served to make the pitch slick, creating ideal conditions for fast passing and moving the ball quickly.

Celtic attacked from kick-off, and within seconds McCloy looked unconvincing in keeping out a John Doyle shot. Only ninety seconds had been played when Glavin fired a free-kick deep into the area. Edvaldsson flicked the ball on to Tom McAdam, who fired a fine low shot into the net. The Celtic players celebrated wildly at their early breakthrough, and the Celtic fans packed on the terraces in the 60,000 crowd joined in.

At this point Celtic were clearly on top with their aggressive, pressing style, putting Rangers off their stride. Celtic continued to push forward, and went 2-0 ahead in fourteen minutes when young George McCluskey cut in from the right hand bye line. He sent a low shot at goal, which McCloy unaccountably let skid under him at his front post in the wet conditions.

Celtic went in at half-time fully meriting their two goal lead. However, their players and fans would have been mindful that the team lost 3-2 at Ibrox, exactly a year to the day, after blowing a 2-0 half-time lead. It could be argued that they did not fully recover from the impact of that defeat for the rest of the 1977-78 season. From a psychological viewpoint it was important that they did not buckle under pressure again.

As expected, Rangers came out with all guns blazing in the second half and it was then Celtic's turn for early nerves. This allowed Parlane the chance to pull a goal back only four minutes after the restart, when he took advantage of defensive hesitancy to score. This was actually Rangers' first league goal of the season and it gave them a new lease of life. With their midfield in control they drove at Celtic. The Celtic centre-backs Edvaldsson and Aitken coped admirably with the pressure, but just when it looked inevitable that Rangers would equalise, Celtic hit them on the break.

In seventy six minutes a clearance down the Celtic right hand side saw substitute Joe Craig, and Tom Forsyth chase the loose ball. Craig got there first, but Forsyth tried to tackle him in a very clumsy manner. Craig wriggled clear to square the ball for McAdam to score his second and Celtic's third. It was an unorthodox move by Craig, but one which proved to be highly effective.

Rangers threw on their precocious winger, Davie Cooper, in an attempt to find some inspiration, and as they grew desperate the game deteriorated into a physical encounter. Alex MacDonald was booked after a confrontation with several Celtic players and was withdrawn by John Greig before he could commit any more transgressions. Following this incident, a deluge of bottles and missiles descended from the Rangers end of the stadium, and spectators fled on to the track side for safety before Police resumed order.

With time running out, Rangers made a final assault to save the game. Smith hit the Celtic bar and in the ensuing scramble Edvaldsson handled in the area and Rangers were awarded a penalty. Substitute Alex Miller took the kick, but to the joy of the Celtic fans, Latchford made a brilliant diving save to retain his side's two goal advantage. The game ended with fierce challenges from players of both sides. At the end of the game five players had been booked but, as the supporters would attest, the most important statistic was that Celtic had won by 3-1.

After the match McNeill was ecstatic at this early boost for his young team. The result gave Celtic an impressive six point lead over their old rivals after only four games played. *'I think we played all the football in the first half, got caught up a bit in the tension and excitement after the interval, but emerged as good winners.'*

For his part Greig lamented the poor start Rangers had made. *'We lost two goals in the first half and then missed a penalty. In these circumstances you can't expect to win matches.'*

The Sunday Mail commissioned ex-England manager Sir Alf Ramsey to watch the match and give his opinion in *'The Ramsey Report'*. He was scathing of the quality of the game, and said that on this display, both sides would struggle to make an impression in English football. He conveniently chose to disregard the tension that surrounds this fixture and which tends to spoil the games as footballing spectacles.

Ramsey did praise Celtic's talented midfield duo of Ronnie Glavin and Tommy Burns. He was also complimentary of Rangers' second half performance, when their passing had improved significantly. Not many fans would have paid much attention to Ramsey's comments over their Sunday breakfast, as he was never a popular figure north of the border.

For twenty one year old Mike Conroy, who had only arrived at Parkhead the previous March from junior football, this was his first appearance on the big occasion, and he recalls being surprised to play.

'I was named in the fifteen man squad on the Friday and it was a one o'clock kick-off so I arrived at the ground at quarter to eleven thinking it would be great if I got a place on the bench as a sub. In those days when you came in the door one of the back room staff gave you an envelope with a number on the postage stamp corner which indicated which number you were playing in and my envelope said eight. So I was surprised but overjoyed to be playing.

Burns (10), Aitken (4), Lynch and Craig, swamp Tom McAdam after his goal clinches victory against Rangers.

When I went into the treatment room I saw Alfie Conn lying there and discovered the reason I was playing was that he had failed a fitness test. I was to be in midfield, directly against Alex MacDonald. He was a fine player but was known to be a wee niggly guy on the field. Alfie spoke to me and told me I had to earn MacDonald's respect by fair means or foul for if I didn't he would be likely to run all over me. I ran out determined to do this and things went well so it was great advice from Alfie. The game was a blur though and I remember asking the ref how long was left and he said four minutes when I thought there was about twenty minutes remaining.'

Joe Filippi was Celtic's right-back on the day and he concurs with Conroy. *'The quickest game of my life'. It flashed by.'*

Young Conroy faced his first test and came through with flying colours. He added a bit of steel to the Celtic midfield and the soft underbelly that had been noticeable the previous season looked to have disappeared. Regardless of what would happen during the rest of the season, it was clear that McNeill's new young Celts would not be found lacking in fighting spirit.

Peter Latchford, whose penalty save had been crucial, remains remarkably modest about his heroic act. *'The penalty was at the Rangers end and I saved it low to my right. It's was a long held secret formula I had - it's what's called pick a side, shut your eyes and dive. I was just lucky that I guessed correctly.'*

Joe Craig, who created Celtic's third goal, played his last game for Celtic in this fixture. Within a matter of days he signed for Blackburn Rovers for £40,000, as Billy McNeill sought to change his squad and raise money for new players. Craig was an enormously popular player with the Celtic fans. They were sorry to see him leave, although happy that his last game had been such a memorable note to depart on.

Unsurprisingly, the early kick-off did not completely avert the hooliganism for which this fixture was infamous.

'Violence erupted at the Old Firm clash after Celtic and Rangers players were involved in a confrontation. Terracing fighting also spilled outside Parkhead. A policeman was hurt by a bottle near an exit and fights broke out in the car park. Early estimates by the police put the number of arrests at 'around one hundred' with many more being made. The 1pm kick-off aimed at stamping out drunken violence brought chaos to city shoppers caught up in the tides of green and blue which swept through streets leading to bus and railway stations. After the match supporters buses were stoned.' Evening Times, 9th September 1978.

Police reported that there were one hundred and sixty arrests and seventy people injured in the course of the match. A policeman who was seriously injured after being struck by a bottle. Glasgow's Lord Provost, David Hodge, felt forced to speak out against the actions of a violent minority, who were not only disgracing the reputations of their clubs, but the reputation of the city itself.

Celtic were then due to travel to the unusual setting of Burnley for an Anglo-Scottish cup tie, and unfortunately the hooliganism which broke out in Glasgow was soon to be seen as product which could be exported.

Celtic - Latchford, Fillipi, Lynch, Aitken, Edvaldsson, Conroy, Doyle, Glavin, McAdam, Burns (Casey), McCluskey (Craig)
Rangers - McCloy Jardine A Forsyth T Forsyth Jackson McDonald (Miller) McLean (Cooper) Russell Parlane Johnstone Smith

12 September 1978: Anglo-Scottish Cup, first leg

Burnley   1-0   Celtic
Kindon 55

Attendance: 25,000

Celtic travelled south to Lancashire to face Burnley in the Anglo-Scottish cup. They were boosted by the selection of their young midfielder, Roy Aitken, for the Scotland squad which would travel to Vienna to play Austria in a European Championship qualifier.

This was testament to Aitken's talents, as he was still only nineteen years old and had only two full seasons behind him. Yet, despite his youth, it was becoming difficult to imagine this Celtic side without him and due to his excellent form this international call up was fully deserved. Apart from Aitken, the St Mirren captain Tony Fitzpatrick was the only other uncapped player to be called up as Scotland manager Ally MacLeod attempted to inject a bit of youth into his discredited squad.

Burnley were managed by the legendary Harry Potts, who was in charge at Turf Moor for the second time. During his first period at the helm in the 1960's he managed them to notable success, winning the first division title in 1960, (then the top tier), and then incredibly taking them to the quarter-finals of the European Cup a season later.

When interviewed, Potts stated that he was a good friend of Jock Stein, but admitted he did not know much about this Celtic side. He did admire the merits of Ronnie Glavin, as he had tried to sign him from Partick Thistle in 1974, but had been beaten to the chase by Celtic. Potts was excited about the prospect of facing Celtic, and said that Burnley anticipated one of their highest attendances for years.

Potts certainly had Burnley on top form, and they were sitting fourth in the second division, (then the second tier). They were coming off the back of an excellent 3-2 home win over title favourites, West Ham United. He could boast several experienced players, notably Alan Stevenson, Peter Noble, Paul Fletcher and Steve Kindon. He had considerable back bone in his team, and also had Glasgow born midfielder Brian Hall, who had been such an influence in Bill Shankly's great Liverpool side in the early part of the decade.

The big news for Burnley was the return of their prodigal son, Leighton James, for a club record fee of £165,000. James had started his career with Burnley in 1969 and in the early 1970's he was said to have been the most talented winger in English football. He then departed for English champions Derby County in 1975, for a record British transfer fee of £310,000. A Welsh internationalist, he shone on the international scene. He played in the Wales team who were most unlucky not to qualify for the 1978 World Cup, losing out narrowly to Scotland.

Coincidentally, James was a left-winger and previously had some fantastic tussles at international level with Celtic's Danny McGrain. The Celtic captain was reported to be in line to return from injury for the game at Turf Moor. McGrain was named on the bench but did not get to reacquaint himself with James in the end.

An estimated 12,000 Celtic fans travelled to Burnley and it was clear that the majority of them had spent the day drinking heavily. As the teams took to the park there was tension in the air and there was growing concern about possible crowd disorder.

Celtic, playing in their traditional strip, but with green socks, started the game brightly with Tommy Burns and George McCluskey inspiring them into attack. The most controversial incident of the evening came when experienced English referee, Pat Partridge, refused Celtic's claims for a penalty after Leighton James had clearly fouled McCluskey in the area.

Steve Kindon gave Burnley the lead in fifty five minutes, when he exposed a lack of pace in the Celtic defence. He ran clear from half way and rounded Latchford, to score a fine goal. Near the end, Stevenson made a fine save to keep out a Tom McAdam flick, and the final whistle left Celtic to make up a one goal deficit in the return leg at Celtic Park.

This game is mostly remembered for reasons other than football and became infamously known as the *'Battle of Turf Moor'*. Drunken Celtic fans scaled railings and crossed a no man's land to get at Burnley supporters, who taunted them with chants of 'Rangers' and 'Argentina', (a reference to the dismal performance of the Scottish national team in the 1978 World Cup finals). Fierce clashes with the police followed, and police dogs had to be deployed to force Celtic fans back into their own area. They then began to throw cans and bottles on to the park, and some even managed to pull up six foot high iron railings to use as missiles.

With ten minutes left the referee withdrew the players for a short period until order was restored. The players did eventually manage to play the game to the finish. Harry Potts stated his admiration for the efforts of the Celtic players. *'But for the action of the Celtic players in appealing to their supporters the match would have been abandoned. Some of the Celtic supporters were so drunk they did not know what they were doing. As far as I'm aware we've never had crowd behaviour as bad as this at Burnley before.'*

The police were more scathing. Superintendent Joseph Henderson of Lancashire constabulary said: *'A small proportion of the fans behaved disgracefully. I know because I was kicked in the stomach through the railings and struck with a can. The violence continued afterwards in the streets and property was damaged. It will be tomorrow before we know the extent of what went on.'*

It was ironic that in the club newspaper, The Celtic View, printed on the day of the game, the Celtic directors had taken the opportunity to praise the behaviour of Celtic fans in the game against Rangers. In the end sixty people required treatment for injuries and twenty arrests were made. This was one of the darkest days in Celtic's history and it would take a long time for the reputation of the Celtic fans to recover south of the border

The English media painted a picture of rampaging Scots travelling south causing mayhem. However, the club were inundated with letters from fans saying that Burnley supporters had been let off lightly in the reporting, especially in the English press. The Celtic Supporters' Association went further by criticising Burnley police for not manning the flashpoint area of the no man's land in the enclosure. They suggested that Glasgow Police, who were far more experienced with this type of situation and big crowds in general, would have nipped any trouble in the bud, and not allowed matters to escalate.

Burnley: Stevenson Scott Brennan Noble Thomson Rodaway Cochrane Hall Fletcher Kindon James Subs: Smith Norman

Celtic: Latchford Fillipi Lynch Aitken Edvaldsson Glavin Doyle Conroy McAdam Burns McCluskey Subs:
McGrain, Baines

Burnley's Leighton James controversially fouls George McCluskey in the area at Turf Moor.

16 September 1978: Premier Division

Celtic   0-1   Hibernian
                    Temperley 25

Attendance: 25,000

Amongst the highlights in Scottish football during the 1970's were the fantastic encounters between Celtic and Hibernian, in what the newspapers used to refer to as the 'Battle of the Greens'. This was before commercialisation enabled kit manufacturers to create a plethora of hideous change strips, spoiling the aesthetics for the fans.

These encounters invariably resulted in plenty of goals, as both teams had an attacking outlook, and a host of fine players graced the fixture. For Celtic, Jimmy Johnstone, Kenny Dalglish and 'The Hammer of the Hibs' Dixie Deans had excelled. Pat Stanton, Jim O'Rourke and Alan Gordon were the most notable performers for the Hi-bees.

Both teams experienced a fair change of personnel and none of the players mentioned above remained in
1978-79. Yet the fans who rolled along to Parkhead still anticipated a rip roaring clash between the two teams. Celtic were nursing their wounds from Burnley. Hibs were in confident mood as they had beaten the Swedish side IFK Norrkoping three days before, in the UEFA cup first leg at Easter Road, by 3-2.

Hibs set out their stall from the beginning, with a disappointing defensive formation. They fielded a back five with Jackie McNamara sweeping up behind aggressive centre-backs George Stewart and Rikki Fleming. Their intention was clearly to intimidate the Celtic ball players, and Alfie Conn in particular was subjected to some ferocious tackles. It was no surprise when three Hibs players were booked in the first half, for successive bad tackles on Conn, McCluskey and Conroy. The Celtic fans, who had admired Hibs' enterprise in previous seasons, reacted to their cynical play by jeering furiously at a succession of pass backs to goalkeeper Mike MacDonald from his defenders, and the spoiling offside tactic that continued to frustrate the Celtic attack.

Hibs showed very little intent to attack but in twenty five minutes they took a shock lead. Johannes Edvaldsson attempted a pass to Andy Lynch in defence, but inexcusably gifted possession to Willie Temperley. He gleefully accepted the blunder and coolly slotted the ball past Latchford. Until then Edvaldsson had been one of Celtic's most consistent players, and the irony was that Temperley had only joined Hibs in the close season, after a free transfer from Celtic. Perhaps it was for this reason that

Temperley thought to overdo it somewhat with his excessive goal celebrations.

In the second half Celtic attacked furiously, and in fifty three minutes they were awarded a penalty when McCluskey was fouled in the area by MacLeod. The normally reliable Ronnie Glavin stepped up and blasted his shot against the post and at that point the majority of Celtic fans feared that it wasn't going to be their day.

Celtic continued to attack, with Hibs content to sit on their lead. McCluskey and Glavin came desperately close to scoring but the match finished with Hibs victorious, despite their negative set up. Celtic fans jeered loudly at full-time, not only because their side lost but because of Hibs' spoiling tactics. The tremendous sight of the battle of the greens earlier in the decade was a thing of the past. Only Arthur Duncan remained from the splendid 'Turnbull's Tornados' side of the early 1970's. Duncan, an excellent left-winger of some renown, had actually been fielded in the right-back position, in what was a total waste of his skills as an attacking player. The frustrating thing was that Hibs had talented players on the field and it was a shame to see the skills of excellent players like MacLeod, Callachan and McNamara not put to better use.

After the match Billy McNeill expressed his frustration at Hibs' tactics, especially at a time when the clubs were trying to entice spectators back to attending matches. A healthy crowd of 27,000 turned out at Parkhead but were not likely to be encouraged back after this display. For his part Eddie Turnbull blamed his defensive tactics on injuries. He claimed that all his fit players were in defence and that his team selection and tactics had reflected this.

The press were a bit more scathing in their criticism: *'These are the kind of tactics one expects from inferior side; not from a team who has a glowing history of attacking football, nor from a side who considers itself one of the foremost in the country.'* Glasgow Herald, 18th September 1978.

The only good news for Celtic fans came at full-time, when it was announced that Aberdeen had taken a point from Rangers at Ibrox, courtesy of a Dom Sullivan goal in injury time.

Because of the defensive system Hibs had honed at Celtic Park, they were able to travel to Sweden ten days later and return with a credible 0-0 draw to go through on a 3-2 aggregate win. So, for Eddie Turnbull, perhaps the end actually did justify the means.

Celtic - Latchford Fillipi Lynch Aitken Edvaldsson Glavin (Doyle) Conn Conroy McAdam Burns McCluskey Sub: Sneddon

Hibs - McDonald Duncan Smith Fleming Stewart McNamara Temperley, McLeod Rae Callachan Higgins Subs: Campbell O'Brien

23 September 1978: Premier Division

Partick Thistle   2-3   Celtic
Melrose 35   Aitken 7
Somner 39 pen   Lynch 48 pen
                        MacDonald 50

Attendance: 22,000

During midweek some of the media focus fell on the Scottish national team. The press reported on the disappointing 3-2 defeat to Austria in Vienna, and it became abundantly clear Ally MacLeod's days as manager were numbered.

However, Celtic stole the headlines that week due to the sensational signing of Kilmarnock winger Davie Provan, from Kilmarnock for £120,000. The signing was Celtic's record transfer deal, and also a Scottish record fee. Provan had been angling for a move from Rugby Park for some time and was said to be delighted with his transfer to Celtic Park.

Billy McNeill had been looking to strengthen his team since his return to Celtic. The supporters were pleasantly surprised to see their normally frugal board of directors show a bit of ambition by signing such a highly rated player, who was said to have been interesting several major clubs in England. It had long been a criticism that Celtic had not invested the £440,000 they received from Liverpool for Kenny Dalglish, and the fans were glad to see a substantial fee paid for a quality player.

Provan had been instrumental in Kilmarnock's sensational Scottish Cup replay victory against Celtic at Rugby Park the previous March. Over the two games the Celtic fans marvelled at Provan's skills on the right wing and he destroyed Celtic's left-backs, Tommy Burns and John Dowie in both games. It should be noted that both Burns and Dowie were midfielders who were playing as auxiliary left-backs, but that does nothing to detract from Provan's great performances in the two games.

Although the Kilmarnock directors stood to gain a Scottish record fee, they did nothing to make the transfer go smoothly. Celtic moved for Provan weeks previously but Kilmarnock were said to be reluctant to let their greatest asset leave. It may have been that they were waiting for a more lucrative bid from an English club which didn't materialise. Provan, who was a part-time player and also worked in a whisky bond, got wind of Celtic's offer and it was only when he threatened to withdraw from football and go full-time with his main employer, that the transfer went through.

Provan, to this day, can still recall when he first heard of Celtic's interest. *'I was still staying with my parents and the phone went and my mother said it was someone from the Weekly News, wanting an interview. I answered and this voice said that Celtic were interested in me and would I be interested in going to Parkhead. I told him I would walk there to sign and there was no problem whatsoever with me signing for Celtic. It turned out it was Celtic assistant manager John Clark, who was testing me out to see if I was prepared to come before they put a bid in.'*

The £120,000 sum was a considerable amount for Celtic to splash out on a player who was plying his trade in the second tier of the Scottish game. However this was an era when such talents as Gordon Strachan, Davie Cooper, Frank McDougall, Frank McGarvey and Billy Stark had all excelled at that level, and shown they were more than ready for a step up. It should be noted that Celtic had recouped £95,000 in transfer fees, from the sales of Paul Wilson and Joe Craig, so Celtic were well able to smash the Scottish transfer record to obtain Provan's services.

Provan only met his new team mates on the morning of his debut, as he had had been training with the youth team under Frank Connor. He was training at night to improve his fitness, whilst working his notice period with his day time employer, before becoming a full-time player at Parkhead.

22,000 fans packed into Firhill, with the Celtic support keen to see what kind of impression their expensive new signing would make on his Celtic debut. If the spectators had been disappointed by the quality of the game against Hibs, they were now to be entertained by what was to be described as the finest game of the season so far.

Provan took his place, wide on Celtic's right wing. With his curly locks, jersey hanging over his shorts and socks flailing around the ankles, he would become an instantly recognisable character on the field of play. Provan was directly up against Thistle's promising young full-back Brian Whittaker. Rangers were said to have made a £100,000 bid for him, but were turned down by Thistle a few weeks earlier.

The spectators were able to enjoy some fine autumnal weather as they watched the game. Provan made a fine start to his Celtic career in only seven minutes, when he lobbed a ball across for Roy Aitken to run on to in the area, and he made no mistake with a fine shot from twelve yards.

The match was played with the fervour of a cup tie and Thistle were keen to attack. They rightly equalised in thirty five minutes when the impressive Bobby Houston crossed for Jim Melrose to head past Latchford. Houston was obviously keen to impress, as he had been linked with a move to Celtic for a number of seasons. Four minutes later, Thistle went in front when Edvaldsson punched a Gibson header on to the crossbar, with Latchford stranded. Justice was then done when Doug Somner scored from the resultant spot kick, to give the Jags a 2-1 half-time lead.

At the start of the second half McNeill sent on Mike Conroy for George McCluskey and Celtic then found their form. In forty eight minutes Whittaker handled a Provan cross in the area and Andy Lynch made no mistake from the penalty spot. Two minutes later and the Celtic fans roared their appreciation when Lynch accepted a short corner from Conn, and sent over an excellent cross for Roddy MacDonald to score with a powerful shot past Alan Rough.

Both teams continued to attack and in eighty two minutes Donald Park was unlucky when he struck the Celtic post with a long range shot. Provan retaliated immediately and Rough made a great save from his shot, before Thistle mounted a final desperate attempt at finding an equaliser.

With minutes remaining, Somner sent in a great header from a Houston cross, which Latchford saved brilliantly. His save was said to have resembled Gordon Banks' magnificent save from Pele in the 1970 World Cup finals. If that wasn't enough, Latchford then threw himself across his goal a minute later to keep out a powerful Melrose shot, and with that Celtic had grabbed the points.

Davie Provan becomes Scotland's most expensive player after signing for Celtic in September 1978.

The media were fulsome in their praise of the talents of Houston, Park and Melrose for the Jags and Conn, Provan and Burns for the Celts. However special mention was given to both goalkeepers, Rough and Latchford, who despite losing five goals between them, played splendidly on the day.

The old cliché, 'It's Firhill for thrills', was never more apt than on this occasion.

Partick Thistle: Rough McKinnon Whittaker Campbell Marr Gibson Houston Love (O'Hara) Somner Melrose, Park Sub: McAdam

Celtic: Latchford Fillipi Lynch Aitken MacDonald Edvaldsson Provan Conn McAdam Burns McCluskey (Conroy) Sub: Lennox

27 September 1978: Anglo-Scottish Cup, second leg

Celtic	**1-2**	**Burnley (Aggregate 1-3)**
Lynch pen 68		Brennan 21
		Kindon 26

Attendance: 27,000

In the lead up to this game it was announced that Ally MacLeod had accepted Ayr United's offer to become their new manager, and thus vacate the Scotland manager's post. This presented the SFA with a huge dilemma as they considered his replacement.

MacLeod had been a victim of circumstance, with some observers subscribing to the fact that had Danny McGrain and Gordon McQueen not been injured and missed the World Cup finals in Argentina, then matters may have turned out entirely different for the likeable Ally. It was a decent argument, as both players were thought to be the best in Europe in their regular positions, and they were sorely missed during that ill fated campaign in South America.

Ally MacLeod had found himself under intolerable pressure, with criticism mounting on an almost weekly basis since Argentina. Scotland's 3-2 defeat in Vienna had been his farewell match as manager. The result is perhaps misleading, as Austria were comprehensively in control at 3-0, before two late Scottish goals gave the score an air of respectability. MacLeod and the SFA came to an agreement and Ayr United's offer gave Ally an opportunity to leave with dignity.

Before the game against Burnley, McNeill announced that Danny McGrain would finally make his long awaited come back, having been missing for almost a year through injury. McGrain had come through several reserve games, and McNeill decided the time was right to push him a bit further, with a game in the first team.

McNeill was optimistic about his side's chances of overcoming the one goal deficit. Burnley had made promising noises about coming to Glasgow to attack and a decent crowd of 27,000 turned up on the night to cheer the Celts on. With McGrain back as captain, and driving them forward early in the match, Celtic made all the running in the first twenty minutes, roared on by the Celtic support. Then the roof caved in on them.

Firstly, Roy Aitken fouled Paul Fletcher at the edge of the box. From the resultant free-kick, Ian Brennan fired in a low shot which trundled into the net past Peter Latchford. Just five minutes later, Fletcher broke free on the right and swept a low shot across goal which Latchford fumbled, and allowed the ever sharp Steve Kindon to score an easy second. It was clearly not a good night for Celtic's big English keeper against his fellow countrymen.

Celtic threw everything into attack, but did not get the goal they craved, although Lynch scraped the Burnley post with a free-kick. Edvaldsson sent a header crashing against the bar, and right on the stroke of half-time the Burnley keeper Stevenson made the save of the tie from a powerful shot by Mike Conroy. In the second half Stevenson saved a good effort from

McAdam, before Lynch finally scored from a penalty after Conn was hauled down in the area. But, as the game progressed, it became clear that Celtic were not going to overcome the deficit, despite the best efforts of the players.

At the end, McNeill was magnanimous in defeat, although he lamented the loss of Roddy MacDonald, which was said to have disrupted his defence. He then hailed the comeback of Danny McGrain, who came through the match unscathed. In truth, McNeill did not seem too concerned that his team had gone out, as this would allow him to concentrate on the Premier Division campaign, which had been his priority from the very start. It was some consolation to know that Burnley were to be the eventual winners of the competition, beating Mansfield Town in the semi-finals and then Oldham Athletic in the final.

Across Glasgow, on the same evening, the continental aristocrats of Juventus had travelled from Italy with a 1-0 first leg lead against Rangers. At Ibrox Rangers played superbly and goals from Alex MacDonald and Gordon Smith on the night gave them a 2-0 win, to take them through on a 2-1 aggregate score. Juventus, with so many experienced Italian internationalists, had been strong favourites to win. This was a stunning victory for Rangers and perhaps the best performance from a Scottish club in Europe since Celtic's win against the much vaunted Leeds United in 1970.

These were days when Glasgow Police were still content to have Celtic and Rangers play at home on the same evening. Celtic fans were tremendously subdued as they made their way home, in sharp contrast to the singing and celebrating going on amongst their rival supporters as they travelled back from Ibrox.

Celtic: Latchford McGrain Lynch Aitken Edvaldsson Conroy Provan Conn McAdam Burns Lennox Subs: Baines Glavin

Burnley: Stevenson Scott Brennan Noble Thomson Rodaway Ingham Smith Fletcher Kindon James Subs: Hall Norman

30 September 1978: Premier Division

Celtic   2-1   St Mirren
Lynch pen 35   Hyslop 81
Conn 75

Attendance: 26,000

Celtic fans could be forgiven for a feeling of trepidation before the game against St Mirren at Parkhead. During the previous season Saints had won three and drawn one of their four league meetings and had been worthy winners in both league games at Celtic Park. St Mirren had been ably managed by their fiery, ambitious manager Alex Ferguson, and it had been a great shock when the up and coming Fergie was sacked by the Saints board during the summer and replaced by the ex- St Mirren player, Jim Clunie.

Clunie continued Ferguson's good work, and his team were lying fifth in the table, having already beaten Rangers at Ibrox on the opening day. They could boast the best two prospects in Scottish football in Tony Fitzpatrick and Frank McGarvey, who were reputed to be valued at a combined figure of £500,000. A host of scouts from the major English clubs filled the Love Street stand every fortnight to watch these players. Both men were said to have leanings for Celtic when they were younger and the hope was that they would end up at Celtic Park at some point in their careers.

The Saints fielded their new goalkeeper, Billy Thomson, who had recently joined them from Partick Thistle. The Jags had been loath to lose Thomson, and had only agreed to his sale as he could not hope to displace first choice Thistle custodian, Alan Rough, who was well established as Scotland's national 'keeper. Thomson was obviously good enough to play elsewhere and St Mirren had taken advantage of the situation to sign him for a reasonable fee.

During the game it was clear to see why the young Thomson was so highly rated. He had a superb game and his athletic saves from a McAdam header and a lob from Conn were top drawer. In the first half he defied Celtic until Tommy Burns was awarded a penalty, after he was fouled by Jackie Copland in the area. Andy Lynch, who was becoming a prolific scorer, slotted home the penalty kick effectively.

With the game delicately poised in the second half, Celtic scored their second goal. Joe Filippi sent a long ball forward which Tom McAdam touched on with his head. Alfie Conn then controlled the ball, swerved past a defender and appeared to have knocked the ball too far forward. As Thomson came out, Conn managed to touch the ball past him and score from a tight angle, all in one flowing move.

It was a magnificent goal, and Conn rightly took the acclaim of the Celtic fans in the Jungle, who chanted his name in admiration. Only a special player could have scored a goal of such quality and Conn, who had been Celtic's main flair player since the start of the season, hoped that his crippling injury problems were finally over. Alfie was a throwback to the old fashioned Scottish inside forward, and was both a maker and taker of goals. It was believed that he had been signed in advance of Kenny Dalglish's departure to be the creative hub of the side, and the fans were glad to see his undoubted talent come to the fore at last.

St Mirren had disappointed in the game, but finally began to attack after Conn's goal. With nine minutes left Hyslop scored, and in the dying seconds Jimmy Bone came close to equalising, after McGarvey had created the chance. Having been in control of the game, Celtic almost threw a point away.

On the last day of September Celtic sat two points clear at the top of the league table. Billy McNeill and the players could be well satisfied with their early season efforts. It was a good start, but the problems of the previous season were soon to resurface.

Celtic: Latchford Filippi Lynch Aitken Edvaldsson Conroy Doyle Glavin McAdam Burns Conn Subs: McCluskey Lennox

St Mirren: Thomson Beckett Munro Fitzpatrick Dunlop Copland Hyslop Stark Bone Abercrombie (Richardson) McGarvey Sub: Young

League table at the end of September 1978

	P	W	D	L	F	A	Pts
Celtic	7	6	0	1	19	7	12
Hibernian	7	3	4	0	6	3	10
Aberdeen	7	3	3	1	15	7	9
Dundee Utd	7	3	3	1	10	6	9
Partick Thistle	7	2	3	2	8	8	7
St Mirren	7	3	0	4	7	8	6
Rangers	7	1	4	2	8	8	6
Morton	7	1	3	3	9	13	5
Hearts	7	1	2	4	7	16	4
Motherwell	7	1	0	6	3	16	2

CHAPTER 4 • THE MOMENTUM ENDS

4 October 1978: League Cup first leg

Celtic   0-1   Motherwell
                    Pettigrew 68

Attendance: 19,000

Motherwell came to Celtic Park without a great deal of confidence given their poor form at that time. The Steelmen were stranded at the bottom of the Premier Division, with ten points separating them from league leaders, Celtic. Given the fact that Celtic had already taken five goals off them in August, McNeill's men were bound to feel confident going into the game.

In the mid to late 1970's Motherwell had several fine players, but it was their half-back line of McLaren, McVie and Stevens which is perhaps best remembered for their robust tackling and aggressive outlook. These players were rugged and uncompromising. They played in an era where defenders were given more scope to commit hard tackles and were often given the opportunity to do so by lenient referees.

From the start this was an ill-tempered affair, as referee George Smith struggled to keep control. In one particular incident, Davie Provan literally had the jersey torn from his back by 'Well defender Jim Boyd. A photo of this made the newspapers, showing a bemused Provan standing in his shredded jersey.

Peter Latchford's brother Dave again kept goal for the 'Well and he chose this game to have his best performance so far. Celtic's forwards were also careless in front of goal and were the architects of their own downfall. Early on, Conn could not hit the target when put through clear on goal. The same player also struck the bar with a free-kick and Aitken, Burns and McAdam all wasted great chances.

Davie Provan's jersey is ripped from his back against Motherwell.

By midway in the second half Motherwell had not even managed a shot at goal. Then, on the sixty four minute mark, the game erupted after McLaren and Conn exchanged kicks when McLaren's close attention became too much for the Celtic forward. Both men were immediately ordered off and the Celtic crowd cranked up the noise in an attempt to inspire their team.

However, as often happens, Motherwell scored after constant Celtic pressure. Captain Andy Lynch was short with a pass back on the slippy surface and Willie Pettigrew nipped in to gleefully tuck the ball away past Latchford.

Late on Celtic did score through McAdam, but referee Smith disallowed it for handball against the Celtic forward. Pettigrew was a fine striker and had been the subject of much interest from bigger clubs. With his own strikers beginning to misfire, it was said that Billy McNeill was interested in purchasing Motherwell's biggest asset.

Although they lost Celtic had not played badly. Their lead up work had been excellent and the feeling was that everything could be sorted if the strikers could find their form for the second leg.

Away from Celtic, the Scottish media were reporting that Jock Stein had been confirmed as Scotland manager, after the SFA reached a settlement with Leeds United. Stein had only been in charge at Elland Road for forty four days. Leeds were said to have been disappointed to lose him but had not stood in his way of a return north.

Celtic: Latchford Filippi Lynch Aitken MacDonald Edvadsson Provan Conroy (Glavin) McAdam (McCluskey) Burns Doyle

Motherwell: Latchford Shanks Boyd Capaldi (Larnach) McVie Stevens Marinello Pettigrew Clinging (MacLeod) McLaren Lindsay

7 October 1978 Premier Division

Aberdeen　　　　4-1　Celtic
Archibald 22, 54　　　　McAdam 43
Harper pen 24
Jarvie 32

Attendance: 24,000

Celtic's visit to Pittodrie was keenly anticipated as both teams were regarded as being the most attack minded in the country, and in view of this, the game was a 24,000 all ticket sell out. Further spice was added to the fixture with Billy McNeill's first return to Pittodrie after leaving Aberdeen for Celtic. The Dons' new manager was Alex Ferguson and he and McNeill had some tremendous encounters against each other as players, particularly when Ferguson had been a Rangers striker in the late 1960's.

McNeill had built a fine side in his short time at Aberdeen and had made excellent signings in Gordon Strachan, Steve Archibald and Ian Scanlon. He had also encouraged the potential of young players Alex McLeish and John MacMaster, and although he was proud to be Celtic manager, he was known to have regretted not being able to see his good work at Pittodrie come to fruition.

Celtic were known to have an injury doubt before the game and when the teams were announced it was found that Andy Lynch had not made it. He was replaced by the inexperienced Alan Sneddon. Alfie Conn was absent through suspension and these were clearly problems McNeill could well have done without.

The game did not disappoint and was a pulsating encounter from the kick-off. Within the first eight minutes Archibald had a goal disallowed, Edvaldsson and McLelland were booked for fouls, and four players required treatment from their physios.

Aberdeen grabbed the initiative and took the lead in twenty two minutes when Latchford couldn't hold Harper's shot and Archibald was on the spot to score. Two minutes later, Harper made it 2-0 from a penalty, after Edvaldsson had scythed down Sullivan in the area. By thirty two minutes Aberdeen had an incredible 3-0 lead, when Jarvie scored with a header after Archibald had headed on a long throw by Sullivan. The Celtic defence had been static throughout and at this stage the Celts were staring at a damaging heavy defeat.

They managed to reorganise themselves and were unlucky not to have a penalty of their own when McLeish handled a Provan cross in the area, but referee JRP Gordon declined to make the award. Provan was Celtic's main inspiration, and he beat two men before setting up McAdam to score to make it 3-1, giving the huge travelling Celtic support something to cheer at last. This goal galvanised Celtic, and before half-time Leighton had to save well from an Aitken header and a Burns shot.

At half-time Glavin replaced the unfortunate Edvaldsson, with Roy Aitken required to move back into defence. When Glavin appeared on the field he was immediately booked, as the referee had been completely unaware of his appearance as a substitute.

Aberdeen still carried the most threat and it was no surprise when Harper's shot on the turn beat Latchford, allowing Archibald to tap in on the goal line. Celtic managed to hold out until full-time without suffering any further damage. The much respected Bobby Lennox came on for Tommy Burns late in the match, to huge applause for his first appearance in his second spell as a Celt.

In this game it was clear that Celtic's problems had been with their defence. *'McNeill needs a paceman in his back four. MacDonald and Edvaldsson were as slow as treacle against Archibald and Harper'.* Daily Record, 9th October 1978.

Afterwards, it emerged that Celtic assistant manager John Clark had been reported to the SFA following an altercation at half-time with referee John Gordon, in which police had seen fit to intervene and separate the two men.

Pittodrie stadium had been renovated during the summer and this was the Celtic fans first experience of the new surroundings. Although described as all seated, it should be noted that the stadium mostly consisted of benches. Some of the ground remained uncovered, which would not be ideal in Aberdeen come winter time.

Despite the result the fans got behind the team until the end, and Billy McNeill's feelings after the match had been succinct: *'I wish some of the players had the same spirit as the supporters.'*

The Celtic fans clearly made a good impression on the day: *'The memories which will live on from this match will be made up from Aberdeen's flowing attacks and those incredible Celtic fans, still singing at the end of a game when their team was totally outclassed.'* Daily Record, 9th October 1978.

Aberdeen - Leighton Kennedy McLelland McMaster McLeish Miller Sullivan Archibald Harper Jarvie Strachan Subs: Scanlon Fleming

Celtic - Latchford Filippi Sneddon Aitken MacDonald Edvaldsson (Glavin) Provan Conroy McAdam Burns (Lennox) McCluskey

11 October 1978: League Cup, second leg

Motherwell	1-4	Celtic (Aggregate 2-4)
Marinello 76		McAdam 17, 32
		Aitken 83
		Lennox 87

Attendance: 17,911

Before the game, Billy McNeill rallied the troops by praising the Celtic fans for their tremendous vocal support in Aberdeen. He called on his players to play as they had done in the first leg, but this time to finish off their fine outfield play with goals.

Backed once again by a large following, Celtic attacked Motherwell from the start and they wiped out their one goal deficit in seventeen minutes. Provan made a sparkling run down the right flank, and fired over a fierce cross which Tom McAdam superbly bulleted into the Motherwell net with his head.

This goal gave Celtic tremendous confidence and they went in front on aggregate in thirty two minutes. McAdam was again the goal scorer, with a vicious shot from the edge of the area, after referee Brian McGinlay had done well to play advantage, when Conn had been fouled in the build up to the goal.

Tommy Burns had been fielded in the unusual role of left back, and was given a torrid time by the experienced winger, Peter Marinello. It was Marinello who was to be the main figure on the field in the second half. Firstly, he had the chance to level the tie but missed a penalty. The drama continued when he recovered his composure to score with his next opportunity, to make it 2-2 on aggregate with just fourteen minutes remaining.

Provan was maintaining his excellent form, and he crossed for Aitken to storm into the area and power home the goal which gave them the lead on the night, much to the delight of the thousands of Celtic fans packed into the tight Fir Park ground.

Alfie Conn was injured and was replaced by veteran Bobby Lennox. Much had been made in the press of Celtic's marvellous record of fourteen successive appearances in League Cup finals, going back to 1964. Lennox had just started out on his Celtic career back then, and it was only fitting that he scored the decisive goal, bringing Celtic to their fifteenth consecutive final. He scored with a low shot after Provan had made the opening, and it showed the wee man's popularity when he was swamped by happy players after scoring, and the fans joyfully chanted his name in praise.

Joe Filippi gets in a challenge against Motherwell at Fir Park.

Billy McNeill had pondered over asking his old pal Lennox to rejoin him at Parkhead. He originally intended that Bobby assist the younger players in the reserves, but in view of the relatively small squad at his disposal he had no alternative but to utilise his talents in the first team.

For his part, Lennox had shown his old team mate and new manager that he was still able to make a contribution to the team. The last of the Lisbon Lions still had a roar in him yet, and he was to be a huge influence on the young players in the Celtic ranks in the months ahead. Celtic midfielder Mike Conroy had been a huge fan of Lennox in his schooldays and he recalls a story of how popular wee Bobby was at his peak. *'When I was nine or ten my pal and I looked up 'R.Lennox, Saltcoats' in the phone book and we phoned the number up and actually got through to his home but Bobby wasn't there. We said to his wife that we were calling to ask for training tips but she said he was out at training. I never had the nerve to tell Bobby that story when I started playing alongside him.'*

Motherwell - Latchford Carr (MacLeod) Wark McLaren McVie Stevens Marinello Pettigrew Larnach (Kennedy) Clinging Lindsay

Celtic - Latchford Filippi Burns Aitken MacDonald Edvaldsson Provan Conroy McAdam Glavin Conn (Lennox) Sub: McCluskey

14 October 1978: Premier Division

Dundee United   1-0   Celtic
Kopel 2

Attendance: 17,700

Bobby Lennox is swamped after scoring against Motherwell at Fir Park.

Celtic had an injury crisis for the difficult trip to Tannadice with McGrain, Lynch, Glavin and Doyle all ruled out through injury. Tommy Burns continued as an auxiliary left-back, and Bobby Lennox made his first full appearance since his return from America.

United caught Celtic cold at the start, and the only goal of the game came on the sixty seconds mark when right back Ray Stewart set up his full-back partner Frank Kopel to score with a firm shot. All this before several Celtic players had even touched the ball.

It was a fine open game with United having the edge, and if the Tannadice strikers had been on form then a repeat of the previous Saturday's debacle at Pittodrie may have been on the cards. Late in the game Celtic pushed Edvaldsson up front, and although matters improved slightly, they could not grab an equaliser.

For a few seasons Jim McLean had been in the process of building an excellent side at Tannadice and it was now felt they were ready to live up to their potential. He had a band of fine young players at his disposal, including David Narey, Graeme Payne, Ray Stewart, Paul Sturrock, Davie Dodds and Billy Kirkwood.

United's master stroke was to play the superb Narey further forward in midfield, rather than in his normal role as sweeper alongside Paul Hegarty. Narey had a fair old tussle with Roy Aitken, who had performed well for Celtic, and this had not gone unnoticed:

'The brightest features were the five star studded displays of two young men who are fast breaking through as Scotland caps – United's Dave Narey and Celtic's Roy Aitken....they are super athletes, tall, powerful, towering and, dare I forecast, it won't be long until they are playing together in Scotland's blue.' Evening Times, 16th October 1978.

United's victory had pushed them level on twelve points at the top of the table with both Hibs and Celtic. Despite this defeat, Celtic were in outright top position due to goal difference, but it was clear that this league race was going to be a close run thing even at this early stage of the season.

Dundee Utd: McAlpine Stewart Kopel Fleming Hegarty Narey Smith Sturrock Payne Kirkwood Addison Subs: Robinson Dodds

Celtic: Latchford Filippi Burns Aitken MacDonald Edvaldsson (Mackie) Provan Conroy McAdam Conn (McCluskey) Lennox

21 October 1978: Premier Division

Celtic   0-0   Morton

Attendance: 24,000

Before the game the new Scotland manager, Jock Stein, took his seat at Parkhead. He was given a standing ovation by the patrons in the main stand, who were still hugely apprecievative of his efforts as Celtic manager over the previous thirteen years.

Stein was sure to have noted the form of Morton sensation Andy Ritchie, who was taking the Premier Division by storm. He had already scored ten goals that season, as Morton gave him a free role on the park in an attempt to maximise his talents - and what a talent he was. He was particularly able in dead ball situations, and had a powerful shot when given sight of the goal.

On the down side, Ritchie was economical with his effort on the park and this was thought to be his major failing. Stein would no doubt have recalled that he sent Ritchie to Cappielow in October 1976, in exchange for Morton goalkeeper Roy Baines. It was said that Stein had eventually tired of Ritchie's lacklustre attitude but the move to the tail of the bank had given Ritchie a new lease of life. Ritchie was now keen to make an impression on his return to Parkhead, especially with Stein now watching from the stand.

No one could deny that Andy Ritchie had enormous talent and there were many Celtic fans who lamented the fact that he was allowed to leave, believing that a place in the team should have been found for his touch and technique. Indeed, Ritchie himself admitted in later years that he hadn't showed the desired commitment to make a success of his career at Parkhead.

Because of a clash of colours, Celtic ran out wearing their new change strip, which was the first time their fans had witnessed them in it. Their smart green tops were made of a modern satin style material, and had a white collar with white diamond piping down the side of the sleeves, identifying the manufacturers as Umbro. The shorts were white with green diamond piping at the side, and the socks green with white diamond piping.

This was a further example of Celtic moving into the modern era and improving their marketing. The new strip had the club badge in the middle of the jersey and the strip was now an official club product to be sold in the club shop. It was only twelve months previously that the club badge had been put on the traditional hooped shirts for the first time, resulting in a storm of protests to the club newspaper. Many traditionalists objected to anything being put on their beloved hoops, even the club badge. However, this new change strip was to find favour with the fans and became hugely popular, particularly with younger supporters.

Celtic were missing first choice full-backs McGrain and Lynch, together with their creative hub of Glavin and Conn, all out through injury. They struggled to make an impression on the Morton defence throughout the game, although McAdam struck the crossbar with a header. Late on, referee Dougie Ramsey infuriated the Parkhead crowd by denying Celtic two reasonable penalty claims, one for handball against Davie Hayes and the other after Evans looked to have tripped McCluskey in the area. Yet it had taken a magnificent save by Latchford to save the day, when the man of the moment, Ritchie, struck a tremendous shot which looked net bound all the way, only for the Celtic keeper to make a great one handed save. This was in sixty nine minutes and it would have been a long way back for the Celts had his shot gone in. Celtic ran out of ideas and lacked creativity. At full-time the majority of fans stood in mute disbelief at another lacklustre performance, although it was hardly surprising that some voiced their displeasure. The fine form of August and September was now a fading memory, and it was only through the good fortune of other results that Celtic remained top of the table on goal difference.

The fans were desperate for more new faces to join the impressive Davie Provan but Billy McNeill refused to be rushed. *'I have said all along that everything could not be sorted out after a few months….if we do move into the transfer market again it will be after careful consideration and in the knowledge that we are getting better than we already have. I will be selective.'* Glasgow Herald, 23rd October 1978.

Celtic then announced they were in talks with crisps manufacturer Smith's over the possibility of sponsorship for the league game against Aberdeen on 9th December. The newspapers made much of Smith's being the firm who produced those crisps with the *blue* bag, but Desmond White confirmed that they were speaking to the company and that the club were actively seeking companies to sponsor future games. These were changing times and the Celtic board were obviously keen to explore new ways of increasing their revenue streams.

Newspapers also reported that Celtic had bid £100,000 for Carlisle's uncompromising Scots centre-half, Ian McDonald. Billy McNeill would not actually name McDonald, the former St Johnstone player, but did confirm that Celtic had bid for an Anglo-Scot, and that no deal would be reached before the Hearts game at Tynecastle.

Celtic - Latchford Fillipi Sneddon Aitken MacDonald Edvaldsson Provan Conroy McAdam Burns (McCluskey) Lennox Sub: Mackie

Morton - Connaghan Hayes Holmes Evans Orr Rooney Russell Miller Thomson Scott Ritchie Subs: Hutchison McNeil Subs: Hutchison McNeil

28 October 1978: Premier Division

Hearts   **2-0**   **Celtic**
Busby 52, 68

Attendance: 19,000

The Hearts match had an earlier kick-off of 2pm, in an effort by the Tynecastle club and the police to avoid any crowd trouble. A fence had been newly erected around the ground in order to prevent spectators from gaining access to the field of play, and strict segregation was now in place inside the ground to keep the rival sets of fans apart, a sight that was to remain in UK football stadiums until the tragic events of Hillsborough in 1989. Traditionalists lamented this new arrangement and recalled happier times when the respective spectators stood together without any commotion.

With Hearts lying second bottom of the table and having failed to win at home in the league so far, Celtic should have been optimistic about their chances. They played reasonably well in a goalless first half and were unlucky not to have been in front after Hearts' keeper Ray Dunlop made two tremendous saves from Joe Filippi and Alfie Conn. There was certainly little indication of the second half collapse that was to follow.

After the break Hearts' midfielders Cammy Fraser and Eamonn Bannon became the most influential players on the field. In fifty two minutes they combined to create a shooting chance for Drew Busby, who cracked a tremendous shot high past Latchford to give Hearts the lead.

In sixty five minutes Hearts' winger Malcolm Robertson was ordered off after a touchline altercation with Andy Lynch, in which he appeared to strike the Celtic man. Referee Bob Valentine consulted his stand side linesman before producing the red card for Robertson, to much protest from Hearts players. With Hearts down to ten men, this gave Celtic an ideal opportunity to fight their way back into the game.

However, Celtic self-destructed and Hearts grew stronger. The Tynecastle men were obviously fortified by their perceived injustice over Robertson's departure. In sixty eight minutes Hearts delivered their 'coup de grace', when Busby scored again. This time the goal was preventable, as Peter Latchford allowed Busby's hopeful, dipping shot to slip under his body, to the obvious delight of the Hearts fans massed behind his goal. This was a tragedy for the big English keeper who, until then, had given a faultless performance.

As time ran out Celtic became desperate and lost their shape. Aitken ran energetically until the end, and Provan and Conn tried hard to create something, but without success. Celtic were all aggression in the closing stages and Conn did manage to score with three minutes left, only to be flagged for offside. If anything, that one incident seemed to sum up Celtic's day. The only bonus for the team was that the fans had still not turned against them. Throughout the game they had tried their best to inspire the players with their encouragement, but as the game closed out there was a mute acceptance of their fate.

'The eerie silence of their terracing legions was a damning testament. Rarely have so many been silent for so long…and with good reason.' Glasgow Herald, 30th October 1978.

After the game, McNeill could no longer hide his anger and he was keen to reassure the supporters that players who settled for second best would no longer be tolerated. He was damning in his indictment.

'There were some players who looked as if they were just along for the ride. If they want to remain Celtic players they will have to contribute – it is as simple as that…..we have too many players just not good enough to play for Celtic and wear that jersey. Were they all fit? Fit...the only way my players could have got hurt was falling out of the bath.'

Davie Provan recalls McNeill lambasting the players afterwards, but the manager also had the presence of mind not to discourage his new signing:

'Billy slaughtered us after that game publicly and privately although I played well that day. In fact Billy came up to me on the Monday and said anything you read in the papers you can disregard it, you did well just keep playing that way and you'll be alright.'

Despite their run of poor form, Celtic still had the small consolation of remaining in second place, two points behind leaders Dundee United. In a ten team league only five points separated the top nine teams, with many observers reckoning that this was the finest league race Scotland had seen for many years.

But, if Celtic were to remain in that league race, then their results, and performances, would have to improve significantly.

Hearts: - Dunlop Brown Jefferies McNicoll Liddell Fraser (Tierney) Gibson Bannon O'Connor Busby Robertson Sub: McQuade

Celtic: - Latchford Filippi Lynch Aitken MacDonald Edvaldsson Provan Conn McAdam Burns (Mackie), McCluskey Sub: Sneddon

League table at the end of October 1978

	P	W	D	L	F	A	Pts
Dundee Utd	11	5	5	1	15	8	15
Celtic	11	6	1	4	20	14	13
Hibernian	11	4	5	2	12	10	13
Rangers	11	3	6	2	12	10	12
Aberdeen	11	4	3	4	21	14	11
Partick Thistle	11	4	3	4	12	12	11
St Mirren	11	5	1	5	12	12	11
Hearts	11	3	4	4	12	18	10
Morton	11	3	4	4	13	16	10
Motherwell	11	2	0	9	8	24	4

CHAPTER 5 • A WINTER OF DISCONTENT BEGINS

4 November 1978: Premier Division

Celtic   **1-2**   **Motherwell**
McAdam 12   Stevens 38
                             McLaren 81

Attendance: 21,000

After the Tynecastle debacle, Celtic fans were delighted to see the club sign the promising twenty year old Dumbarton midfielder, Murdo MacLeod, for a considerable fee of £100,000. MacLeod was a much sought after prospect, with many English sides hovering in the back ground, and the feeling was that Celtic had done well to acquire him. He was reported to be a robust midfielder, who was a good passer of the ball, with a rocket shot in either foot.

On the other hand, the offer for Carlisle's Ian McDonald ended in acrimony with the English side declining Celtic's £100,000 offer, and stating it was their intention to report Celtic to the authorities. They maintained they had not received an official approach and that the player had learned of Celtic's bid before his club had. This was strenuously denied by McNeill, who said that Carlisle's manager Bobby Moncur had been kept informed of Celtic's intentions at all times.

Newspaper reports indicated that McNeill had also been close to signing Spurs' Scots midfielder Neil McNab, but he opted to sign for Bolton Wanderers for £250,000. However, McNeill was happy with his new purchase. *'It's no longer a case of old favourites getting their places....there will now be competition, genuine competition.'*

McNeill called a team meeting earlier in the week to personally make his displeasure known to the players in no uncertain terms. He had no doubt considered dropping certain players in an attempt to show that declining levels of performance would not be tolerated, but with such a small squad at his disposal his options were limited.

It was, however, a major surprise when his team to face Motherwell was announced, to find that goalkeeper Peter Latchford had been dropped, with Roy Baines taking his place. Baines hadn't played a game for Celtic since April 1977 and had actually asked for a transfer only a few weeks earlier, in order to play regular first team football. His request had been granted by the club. Latchford had blundered at Tynecastle but he had still been one of the team's most consistent performers, and he could consider himself unlucky to take the fall for the Hearts defeat.

Ex-Celt Paul Wilson made a quick return to Celtic Park after his move to Motherwell, and having given the club ten years of good service he was given a warm welcome by the Celtic supporters. As a mark of the man, just before the game started, Wilson ran across to the young debutant Murdo MacLeod to shake his hand and wish him all the best in his new Celtic career. This was a tremendous gesture by Wilson and was greatly appreciated by the new Celt and the Parkhead crowd. Motherwell were rooted at the foot of the league with only four points and manager Roger Hynd had recently been sacked. Assistant manager John Hagart had taken the team to Celtic Park as interim manager, as the 'Well board debated over the merits of a new appointment.

Celtic started strongly, obviously keen to make amends for poor results. They took the lead in twelve minutes, when Tom McAdam scored. New signings Provan and MacLeod combined to set up the chance for the Celtic striker, who scored with a powerful header for a fine goal. McAdam had represented the Scottish League against the Irish League the previous midweek, as a testament to his fine form for his club. In the first half he could have claimed four goals and only a mixture of bad luck and careless finishing had prevented him from doing so.

Motherwell came into the game as the first half progressed, although they had the ever dangerous Willie Pettigrew wasted in an unusual midfield role. Pettigrew actually set up Wilson to score, but the goal was disallowed for a marginal offside decision. Celtic did not heed the warning and in thirty nine minutes 'Well equalised when Wilson, revelling on his return to his old stomping ground, set up Gregor Stevens to score from close in. Stevens was arguably the best man on the park, with his reading of the game in defence and ability to break into attack from the back. It was rumoured that McNeill strongly fancied the Motherwell defender as a future Celt.

Celtic attacked throughout the second half but became increasingly desperate as the game wore on, and lost their shape as they chased the game. There was an air of predictability in eighty one minutes, when Pettigrew set up Stewart McLaren for a late winning goal.

Disappointment reigned again at Parkhead, although Celtic's new midfielder had made a fine impression in his first game. *'MacLeod tired in the second half but his early play brought a lot of satisfaction to Parkhead fans, in particular his ability to split the Fir Park defence with passes from midfield.'* Glasgow Herald 6th November 1978.

'Celtic came in like lions but went out like lambs.' Sunday Express, 5th November 1978.

Statistics often throw up little curiosities and this is a decent trivia question - Which opposition team won the most games at Celtic Park during the 1970's? Rangers had a poor record at Parkhead and that discounts them, so you may then think of the likes of Hibs or Aberdeen who both had fine teams during that era.

The answer to this poser is actually Motherwell, who can boast an astonishing seven victories on Celtic's home soil, all achieved within the period October 1973 to November 1978. With the 'Well still rooted to the foot of the table even after their latest win, Celtic fans were hoping they would not remain around for much longer to inflict even more damage on their team.

Staying with a statistical theme, only Aberdeen had scored more goals than the Celts, but only bottom team Motherwell had lost more. The only plus point on the day was that Rangers indifferent league form continued, as they lost 2-1 to Partick Thistle at Firhill.

Celtic - Baines Sneddon Lynch Aitken MacDonald Edvaldsson Provan, MacLeod McAdam Burns Conn Subs: McCluskey Casey

Motherwell - Rennie Carr Wark McLaren McVie Stevens Marinello Pettigrew Larnach Clinging (Lindsay) Wilson Sub: Shanks

8 November 1978: League Cup Quarter-Final, first leg

Montrose   1-1   Celtic
Hair 23   Lynch pen 28

Attendance: 3,872

The draw for the League Cup quarter-finals paired Celtic up against first division side Montrose. Celtic travelled to the tiny Links Park ground for their first competitive game since 1939, although it was ironic that Billy McNeill's first game as manager was a friendly at that very ground in late July.

With Celtic having won only one of their last seven games, the Montrose manager, Kenny Cameron, made optimistic noises about his team's chances on the night. Ronnie Glavin was required to replace Murdo MacLeod, who was cup tied from his days at Dumbarton.

The score line may give the misapprehension that this was a close game, but this was far from the case. Celtic attacked from the start, but it was Montrose who struck first. Edvaldsson partially cleared a cross ball and the ex Aberdeen player, Ian Hair, sent a fine lob over Roy Baines and into the net.

The influential Davie Provan was carried off injured early on, and Celtic were fortunate to have an ideal replacement in winger John Doyle. In twenty seven minutes Doyle anticipated a pass back from Lowe, and Montrose keeper Dave Gorman had to bring down Doyle in the area to prevent him from scoring. Andy Lynch dispatched the resultant penalty and the Celts were level.

After that, the amount of Celtic pressure on the Montrose goal bordered on the ridiculous, and Celtic had four goals disallowed, the worst being when Roy Aitken's effort was chalked off for a mysterious infringement. There were also two decent penalty claims for hand ball which would have been awarded on another day. Late in the game Montrose were happy to string every player along the eighteen yard box, in a desperate bid to hold out, but although the game was fiercely competitive, there was no malice from either team.

Celtic fans leaving Links Park may have allowed their thoughts to turn towards their next game, against Rangers. Celtic had only one victory in their previous eight games and Glasgow bookmakers gave odds on a Celtic victory at 9/4, which was a fair reflection on their poor form. Rangers were clear favourites at 11/10, and the game was not a pleasant prospect for those who favoured the green and white.

Montrose: Gorman Lowe B D'Arcy Ford D D'Arcy Taylor McIntosh (Georgeson) Robb Livingston Hair Miller Sub: Murray

Celtic: Baines Filippi Lynch Aitken MacDonald Edvaldsson Provan (Doyle) Glavin (Casey) McAdam Burns McCluskey

11 November 1978: Premier Division

| **Rangers** | **1-1** | **Celtic** |
| Forsyth pen 55 | | Lynch 52 |

Attendance: 52,330

Since the first Old Firm clash in September, Rangers had eliminated the much vaunted Juventus from the European Cup, and were rewarded with another glamour clash against the Dutch champions PSV Eindhoven. Although not as famous as their Dutch counterparts, Ajax and Feyenoord, PSV were stiff opposition and were strong favourites to go through to the quarter-finals. This was largely due to the quality of several of their players, who had given impressive performances for the Dutch national team in the World Cup finals.

The Van De Kerkhof twins, Van Kraay, Lubse, Poortvliet and Brandts had all enhanced their reputations in South America, with some wonderful performances for Holland, and the feeling was that PSV would be too strong for Rangers, especially when the first leg at Ibrox ended in a dull 0-0 draw.

In Eindhoven Rangers played a clever tactical game of sitting in and hitting on the break. They also showed great resolve in twice coming back from a goal down, particularly after Lubse had opened the scoring for PSV within the first minute. With only three minutes remaining, and the score at 2-2, Rangers were destined to go through on away goals. PSV were hammering away looking for a decisive winning goal. Rangers won possession, with Tommy McLean cleverly holding the ball in the centre of the pitch, until Bobby Russell made a forty yard sprint from midfield. McLean then released a perfect pass for Russell to run on to, and he tucked the ball past the PSV goalkeeper. Rangers were through to the quarter-finals and they thoroughly deserved to be. It was a sensational effort and the winner was arguably the greatest goal ever scored by a Rangers player.

It's no exaggeration to say that this result sent shockwaves throughout Europe. Rangers had beaten two of the sides who were favourites to lift the European Cup, and with the holders Liverpool having been defeated by an inexperienced Nottingham Forest team, there was no one left in the competition that Rangers needed to fear. This was the best result from a Scottish club playing away in Europe for many a long year. The notable PSV coach, Kees Rijvers, had been forced to comment that the Rangers' victory had been a revelation to him, *'because they played imaginative and stylish football, the likes of which I didn't expect from a British side.'*

John Greig gained himself a reputation as a fine tactical manager, and the esteemed football journalist Brian Glanville raved about Rangers victories over the Italian and Dutch champions. Previously, under Jock Wallace, Rangers had a reputation for a direct style of play, but Greig had changed that totally and had them playing a patient game of possession with swift breaks from midfield, perfectly illustrated by Russell's wonder goal in Eindhoven.

Although their domestic form had been patchy, Rangers went into the game against Celtic as strong favourites. The game was to be played at Hampden Park due to renovation work taking place at Ibrox, as the new Copland Road stand was in the process of being built. As with all Old Firm clashes of the period, there was an early kick-off at 1pm, in an effort to minimise the risk of drunken behaviour amongst the all ticket crowd.

Celtic fielded an inexperienced side with Baines, Filippi, Provan, MacLeod and McAdam, all playing at Hampden for the first time in a Celtic jersey. Despite their poor form, Billy McNeill was publicly optimistic and promised to take the game to Rangers. He was true to his word.

There was a contrast in styles throughout. Celtic fielded two wingers in Provan and Doyle and they were a constant threat in the wide areas. Rangers opted for their European containing game, but were nonetheless dangerous with quick counter attacks. There was slight confusion for the spectators when John Greig sent out Jardine at number two, Johnstone at number five and Miller at number eleven. When they actually lined up, Jardine played as sweeper, Johnstone was up front as centre forward and Miller was at right back.

Celtic had enjoyed the better of the play in the first half, and opened the scoring in fifty two minutes when Andy Lynch played a beautiful one-two with Murdo MacLeod, and strode through to score with a low shot. Celtic fans were still noisily celebrating, when Edvaldsson punched the ball away on the goal line from a Johnstone header. It had looked as if the ball was going over the bar, and Edvaldsson may have blundered, but Alex Forsyth took full advantage to score with the resultant penalty.

After the goals, both sides had chances to win the match within seconds of each other. Firstly, McCloy fumbled a cross after a great run by Doyle, and with several Celts waiting to pounce, McCloy was fortunate to retrieve the ball right on his goal line. Then, at the other end, Kenny Watson shot past from inside the area when it seemed certain he would score.

Honours were even at the end. The game had generally been played in a good spirit, although Celtic were angry that Miller only received a booking for a waist high assault on Doyle, as the Celtic winger was tearing in on goal in the second half.

This game was remarkable for the change in fortunes for John Doyle. After the arrival of Davie Provan in September, there had been speculation that Doyle would move on, as he was seen to be surplus to requirements. Perhaps he felt that he was fighting for his Celtic career, as this game was easily his best performance in the Hoops for some considerable time, and many observers rated him as the man of the match. He had spent a fair time on the sidelines waiting for his chance, and he grabbed it. He also showed his versatility, by giving Celtic balance on the left hand side of the field, with Provan now the more popular choice on the right flank.

This game had given Billy McNeill some respite. It may not have been a victory, but the team had risen well to the challenge of the big occasion, and McNeill seemed satisfied with the outcome at the end. *'I could sense yesterday talking to the lads that there was a certain air of confidence about them and they showed that today.'* Evening Times, 11th November 1978.

Rangers - McCloy Jardine A Forsyth T Forsyth Johnstone MacDonald McLean Russell Smith Watson Miller Subs Parlane Cooper

Celtic - Baines Filippi Lynch Aitken MacDonald Edvaldsson Provan MacLeod McAdam Burns Doyle Subs Lennox Casey

15 November 1978: League Cup Quarter-Final, second leg

Celtic	**3-1**	**Montrose (aggregate 4-2)**
McAdam 5		Georgeson 54
Lynch pen 11		
Edvaldsson 37		

Attendance: 10,000

Danny McGrain's recuperation from injury had been an exasperatingly slow process. Although McGrain played against Burnley at the end of September, Billy McNeill had refused to rush his captain back too soon and chose to heed the medical advice that he had been given, that Danny should come back slowly and carefully.

It was with great satisfaction that McNeill announced that Danny would not only return to the side against Montrose, but would also take his rightful place as captain. He was quick to point out that this was no slight against right-back Joe Filippi, who had been in fine form, or of Andy Lynch, who had proved to be a capable captain in Danny's absence. But, when a player of the calibre of Danny McGrain came back to fitness, then he had to play.

A meagre crowd of 10,000 turned out on a night of cold weather which was described by one hack as 'despicable'. Within the first minutes McGrain had a fine start and raised the spirits of the supporters with two great crosses into the area. In only five minutes he started the move that led to Tom McAdam scoring, after defender Denis D'Arcy had miskicked.

The outcome of the game was never in any danger after that. By half-time Celtic had scored again, from a Lynch penalty after Doyle was brought down, and then through an Edvaldsson header. In the second half there was little of note as Celtic went down the gears, apart from Georgeson scoring a consolation goal. The good news was that McGrain came through unscathed, although he would not be needlessly hurried along.

This game took Celtic through to their fifteenth consecutive League Cup semi-final and in the draw the next day they came out of the hat against Rangers. Another thrilling chapter in the season awaited them at Hampden Park on 13th December.

Celtic: Baines McGrain Lynch Aitken MacDonald Edvaldsson Provan Casey McAdam (McCluskey) Lennox Doyle Sub: Filippi

Montrose: Gorman Lowe B D'Arcy Ford D D'Arcy Hair McIntosh Robb Georgeson Walker Livingston (Murray) Sub: Taylor

18 November 1978: Premier Division

Hibernian   2-2   Celtic
Hutchison 31   Provan 39
Callachan 83   MacLeod 81

Attendance: 22,000

After the 1978 World Cup finals there had been an influx of foreign players appearing in English football. The Argentinian pair of Ardiles and Villa had been an outstanding success with Tottenham Hotspur, and others sought to copy Spurs' lead. Tarantini (Birmingham), Deyna (Man City) and the Dutch pair of Muhren and Thijssen (Ipswich), all arrived to play in England, with mixed results.

Hibernian were the first Scottish club to attempt to go foreign with their Norwegian pair of Isak Refvik and Svein Matheison. Both players were making their league debuts for Hibs against Celtic, which was sure to put a few thousand on the gates at Easter Road on the day. Mathieson was said to be a skilful midfielder and Refvik a hard working striker. Hibees' fans hoped these new faces would give their team a new dimension from the dismal days of September, when they had stolen two points from Celtic with an ultra defensive display.

There was a bright start to the game, with both teams happily showing their commitment to attack. Provan went on a tremendous run down the Celtic right flank in which he beat four defenders, but couldn't deliver a precise cross at the end. Hibs replied with a good move of their own in which their two new Scandinavian imports combined to set up Des Bremner, who shot wastefully high over the bar.

Hibs soon settled, and in thirty one minutes McNamara played a fine long ball over the Celtic defence for Hutchison to chase. As Edvaldsson moved to cover, Roy Baines came out to collect the ball and as both Celtic men dithered, they allowed Hutchison to nick the ball from them and slide the ball into the net. It was a disastrous goal for Celtic to lose.

Celtic responded well and equalised within eight minutes. Young George McCluskey was the architect, and he showed deft footwork, beating one defender and then cutely lobbing the ball over another Hibs player, for Davie Provan to score with a well struck volley. It was a goal full of invention and opportunism, brilliant in its creativity and swift in its execution.

In the second half Hibs were kicking down the slope and forced Celtic back. All the action was around Baines' goal mouth, but Hibs could not break through, although they almost did when Lynch came to Celtic's rescue by clearing a Refvik effort ball from his own goal.

The energetic Roy Aitken managed to bring Celtic upfield at last, with some surging runs through the middle of the park. Celtic protested vigorously for a penalty after Duncan handled at the near post. It should have been a penalty, but Duncan's ruse to lie prostrate holding his abdomen, had the desired effect for Hibs, and no award was given. From the resultant corner the ball was cleared to Murdo MacLeod twenty five yards out. He had already been thwarted twice by Hibs' keeper McDonald, but this time he was not to be denied. He fired a glorious shot high into the Hibs net, behind that goal where the majority of the Celtic support were situated. This kind of power shooting was to become MacLeod's trademark and he was to entertain the Celtic fans with many such goals in the coming years.

Sadly Celtic could not keep hold of their lead. In eighty three minutes Ralph Callachan scored a goal to match MacLeod's, when he ran across the edge of the Celtic area before swivelling and hitting a marvellous high shot, which gave Baines no chance of saving. The last two goals had been worth the admission money alone, both being spectacular efforts.

Honours were even at the end and both sets of fans in the 22,000 crowd left relatively happy. Billy McNeill was glad to see the Celtic fans had taken to their new players, Provan and MacLeod, and there had been perfect symmetry in that they had both scored their first goals for the hoops with tremendous shots. However, it was another of Celtic's youngsters who stood out most.

'My man of the match was Roy Aitken, whose skill now almost matches his strength, whose surging raids brought back memories of Duncan Edwards, whose inspiration is that of Bobby Evans. In a match where there were more incidents than in a Western, where it was so often hell for leather, Aitken was immense.' Glasgow Herald, 20th November 1978.

Quite a compliment indeed for the young Roy.

Hibs: McDonald Duncan Smith Bremner Fleming McNamara Mathieson MacLeod Refvik Callachan Hutchison Subs: Higgins Rae

Celtic: Baines Filippi (Casey) Lynch Aitken MacDonald Edvaldsson Provan MacLeod McAdam McCluskey (Lennox) Doyle

25 November 1978: Premier Division

Celtic   1-0   Partick Thistle
McAdam 47

Attendance 26,000

In midweek, a Celtic side travelled to London to take part in the annual Daily Express five a side tournament in the Wembley arena, where they were represented by the six man contingent of Latchford, McGrain, Lumsden, Casey, Lennox and Mackie.

The competition itself was a simple knock out format, the highlights of which were shown on Sportsnight that night. In their first match Celtic defeated Millwall 3-2, through two goals from Lennox and one from McGrain. However in the next round the Celts lost out by 2-1 to West Bromwich Albion, with Lennox scoring Celtic's goal. Peter Latchford enjoyed meeting up with several old team mates from his West Brom days, and in the end Crystal Palace won the trophy by beating Chelsea in the final.

Partick Thistle, under the shrewd stewardship of Lisbon Lion Bertie Auld, were experiencing a fine season. They were sitting joint top of the Premier Division on seventeen points, narrowly behind Dundee United on goal difference. Celtic were in fourth place, only two points behind them. It was so tight in the league table that only ten points separated all ten teams in it.

Thistle had some fine young players in Brian Whittaker, Jim Melrose and Ian Gibson and they had journeyman striker Doug Somner playing in a rich vein of form. However, their main inspiration, as always, was Alan Rough, their Scottish international goalkeeper. Rough was the only full-time player in the Firhill set up and Auld had declined several bids from English sides and, it was rumoured, both halves of the Old Firm. Although Rough's stock had fallen slightly since Scotland's lame performances in the 1978 World Cup finals, he was easily regarded as the best 'keeper in the country and it seemed only a matter of time before a major club swooped for his signature, providing a substantial fee for Thistle in the process.

Auld had promised to come to Parkhead and take the game to Celtic. He was true to his word and in the opening exchanges Thistle could have scored three times. Roy Baines was forced into a great save from Alex O'Hara after a Somner cut back, and from a corner he was fortunate to block a strong Somner shot with his body. During the early stages Celtic's defence looked desperately uncertain. Baines came to the rescue again when he saved from the on rushing Somner, and then relied on Edvaldsson to complete the clearance from the Celtic goal. The Parkhead fans were beginning to become restless.

Celtic pressed into the game through their wide men Provan and Doyle, and then Celtic Park found itself engulfed in a snow storm on a bitterly cold day. The fans stood huddled on the freezing terraces, struggling to watch the action through the blizzard conditions.

MacLeod, having opened his goal scoring account a week earlier at Easter Road, was again keen to show his shooting prowess. Rough made a great save which would have pleased him enormously, as Scotland manager Jock Stein was seated in the Parkhead stand viewing the action.

The fans were hoping for something to warm both their hands and their hearts in the second half, and Celtic provided a goal for them right after half-time. MacLeod surged forward from midfield and tried a shot from twenty five yards. It was a miscued effort, and the ball fortunately landed at the feet of striker Tom McAdam, who gleefully took a couple of steps forward before placing a fine shot past Alan Rough.

MacLeod was now in his element in the heavy conditions and he powered forward again, only for Rough to deny him with another fine save. Thistle may have had the better of the first half but Celtic had the better of the second period, and the Jags rarely threatened again before full-time.

Incredibly, this was Celtic's first league win since 30th September. Billy McNeill could at last have an enjoyable weekend, after a decent result at the expense of his old team mate Bertie Auld. He would have been very satisfied with the two points, given the fact that injuries had decimated his fragile squad with McGrain, Conroy, Burns, Conn and Glavin all missing with various ailments.

Despite their indifferent form, Celtic moved up to third place, level on points with second place Aberdeen, and just one point behind leaders Dundee United. The feeling was that if they could get their injured players back and find a bit of form, then this could still be Celtic's season.

New Bhoy Murdo MacLeod had made a fine start to his Celtic career and had been in most impressive form. In a newspaper article he confessed to being a boyhood supporter of Celtic's main rivals Rangers, and told how his father and brother enjoyed teasing him: *'They keep ribbing me about having to learn new songs instead of Follow Follow. However I'm just glad to be playing with such a great club like Celtic.'* Sunday Mail, 26th November.

MacLeod had made a fine impression at Parkhead, although there was one Celtic player who was not entirely enamoured with his arrival, as Joe Filippi points out. *'Murdo was very fast and after training we would often have a sprint competition and he could beat Johnny Doyle, who was also quick, nine times out of ten. I travelled from Ayrshire with Johnny and that didn't please him at all. Johnny was very competitive and liked to win at everything'*

Celtic: Baines Filippi Lynch Aitken MacDonald Edvaldsson Provan MacLeod McAdam Casey Doyle Subs: McCluskey Lennox

Partick: Rough McKinnon Whittaker Anderson Campbell (Love) Marr Houston Melrose O'Hara Somner Park Sub: Gibson

League table at the end of November 1978

	P	W	D	L	F	A	Pts
Dundee Utd	15	6	6	3	19	14	18
Celtic	15	7	3	5	25	19	17
Partick Thistle	15	7	3	5	16	14	17
Aberdeen	14	5	5	4	24	15	15
Morton	14	5	5	4	19	19	15
St Mirren	15	6	3	6	15	15	15
Rangers	14	3	8	3	13	12	14
Hibernian	14	4	6	4	15	15	14
Hearts	14	3	4	4	13	16	10
Motherwell	14	3	1	10	8	24	7

CHAPTER 6 • FESTIVE DESPAIR

2 December 1978 Premier Division

St Mirren v Celtic (match postponed)

In midweek Scotland travelled to Portugal for their European championship qualifying games in Lisbon. Celtic had no representation in the full international team, but had Roy Aitken and George McCluskey in the under 21 line-up, with Murdo MacLeod as an unused substitute. Scotland's youngsters romped to a fine 3-0 win in the Portuguese capital, with McCluskey scoring a fine solo goal, and Aitken enhancing his growing reputation with a fine game in midfield. Sadly, the senior Scots' side went down tamely by 1-0, and that defeat meant their chances of qualifying for *Italia 1980* looked painfully slim. Jock Stein was realising that he was not immune to intense scrutiny from the critical Scottish media corps.

Celtic's visit to Love Street was keenly anticipated as both sides were capable of producing tremendous performances on their day. The weather had been bitterly cold in the week leading up to the game, and when the entire country was struck by freezing sub zero temperatures on the Friday night this devastated the sporting card. It was so bad that every Premier Division game was postponed as clubs struggled to find ways of overcoming the frozen conditions. At least the St Mirren v Celtic game was called off early on the Saturday morning, thus preventing fans from making needless journeys.

Over the weekend Celtic fans were amused to learn of the demise of one of their old adversaries, the Scottish grade one referee John Gordon. Gordon was better known by the moniker J.R.P. Gordon to which the Celtic fans had christened him '*John Right Protestant'* given some of the controversial decisions he had made against Celtic over the years. He was a noted adversary of Jock Stein who had been enraged by Gordon's sometimes eccentric refereeing.

Gordon had a career of some distinction. The previous summer he was involved in the World Cup finals in Argentina, when he took charge of the Holland v Austria and Tunisia v Mexico fixtures. At that time the Scottish press had caustically stated that he was the only Scotsman who had actually performed well during that tournament, given the dreadful performances of the Scottish players in their matches.

Gordon and his linesmen, Rollo Kyle and David McCartney, had been given control of the AC Milan v Levski Sofia UEFA cup tie on 1st November. They then accepted gifts from the Italian club, described as a significant amount of 'expensive clothing', worth an estimated £300 to each official, which was a fantastic sum of money in 1978. It has to be said that all three were guilty of gross stupidity, rather than corruption, but this case was very much an embarrassment to the SFA and Scottish football in general.

The only satisfaction which could be taken was the fact that the SFA acted quickly by dealing with a difficult situation not of their making, and they earned great credit by doing so. Ernie Walker was often maligned, but on this occasion he took swift and effective action to limit any damage to Scotland's reputation, and this is something his successors in the Association could very well learn from. All three officials were suspended until April 1981, and given their ages their careers were considered to be as good as over.

AC Milan won the tie 3-0 and no impropriety was suggested from the defeated Bulgarians. Nevertheless, there were strict rules forbidding match officials from accepting gifts from clubs, and they had been broken. For their part, AC Milan were given what was described as a 'paltry' £8000 fine, and the reward of a lucrative tie against Manchester City in the next round.

There was controversy too as tickets went on sale for the League Cup semi-final ties between Celtic and Rangers, and Hibs against Aberdeen. Ticket prices ranged from £1.20 for the ground, up to £2.50 for the stand. Printed on the tickets was the price, 'inclusive of VAT and a donation of 20p towards the Hampden stadium fund.' Fans of all four clubs were incensed at the thought of having no choice in making a donation, and had flooded the newspapers with protests. Scottish League secretary Les Michie was at pains to point out that even if there was no donation towards the fund, then the prices would still have been the same, so it was actually the clubs who were taking the hit, with the money going towards the renovation of a new national stadium. Apparently, the wording on the tickets had to be there for tax reasons.

9 December 1978: Premier Division

Celtic   0-0   Aberdeen

Attendance: 24,000

Billy McNeill often remarked in later years of how difficult it was for him to turn his back on the Aberdeen team he had built during his short time at Pittodrie. Gordon Strachan and Steve Archibald were McNeill signings and both were now blossoming at Pittodrie, alongside the experienced back bone of the Dons' side, Bobby Clark, Drew Jarvie, Joe Harper, and their inspirational captain Willie Miller.

Alex Ferguson had taken over from McNeill at Aberdeen and he was in the early throes of putting together one of the most impressive teams in Scottish football. The basic elements were already there and Ferguson's aggressive, competitive nature would prove to be the final part of the jigsaw for this Aberdeen side, although it would be another eighteen months before the Dons' would come to the fore as a major force. However, the fact that much of the ground work had already been done by Billy McNeill, and Ally MacLeod before him, was often overlooked.

Aside from McNeill's Aberdeen connection, competition between the two managers was sure to be fierce. McNeill had been a resolute Celtic centre-half and had come up against Ferguson, a combative centre-forward, in direct opposition many times during his spells at St Johnstone, Dunfermline, Rangers, Falkirk and Ayr. Ferguson earned a dream move to Rangers in 1967, but things turned sour after the 1969 Scottish Cup final, in which Celtic thrashed Rangers 4-0. Unusually for that time, Rangers had been strong favourites to win, but in the early stages of the match Ferguson lost McNeill at a corner kick, allowing him to score Celtic's vital opening goal in only two minutes, which was the first step on the way to one of Celtic's most famous victories.

Afterwards the Rangers fans were most unforgiving and Ferguson was made the scapegoat for that Hampden defeat. He was ignominiously moved out of Ibrox shortly afterwards, having fallen out of favour with the Rangers hierarchy. What both men had in common was a tremendous competitive spirit and a fierce desire to win. When their teams came to together in opposition it was sure to be a contest not for the faint hearted.

Ferguson did not travel to Glasgow in the best of spirits. He had just lost an industrial tribunal against St Mirren for constructive dismissal, after the Saints' directors had sacked him in May 1978. During the tribunal, elements of Ferguson's behaviour as Saints' manager had been called into question and it had not been a pleasant experience for him. Losing the court case had also hit him financially. Worse still for Ferguson, was that his father Alex senior, to whom he was very close, had passed away suddenly, and this period was perhaps the most difficult time of his personal and professional life.

The Aberdeen game promised much but, as often happens, it delivered very little, and was marred by nasty fouls and petty feuds all over the field. There were five bookings and no goals, and it has to be said that the number of bookings could have been doubled. Both centre-back pairings had been in full control, MacDonald and Edvaldsson of Celtic, and Rougvie and

Miller of Aberdeen, so much so that their respective goalkeepers had very little to do.

In the second half, Celtic brought Conn on for the ineffective McAdam, and at last Celtic had some life breathed into them. In eighty four minutes came the main talking point of the game. Conn neatly beat Kennedy, and was shaping to shoot a yard inside the penalty area, when the Dons' full-back clumsily tackled him from behind. A huge roar went up from the Celtic crowd for a penalty kick.

Yet referee Bill Anderson controversially waved play on, to a storm of protest from Celtic players and fans alike. Television pictures the following day proved the legitimacy of Celtic's claims, and Conn, who was particularly aggrieved, was booked for his protests. At full-time the Celtic fans howled their frustrations at the referee, with Conn still remonstrating with him. It took both Edvaldsson and Harper to turn the furious Celtic man away from Anderson, to allow the referee to eventually depart up the tunnel to a storm of jeering.

Despite the lack of excitement on the day, one player managed to rise above the mediocrity on show. *'The skills of the game were almost non-existent on the heavy, greasy surface but I admired the persistence of Celtic's Tommy Burns who at all times tried to do something with the ball.'* Sunday Mail, 10th December 1978.

Dundee United had been surprise league leaders for a number of weeks, and Rangers travelled to Tannadice intent on bringing United's fine run to an end. To the surprise of most observers, United ripped Rangers apart to win 3-0, and although Celtic fans were heartened by that result, it was clear that United's challenge would be no flash in the pan and they were now a team to be taken seriously. It was shaping up to be the most competitive of league seasons.

Celtic: Baines Filippi Lynch Aitken MacDonald Edvaldsson Provan Conroy McAdam (Conn) Burns Doyle Sub: Casey

Aberdeen: Clark Kennedy McLelland MacMaster (Archibald) Rougvie Miller Strachan Fleming Harper Jarvie Sullivan Sub: Cooper

13 December 1978: Scottish League Cup, semi-final

Rangers	**3-2**	**Celtic (after extra time)**
Jardine pen 26		McAdam 10
Jackson 80		Doyle 65
Casey (og) 113		

This was Celtic's 154th consecutive tie in the tournament, and although they lost the odd section match along the way, they had always managed to win their group and play their way through to the final. The Celts were looking to qualify for the final for an incredible fifteenth successive year. Coincidentally, Bobby Lennox who was in the Celtic squad, was also at the club for the first game of this remarkable cup run, against Partick Thistle on 8th August 1964. This tie took place at Celtic Park when Jimmy McGrory was the manager.

Celtic, as always, prepared for this important game by spending some time at their traditional Seamill base on the Ayrshire coast. The players enjoyed a well earned break from what had been a most demanding season. Murdo MacLeod was ineligible for the semi due to previously appearing for Dumbarton, so Mike Conroy and Jim Casey were drafted into the squad as possible replacements.

For sponsorship reasons, the match ball was a black and white panelled World Cup style Adidas 'Telstar' football, and both teams felt it was much lighter than the normal Mitre footballs used during Premier Division games.

Celtic were first to settle, and scored the opening goal in ten minutes, with what was described as the goal of the season. Tommy Burns intercepted an Alex MacDonald pass in midfield and ran fully fifty yards into the Rangers half. He then split the

Rangers defence with a glorious pass, to allow John Doyle to score past McCloy.

Celtic were performing well when Miller was booked for a crude foul on Conroy, before Rangers equalised with a disputed penalty. Rangers' Davie Cooper went down very easily in the area after a tackle by Celtic defender Edvaldsson, and Celtic players protested furiously at this perceived injustice. Doyle was booked for over stating his case, and before the penalty could be taken, Burns was called over and sensationally ordered off, presumably for saying something out of turn to the match official. This was a severe blow to Celtic, as Burns had been the game's best player by far until that incident. There were more angry scenes on and off the park, but when order was restored Jardine equalised for Rangers from the penalty kick.

It was hoped that tempers would be reduced after the half-time break, but in forty seven minutes the teams were level with ten men, after Miller was given a second yellow card following a clash with Doyle. With both teams a man down the players began to find more space to play, and the game became a better spectacle. Rangers' goalkeeper McCloy made a brilliant save from a Provan free-kick, and Celtic, with some momentum behind them, then took the lead. Doyle created a shooting chance for Aitken, and after McCloy made another fine save, Tom McAdam scored from the rebound.

Celtic appeared to grow more nervous as the game wore on, and Rangers equalised with ten minutes remaining. Russell found Jackson in the area and the big centre-half hit a shot which was deflected past Roy Baines for a soft goal. This was most unfortunate, as the Celtic keeper appeared to have the ball covered before the deflection. With time running out, Johnstone had the chance to win the tie, but hit the side netting when it looked easier to score, much to the frustration of the Rangers fans behind the goal. They roared loudly as they thought the ball had gone in, when it had actually hit the side netting.

If the players were breathless after their exertions during the ninety minutes, then the fans were desperate for more as the game moved into extra time. With only seven minutes remaining, came the deciding moment of the game. Derek Johnstone appeared to be offside as he moved in on Baines, and the Celtic keeper did well to save his shot. Unfortunately, the ball rebounded off Baines and hit the in rushing Jim Casey, and slid into the Celtic net.

It was a devastating blow, and very unfortunate for the young Celt who inadvertently caused Celtic's defeat through this freak goal. He had not been on the field for long after replacing the injured Mike Conroy, and he could not be faulted in causing the goal. Jim Casey was a player of great potential, but he didn't quite make the grade. His contemporaries in the Celtic youth squad were Tommy Burns, Roy Aitken and George McCluskey. His Celtic career would ultimately centre around three Old Firm games, in which he had carried no luck whatsoever.

In September 1977, as an inexperienced twenty year old, Casey was a surprise choice at sweeper, in place of the injured Pat Stanton, as Celtic took on Rangers at Ibrox. At half-time, Celtic had a comfortable two goal lead, but in the second half the defence capitulated as Rangers roared back to win by 3-2. Jim then found himself out of favour.

In December 1978 he was desperately unlucky in scoring a freak own goal. Later, in May 1980, he was due to play in the Scottish Cup final against Rangers, but injured his foot in training, only a matter of days before the game. This allowed Mike Conroy to be a most unlikely hero, in an unusual centre-half role, as Celtic triumphed by 1-0. Had fate been kinder to Jim Casey, then this game could have been the turning point in his Celtic career. As it was, he was faded into obscurity after that. He deserved better for his efforts.

Billy McNeill refused to speak to the waiting press after the semi-final such was his anger, when several important refereeing decisions had gone against his side. The next day he did state that Doyle had been reprimanded for his booking at the Rangers' penalty, and that Burns had been severely reprimanded and fined over his sending off which, it was announced, was due to swearing at the match officials. Davie Provan sums up referee Hugh Alexander's performance that night quite succinctly - *'The worst refereeing display I've ever seen in my life'.*

Tommy Burns (second right), is sent off by referee Hugh Alexander, as John Doyle, Andy Lynch and Roy Aitken protest.

When the dust had settled, Celtic were left to lick their wounds. They felt a sense of injustice and a feeling that fate had not been kind to them. Their fine League Cup run had ended and was consigned to the history books. A defeat to Rangers is always a major blow to any Celtic team, but it was hoped that the side would recover quickly from such a disappointment.

Mike Conroy recalls being at Parkhead the next day and experiencing something which would put the disappointment of losing to Rangers into context:

'The following afternoon I was in the dressing room alone with Tommy Burns after training. I had treatment on a knee injury that I had picked up, and Tommy was still very upset after being ordered off the night before. Both of us were feeling low. He asked me what I was doing that afternoon and I said 'Nothing', and he said, 'Come with me and I'll guarantee you will feel much better afterwards than you do now.'

I wasn't sure what he meant but we jumped in his car and ended up in the children's ward in the Glasgow Royal Infirmary. I noticed straight away that Tommy was on first name terms with the doctors and nurses, and the kids were delighted to see us, especially the wee Celtic fans.

We stayed for a good while and after we left I asked him how often he went there and he said he visited on a regular basis and I know he had never mentioned this before to anyone at the club. Tommy was a real caring guy and he was right about one thing. I was glad I had gone with him and it put the defeat against Rangers in a football match totally into perspective.'

Celtic: Baines Filippi Lynch Aitken MacDonald Edvaldsson Provan Conroy (Casey) McAdam Burns Doyle Sub: Conn

Rangers: McCloy Miller Dawson Jardine Jackson MacDonald McLean Russell Johnstone Watson Cooper (Smith) Sub: Parlane

16 December 1978: Premier Division

Celtic   **1-1**   **Dundee United**
Lynch pen 45   Narey 74

Attendance: 21,000

After their midweek cup disappointment, Celtic were keen to make amends against Dundee United. Jim McLean proudly brought his young United side to Parkhead as league leaders, and they were on top on merit, having been on a fine run of form. McLean had been manager at Tannadice since 1971, and had worked hard to build a side to compete at the highest level in Scotland, and to challenge in Europe.

He had suffered some setbacks along the way. He had been forced to sell his greatest asset, Andy Gray, to Aston Villa in 1975 for a huge transfer fee, due to financial reasons. However he was optimistic about this side, given the fact that United had rebuffed considerable interest from Derby County for the highly rated David Narey, Derby being a major outfit in the top English league at that time.

Celtic were without the suspended Burns, and the Parkhead faithful wondered how their team would react after the bitter disappointment of the defeat to Rangers at Hampden.

Happily enough, they need not have worried. Celtic roared into action and pressed United back from the first whistle. In five minutes, the returning Ronnie Glavin hit the bar with a header from an Alfie Conn corner, and McAdam saw his follow up effort saved by McAlpine. Minutes later, and another Conn corner saw MacDonald crash a header off the post, and McAdam's header was then cleared off the line by Kirkwood.

Celtic were quicker and more aggressive throughout the opening half. Conn had a goal disallowed after McAdam was deemed to be offside. There then followed a series of near misses in front of McAlpine's goal, as desperate defending and bad finishing prevented Celtic from scoring.

The goal finally came in injury time, shortly before the break. Aitken laid on a chance for Conn, and he hooked in a vicious shot, which appeared to strike United captain Hegarty on the body. The Celtic players appealed the ball had struck Hegarty's arm, but the referee played on until he saw his linesman flagging and then awarded a penalty. Andy Lynch duly struck the ball strongly past McAlpine to give Celtic a 1-0 half-time lead.

All changed in the second half when United found some form and forced themselves into the game. From the kick off, Holt fired in a shot which Baines saved well, and minutes later Baines made another good save from Payne's free-kick.

Celtic were still dangerous from set pieces and both MacDonald and Edvaldsson came close with headers. United however, had more of the play and were stretching Celtic on the flanks. They finally equalised in seventy four minutes, when Lynch only succeeded in clearing a Payne corner to Narey, who sent a fine high shot past Baines from twelve yards. Tom McAdam was booked for protesting that Baines had been impeded by a United player when the corner was taken.

After that Celtic's confidence wilted, and United attacked at will. In the closing minutes Baines made two wondrous saves, a one handed effort from Holt's thunder bolt shot, and then a reflex save when he turned over Addison's close range effort.

This was to be another frustrating afternoon for Billy McNeill. He had seen his side play extremely well in a game they should have won comprehensively in the opening period, but in the end they had been fortunate to hang on for a point. McNeill's biggest cause for concern was the lack of composure in front of goal.

'United's goal didn't merely lead a charmed life. It seemed that every fairy from every Christmas tree in Scotland had waved

her magic wand over it. Anyhow, the post was struck, the bar was hit and the ball miraculously cleared off the line, a United body was in the way of a certain goal – and it looked as though the Parkhead forays were all going to fail.' Evening Times, 18th December 1978.

It was with great delight that McNeill discovered that his reserve side achieved a 3-1 win at Tannadice that afternoon, in which young striker George McCluskey had scored all of Celtic's goals with a fine hat trick. Despite rumours of Celtic chasing a striker in the transfer market, it seemed as if the solution to their goal scoring problems could be found closer to home, in young McCluskey.

Sadly, it was not all good news for the McCluskey family as George's brother, John McCluskey, received devastating news regarding a blood clot in his foot. Sadly this would force him to retire prematurely from the game at the tender age of nineteen. John was a left-sided forward, with tremendous skill, and had been rated as one of Scotland's finest prospects for years. Both brothers were tremendously talented, and it was a great disappointment to everyone concerned that they could not go on to star together in future Celtic teams.

Celtic: Baines Filippi Lynch Aitken MacDonald Edvaldsson Conn MacLeod McAdam (Lennox) Glavin Doyle Sub: Casey

Dundee Utd: McAlpine Stewart Stark Fleming Hegarty Narey Dodds (Phillip) Addison Holt Payne Kirkwood Sub: Milne

23 December 1978: Premier Division

Morton   **1-0**   **Celtic**
Ritchie pen 89

Attendance: 16,000

The dust had barely settled from Celtic's controversial Hampden defeat to Rangers, when it was announced that the referee from that game, Hugh Alexander, was now to take charge of Celtic's forthcoming league game at Cappielow against Morton. Ironically the loudest complaint against Alexander being given control of the game came from the Morton manager, Benny Rooney.

'I have no complaints about his refereeing in the past but after the way things went for him last week he can't be happy about handling a Celtic game so soon. I have a lot of sympathy for the man but I feel that someone should point out to the Scottish League that he must be under a lot of pressure.'

Stern stuff from Rooney, who stopped just short of requesting Alexander's withdrawal. Celtic, for their part, held their own counsel, and stated that they were still discussing the matter internally, and that they were considering a written complaint to the Scottish League regarding Alexander's display at Hampden. The Scottish League then made a statement, saying that Alexander would referee the game, regardless of protest by either side.

The foreign invasion of Scottish football had continued and Morton fielded their new American goalkeeper, Dave Brcic, (pronounced Bir-chick), who made an impressive debut the week before against Motherwell. Brcic was seen as a novelty signing, but had a certain pedigree in that he had previously been with America's premier club, the New York Cosmos. He was only to stay in Scotland for a short period, but would make a huge impression with his acrobatic displays, as Celtic were about to find out.

In 1978 Cappielow was one of a number of Scottish grounds which had fairly confined surroundings. This created a fantastic atmosphere, which more often than not, led to highly competitive, cup tie style matches. The huge Celtic support packed Cappielow in their thousands, and when referee Alexander led out the sides to a storm of jeering from those fans bedecked in green and white, he knew he was in for a difficult afternoon.

Morton keeper Brcic started the game as he meant to go on, with a good save from a Tom McAdam header. Provan and Conn were in fine form and created most of Celtic's early good play, with Morton's Yankee goalie again impressing, with another save from Conn. In twenty five minutes, Morton gave Celtic a timely reminder that they were still in the game, when Thomson and McNeil collided with each other after a fine pass by Hayes set up a tremendous chance.

After the break, McNeil had a goal correctly disallowed for offside before Celtic had the chance of the game. A shot from MacLeod at last beat Brcic, but rebounded from the cross bar to Alfie Conn who, with the goal at his mercy, headed the ball tamely past the post. MacLeod was a dynamo in the Celtic midfield, and fired in several long range shots in an effort to inspire his team mates, but as the game wore on a draw seemed certain.

With only minutes remaining, Morton pressed Celtic back and Ritchie saw a shot go just wide, before Lynch cleared a McNeil shot to safety from the Celtic goal line. With full-time rapidly approaching, McNeil trailed the ball to the bye line, only for Edvaldsson to barge him to the ground, giving the opportunity for Hugh Alexander to award Morton a dramatic penalty. Andy Ritchie gleefully drove the ball past Roy Baines. There was a certain irony in this, given the fact that both players had been part of swap deal in 1976 between Celtic and Morton, in which the players had changed clubs.

As it was, Benny Rooney was to have no concerns about Alexander's decision making after all. Despite Alexander awarding the penalty, Celtic players had remained disciplined:

'It must be said to Celtic's credit that, irrespective what they felt about the last minute award, they accepted it in exactly the right manner.' Sunday Mail 24th December 1978.

To put it mildly, defeat was tough to take for the Celtic players and the large support, but this was another game they should never have lost. The fans trooped wearily out of Cappielow on that cold, dark night and they could only fret about what the future would bring for their team. The supporters buses, decked with banners and flags from such faraway places as Grampian, Perth, Edinburgh, Lochee, Ayr and every part of the West of Scotland, travelled home from the Clyde coast in the sad knowledge that their team was now a very ordinary one indeed. It was just over ten years since Lisbon and Celtic's greatest success, but the league table that night made for sobering reading, with Celtic lying way down in fifth place.

The newspapers and media talked of a *'winter of discontent'* in political circles as James Callaghan's embattled Labour government sought to stay in power, and strikes and discord took hold all over the country. Callaghan was under attack from Margaret Thatcher's Conservatives and from the Trade Unions on his own side. Celtic now faced their own winter of discontent, as the fans, weary of failure and mediocrity, made their displeasure known.

Christmas 1978 was not to be a happy one, and the future appeared desperately bleak. In their previous eleven league games, Celtic had emerged victorious in only one match, and there seemed little to be optimistic about. The Celtic fans who attended Christmas Masses and religious services would no doubt have prayed for divine intervention, and although they were not to realise it at that time, their petitions were about to be answered in the most unusual fashion.

The winter weather had been bitterly cold, but conditions were now about to take a severe turn for the worse. Heavy snow and freezing temperatures, on a scale which the country had not experienced since 1963, were about to take hold. Although no one could have forecast it in late December, Celtic were not able to play another league match until March, ten long weeks away. Arctic conditions prevailed and they were to be Celtic's saving grace.

Morton: Brcic Hayes Holmes Rooney McLaren Orr McNeil Hutchinson Scott Thomson Ritchie Subs: Evans Russell

Celtic: Baines Filippi Lynch Aitken MacDonald Edvaldsson Provan MacLeod McAdam Burns (Lennox) Conn Sub: Conroy

30 December 1979: Premier Division

Celtic v Hearts (match postponed)

In the days following Christmas it snowed heavily and it was clear that this game would be postponed. Officials were resigned at an early stage that there would be a call off, with the Parkhead pitch covered in deep snow. The fans were disappointed, and this would be a feeling that they would become well acquainted with in the weeks ahead.

The Christmas edition of the club's newspaper, The Celtic View, created quite a stir, with a number of celebrities and personalities sending their best wishes to Celtic and their supporters. It transpired that Celtic fan, John McFadyen, had contacted a diverse range of personalities to ask them to send Season's Greetings to Celtic and their fans. Here is a selection of the replies.

Pete Murray (Radio 2 DJ) – *When I worked on STV on Hope Street I watched Celtic as often as I could. Even today I look out for the score of the boys in green and white. I am still a Celtic supporter. Please pass on my good wishes for a Merry Christmas and a Happy New Year to my fellow Celtic supporters.*

Denis Healey (Labour MP, Chancellor of the Exchequer) – *The green and white hoops of Celtic are world famous for attacking and entertaining football. A Merry Christmas and a Happy New Year to all Celtic fans from a Leeds United supporter.*

Cardinal Basil Hume (Spiritual leader of the Catholic Church in England and Wales) – *I have been a keen follower of football all my life and I support Newcastle United my home team. Unfortunately I never had much chance to watch Scottish football nevertheless I am very much aware of Glasgow Celtic. Please wish all the Celtic fans a happy and a holy Christmas.'*

Terry Wogan (TV personality and Radio 2 DJ) - *Celtic are certainly the most successful team in Scottish football and of course the first team from these islands to win the European Cup. My own team, Limerick, play in the League of Ireland. Celtic, of course, also play in my national colours. My best wishes for a Happy Christmas to all Celtic fans.*

Margaret Thatcher (Conservative MP, Leader of the Opposition) – *Unfortunately in England we do not have the opportunity to see top Scottish teams like Celtic very often. However, over the years I have seen Celtic in their famous green and white hoops. They have such a great reputation both in this country and also in Europe. Seasonal Greetings to all Celtic fans.*

And as 1979 rapidly approached, everyone turned their attention to the traditional Old Firm New Year fixture, due to be played on 6th January.

League table at the end of December 1978

	P	W	D	L	F	A	Pts
Dundee Utd	18	8	7	3	25	16	23
Partick Thistle	18	8	5	5	19	16	21
Aberdeen	19	6	8	5	30	19	20
Rangers	18	6	8	4	22	18	20
Morton	19	7	6	6	19	19	20
Celtic	18	7	5	6	26	21	19
St Mirren	18	7	4	7	20	17	18
Hibernian	18	4	8	6	19	23	16
Hearts	18	5	5	8	22	34	15
Motherwell	18	3	4	11	18	24	10

CHAPTER 7 • THE BIG FREEZE

6 January 1979: Premier Division

Celtic v Rangers (match postponed)

The annual New Year Old Firm match was one of the highlights in the Scottish football calendar, but with a heavy covering of snow on top of a layer of ice on the Parkhead pitch, this game looked certain to be postponed. However, the newspapers optimistically reported that tickets were still available to purchase from the Celtic Pools office in West Nile Street.

After the festive period, many Scottish clubs faced the problem of severe flooding, due to burst pipes caused by the freezing temperatures. It was reported that Cappielow, Easter Road, Love Street, Tynecastle and East End Park all had flood damage to their offices and dressing rooms, with the Cappielow board room also badly affected. Hibs' chairman Tom Hart described the inside of Easter Road as, 'a disaster area'. The clubs also experienced problems when training their players, due to lack of washing facilities. A major concern was that a sudden thaw would cause even more disruption to clubs all over the country.

Because of the severe cold weather, Celtic and Rangers took advantage of local facilities. Celtic trained at Baillieston sports centre, whilst Rangers worked out at Bellahouston sports centre on the south side.

Scottish League secretary Tommy Maule was pessimistic about any football being played and arranged for referees to make early inspections to prevent fans making unnecessary journeys. An added problem was that in 1979 no Scottish football ground was entirely covered, and all of them were open to the elements to some degree. Even if pitches were playable, the clubs faced the enormous task of clearing snow and ice from the open terraces before conditions would be considered safe for spectators.

On Friday 5th January, the Scottish League announced that twenty of the fixtures for the following day were already postponed, with the Celtic v Rangers clash being one of the first games to be called off. Despite the snowy conditions, Billy McNeill had the players out on the pitch for a short training session, and this gave the press photographers some unusual photo opportunities, as the players larked about throwing snowballs.

As it was, no games were played in Scotland on 6th January, with only five English games going ahead, and one of those had to be abandoned at half-time. There was some football news to report when the Scottish Cup draw was made, and Celtic were given another trip to Montrose, following their League Cup fixture in November.

Ex-Celtic goalkeeper Ronnie Simpson was required to take part in the pools panel on the day. The pools panel consisted of a group of ex-footballers, who came together on Saturday afternoons to decide the outcome of any postponed fixtures for the big pools companies, such as Littlewoods and Vernons. Despite being a Lisbon Lion, the Celtic legend had no influence over his colleagues, who forecast a Rangers away win in the big Glasgow derby. The panel were to find themselves very busy in the weeks ahead.

The early postponement allowed Billy McNeill to travel to Ireland to watch the match between Dundalk and Home Farm. It was believed he had an interest in signing Home Farm's promising young midfielder, Ronnie Whelan. Celtic ultimately missed out on the young Irishman, who signed for Liverpool, and became an Anfield great in the 1980's. It is still a source of regret that Celtic could not convince the young Ronnie to come to Glasgow.

Newly published attendance figures showed that Celtic had the highest attendances in the league, with an average of 27,777 passing through the Parkhead gates at each home game. Rangers were narrowly behind in second place, with an average of 26,083. Despite the trials and tribulations of the season so far, it was clear that the Celtic fans had shown a great deal of faith by standing by their side during an enormously difficult and trying period.

13 January 1979: Premier Division

Celtic v Hibernian (match postponed)

With the weather showing no signs of improvement, football clubs began to look further afield in order to find suitable conditions to play. Celtic actually considered travelling all the way across the Atlantic for a fixture against the Houston Hurricanes, the club which Bobby Lennox and John Dowie had played for the previous summer.

However, the Hurricanes played in the Astrodome and the astroturf in the stadium had been lifted to allow a rodeo competition to take place there, leading to sarcastic suggestions that Celtic had been given a 'bum steer'.

Billy McNeill also made enquiries about a trip to Malta, but a lack of seats on flights at short notice put paid to that suggestion. Hibs showed great initiative by arranging a match against Tel Aviv, and travelled to Israel via London to get there. It was a worthwhile exercise as the Hibees enjoyed sixty five degree temperatures, in pleasant sunshine, as the citizens of Edinburgh shivered under six inches of snow. Celtic eventually played a game against Clyde at Shawfield, over three half hour periods, to allow as many players as possible to have a run out. The conditions were said to be 'heavy.'

With the country still under a blanket of snow, the Scottish League moved quickly to cancel fixtures early for the second consecutive week, and Celtic's game scheduled for Saturday

13th January was postponed. The only game to beat the weather was played at Stairs Park, when Stranraer drew 1-1 with Dunfermline.

However, if the weather was causing short term problems for the Scottish game, a more serious threat to the future of Scottish football now emerged. The European Economic Community, (E.E.C.), declared that under forthcoming changes in employment law, footballers within the European community would soon be able to move under 'freedom of contract.' This new phrase meant that if a player chose to let his contract run out, then he could move to a new club of his choice, and the old club would have no say in this. At this time, clubs held on to player registrations, even when contracts ran out and they could demand a transfer fee before allowing a player to leave. Clubs held total power and they could choose to freeze a player out of the game if they were inclined to do so.

Scottish football had long relied on incoming transfer fees to prosper, especially when big money was paid by English clubs for the best talent Scotland had to offer. Under this new proposal, if a transfer fee could not be agreed between the selling and buying clubs, then a tribunal would sit to decide the fee. It was proposed that in most cases fees would be settled at approximately ten times the yearly salary of the out of contract player. Since Scottish clubs were not noted for paying large salaries in 1979, this was a proposal which horrified the chairmen of clubs all over the country. Kenny Dalglish's £440,000 transfer from Celtic to Liverpool in August 1977 was cited as an example. Under the new rules, if Dalglish had been out of contract, Celtic would only have been entitled to £100,000, unless Liverpool agreed to pay more.

It is curious to note that the Scottish players union were not enthusiastic about this new change in conditions. This seemed strange, given that their members would be the very people who would benefit, and the recently retired ex-Celtic player, Harry Hood, was most vociferous in his public criticism of his old union's stance.

There was the usual knee jerk reaction from club chairmen and there was much discussion of protests to be made to the European authorities. SFA secretary Ernie Walker wisely advised clubs against this, fearing if the E.E.C were provoked, then they may go further and deem that no transfer fee should be paid for an out of contract player. Ultimately this did not happen until 1995, when the ground breaking 'Bosman' ruling came into place.

January 16 1979: Friendly

Estoril   0-4   Celtic
MacDonald 23
Doyle 30
McAdam 81
Edvaldsson 86

Attendance: 2,000

Celtic at last managed to arrange a game abroad, and travelled to Portugal to play the Portuguese first division side, FC Estoril. In 1967 Celtic stayed in the pleasant coastal resort of Estoril, due to its close proximity to Lisbon, before their momentous European Cup final win. One can only wonder at the memories running through the minds of Billy McNeill, John Clark and Bobby Lennox as they returned for another visit.

However, they realised they were not there for nostalgic reasons, and that a good work out for the players was the desired objective. Peter Latchford remained at home after his wife gave birth. Celtic brought sixteen players for a run out in the pleasant Portuguese climate, and an opportunity to enjoy training facilities which they had not experienced since before Christmas.

Estoril were a decent side and had just beaten Porto 3-0. Their player-manager was the great ex-Benfica centre forward Jose Torres. He was a giant, at six foot three inches tall, and had been a player of considerable talent for Benfica and Portugal in the 1960's. He was a notable opponent of Billy McNeill's in 1969, during the epic European Cup ties between Celtic and Benfica. McNeill was said to be looking forward to renewing his acquaintance.

Celtic won the game 4-0 through goals by MacDonald, Doyle, McAdam and Edvaldsson. Although the game was not particularly competitive, it gave the players a good ninety minutes in decent conditions, in front of a crowd of 2000. The hope was that the Lisbon air would work its magic on the Celtic players once again. The only down side to the trip was that the Celtic party had to extend their stay by twenty four hours, as the cold weather created problems for airports across the UK.

The trip to warmer climes appeared to have been a success and Mike Conroy recalls that Celtic were to reap long term benefits.

'The trip to Estoril was great because we were able to get away to better weather and have better training facilities, although the pitch we played on was terrible. But more than that I believe that is when the team really bonded together. Myself, Davie Provan and Murdo MacLeod weren't at the club that long and Bobby Lennox had just returned. That trip gave us the chance to really get to know each other's strengths and weaknesses and after we returned you could tell that we had now bonded together as a real team, as a unit. The success that we achieved later in the season really all started in those few days in Estoril.'

Davie Provan fondly remembers visiting the Estadio Nacional for the first time, and has an interesting take on the future of the famous old Lisbon stadium.

'That was my first trip to the Estadio Nacional when Billy took the players there on a trip and it was great to see where it all actually happened. Celtic should actually buy that stadium now because they'll knock it down one day, it's a relic. It should be

preserved and that's why Celtic should buy it. Imagine one day the bulldozers go in to knock it down it would be like destroying a place of pilgrimage. Celtic should come to a deal with the local council to maintain its upkeep.'

20 January 1979: Premier Division

Partick Thistle v Celtic (match postponed)

Partick Thistle manager Bertie Auld reported earlier in the week that he was optimistic the Celtic fixture at Firhill would go ahead. Thistle had a small army of volunteers working tirelessly to clear the terraces of snow, laying salt on the steps for safety reasons.

A pitch inspection took place at 9am on the day of the game, and although the pitch was clear of snow, another night of sub zero temperatures had caused a severe frost. The pitch was deemed to be unplayable, much to the frustration of both McNeill and Auld, who were desperate to get the game played. What made their frustrations worse was that all four of the other league games had gone ahead at Easter Road, Cappielow, Fir Park and Love Street. Rangers were the biggest winners on the day, and their 2-0 away win against Morton put them in second place, one point behind leaders Dundee United. A further suggestion to play the Partick v Celtic game in midweek was also scuppered, when the condition of the Firhill pitch deteriorated further.

There was another story in the media which was not related to football, but was of huge Celtic interest. Celtic fans were to read of a scandal involving one of the team's highest profile players, Scottish international, Ronnie Glavin.

Glavin found himself in Hamilton Sheriff Court. He was charged with wilfully setting fire to his sports shop in East Kilbride, on 2nd July 1978, in order to defraud the Guardian Royal Exchange insurance company of a sum of £20,760.

He pled not guilty to the charge. It was reported in court that he brought a butane gas cylinder on to the premises before the fire started. Glavin and his business partner, Ralph D'Ambrosio, had a small bank overdraft, but the Celtic stars annual earnings were said to be between £10,000 and £11,000, which far exceeded any debt on the overdraft facility. For five days the court proceedings played out on the front pages of the Glasgow newspapers. It was claimed that Glavin confessed to the police in July 1978 that he had started the fire. Glavin said that this was true, but that he had only done so after being intimidated by rigid police interrogation.

Glavin was granted bail for the proceedings, but this was controversially withdrawn three days into the trial. Procurator Fiscal depute, James Kelman, claimed to have received information that Glavin would try and abscond and flee the country before the end of the trial. Glavin was then remanded in Glasgow's notorious Barlinnie prison for the duration of the trial, which must have been a terrible ordeal for the player.

On the fifth day of the trial, the jury adjourned to consider their verdict. They returned after only an hour and a half, and informed the court that the charges against Ronnie Glavin were not proven. Applause rang out in the packed public benches, where some Celtic players were in attendance, lending some much needed support to their under pressure team mate.

Glavin was understandably relieved that his ordeal was over, and gave an interview afterwards to the press. He was photographed at home celebrating with fifty members of his family and close personal friends:

'This was a nightmare which will live with me all my life. My fellow players with Celtic have been on the phone non-stop to me, congratulating me and wishing me all the best.

I am very bitter over my terrible ordeal in prison which was a humiliation no innocent person should be asked to endure. I have lived for seven months with this stigma hanging over me.

At times it was proving intolerable but it is ridiculous to suggest I would have fled the country if my bail had not been withdrawn. If I'd wanted to do that I would have done it a long time ago.

I cannot say what my future plans will be. I have not been in communication with the Celtic board, nor they with me. I will just have to wait. It is terrible to be sitting in the dock whilst knowing that one has a future and a past which is not tainted with anything criminal.' Glasgow Herald, 23rd January 1979

Billy McNeill was most concerned about his team's lack of match practice and with a difficult cup tie at Montrose approaching, he arranged two friendly games within twenty four hours against Clyde at Shawfield, and Queen of the South at Palmerston Park.

At Shawfield Celtic put out a strong line up, and won 3-0 through two goals from John Doyle, and a Turnbull own goal. The one thousand hardy souls who braved the elements on a freezing cold night had the pleasure of witnessing Danny McGrain having a fantastic game. McGrain was said to be approaching match fitness and it would be difficult for his manager to leave him out for much longer. The biggest bonus came when McGrain survived a couple of bone crunching tackles, which hopefully proved the troublesome right ankle had now recovered completely.

For the second game, in Dumfries, McNeill chose eleven different players, giving an opportunity to youngsters, Billy Russell, David Young and John Weir. Despite playing with an under strength team, Celtic won well against Queens' first eleven, playing some fine football in the process. Ronnie Glavin was back in the squad following his harrowing court experience, and managed to get on the score sheet. Roy Aitken scored the other goal in a 2-1 win, and McNeill could be satisfied with the performances in both friendlies, which had proved to be very worthwhile.

27 January 1979: Scottish Cup

Montrose v Celtic (match postponed)

Montrose officials were optimistic that this game would go ahead, but the more cynical observer would have noticed that Partick Thistle officials had said the same seven days earlier.

On the Friday before the game, the match referee, George Smith, travelled to Links Park to declare that the pitch was playable. Three inches of snow then fell overnight, and a local referee had to be summoned early on Saturday morning to announce that the game was off. By the time this announcement was made, many supporters buses had already set off, with the Ardrossan Garryowen and Peter Scarff Linwood clubs being cited as cases in point. Celtic were at pains to point out they had done all they could to notify their supporters, and had immediately contacted the police and local radio stations to get word out to travelling fans.

This postponement meant Celtic had not had a competitive match since 23rd December, an astonishing thirty five days. In view of the horrendous numbers of postponements, the SFA insisted that Celtic travel to Montrose the following Wednesday, and the hope was that at last a game would actually be played. The football authorities confirmed that the number of postponements had far exceeded anything that had gone before, even during the severe winter of 1962-63.

On the eve of this game, it was reported that Celtic had made a substantial bid for Gregor Stevens, Motherwell's highly rated defender. It was thought that this was a player plus cash deal, but the Fir Park club refused Celtic's offer. It was reported that they had also declined a previous offer of £100,000 offer from Rangers.

Latchford, Glavin, McAdam and McGrain finally manage to train during the bad winter weather.

31 January 1979: Scottish Cup

Montrose   2-4   Celtic
Miller 13   McCluskey 46, 55, 84
Murray 85   Lynch pen 88

Attendance 3,060

Following an afternoon pitch inspection, this game went ahead in front of a crowd of only 3,060 in freezing conditions. Many Celtic supporters' buses heeded the weather warnings from the authorities and refrained from travelling. Those fans who did travel were surprised to see the return of popular goalkeeper, Peter Latchford, in place of Roy Baines. Captain Danny McGrain also made an appearance.

The fans listening to radio updates at home were shocked to hear that their favourites were 1-0 down at half-time, courtesy of a goal by Bertie Miller. They would have been comforted to know that this was a misleading scoreline. Miller had scored in three minutes, before Latchford had even touched the ball. After that, Celtic laid siege to the Montrose goal, which was said to have resembled the Alamo. Edvaldsson headed just past and MacLeod went close twice. MacDonald and McCluskey both saw headers cleared off the line, and MacDonald hit the side netting with a firm header.

Happily for Celtic, they equalised in the first minute of the second half, before any nerves could set in. McCluskey got a fine touch to a Lynch free-kick, sending the ball past keeper Gorman. In fifty five minutes, Celtic scored the goal of the game. McGrain attacked on the break down the right hand side, as he approached the area he feinted left, sending a pass to the right to the unmarked McCluskey, who then scored with an angled shot.

The veteran Bobby Lennox also scored, only to be ruled offside, before Celtic scored the clincher. MacLeod went off on a tremendous mazy run. He then smashed a shot off the bar for McCluskey to head home the rebound, for a well earned hat trick. Montrose refused to lie down and Murray scored with a fine header, before Lynch rounded off the scoring with a penalty, after Doyle had been downed by D'Arcy.

This was the third competitive match between the teams that season, and Montrose gave Celtic another difficult game. Celtic played well in the strength sapping, heavy conditions, which were far from ideal. Both sets of players came off the field covered in mud, having given their all in a game which was a credit to the fine traditions of the Scottish Cup.

Montrose: Gorman D D'Arcy Ford B D'Arcy Hair McIntosh Robb Livingston (Murray) Lowe Miller Subs: Joss

Celtic: Latchford McGrain Lynch Fillipi MacDonald Edvaldsson Provan MacLeod McCluskey Lennox Doyle Subs: Conroy McAdam

League table at the end of January 1979

	P	W	D	L	F	A	Pts
Dundee Utd	19	8	7	4	26	18	23
Rangers	19	7	8	4	24	18	23
Partick Thistle	18	8	5	5	19	16	21
Aberdeen	20	6	9	5	31	20	21
Morton	20	7	6	7	24	23	20
St Mirren	19	8	4	7	22	18	20
Celtic	18	7	5	6	26	21	19
Hibernian	19	4	9	6	20	24	17
Hearts	19	5	5	9	24	37	15
Motherwell	19	4	4	11	21	36	12

CHAPTER 8 • FRUSTRATION CONTINUES

3 February 1979: Premier Division

Celtic v St Mirren (match postponed)

Twenty four hours before this game Billy McNeill was hopeful that it would go ahead, but he was perhaps being overly optimistic, given the fact that the other four Premier Division fixtures had already been postponed.

Billy was ultimately disappointed as heavy overnight rain fell on an already heavy surface. This led to flooding, resulting in the referee postponing the game after the 10am pitch inspection. The temperatures had improved, but rain was now falling, and pitches all over the country had taken a battering from ice, snow and frost, so were in no condition to absorb the heavy downpours.

Much debate was had in the media regarding the clubs' efforts to get matches played during the worst spell of weather since the winter of 1962-63. It was reported that more Scottish games had been postponed than in any other season in the history of the game.

Clubs in Scotland traditionally put down bales of hay to protect the pitch from heavy frost, but were unable to cope with the heavy snow which landed on the pitch and on the terraces. In England some clubs used heated air balloons with mixed results, but again they were of no use against snow. From the USA came news of under soil heating, which helped protect pitches against frost and snow. It was a system which required the playing surface to be ripped up and pipes placed underneath, through which hot water flowed, preventing ice and frost from forming on the surface. England's rugby authorities had installed such a system on their Twickenham pitch, but it had cost them in excess of £100,000 to install, and a small fortune each time they used it. The big football clubs in England were said to be interested, although the initial outlay was obviously a big drawback, and certainly no Scots club could hope to afford it at this time. As it was, Rangers eventually persevered, and had such a system in place for the 1981-82 season.

The Sunday Mail newspaper held a survey of all thirty eight senior clubs, regarding a possible winter shutdown. They voted in favour of a winter shutdown, by twenty two votes to sixteen. However, the down side of any shutdown would be the loss to each club of £13,000, paid by the football pools companies each year, to help subsidise Scottish football. For clubs in the lower reaches of the league, this money was a life line, and they would struggle to survive without it.

Celtic's representative in the survey, Chairman Desmond White, showed a bit of foresight with this suggestion. *'There is no point having a definitive close down if the weather is good. I'd rather extend the season into May, week by week, when the fixture list is wiped out.'*

10 February 1979: Premier Division

Aberdeen v Celtic (match postponed)

Unbelievably, more heavy snow fell in the west of Scotland in midweek, and this caused the postponement of Scotland's European Championship fixtures against Belgium, at senior and under-21 level.

The vast majority of the Scottish side at that time were 'Anglos', who played their football in England and travelled to join the squad, many of them having difficult journeys to travel north. An estimated 50,000 Scotland supporters were also left disappointed as they had purchased tickets for the game. They were reassured that their tickets would be valid for the new date, but the point was made that some of them would not be able to attend the rearranged fixture, and there were no refunds for such cases.

The postponement of this match caused great disappointment and led to fixture congestion at international level. It was decided that because the tournament was not taking place until the summer of 1980, there was no rush to play the game and it would be arranged for the following season. It was eventually played in December 1979, with Belgium winning convincingly by 3-1. This was regarded as a bad result at the time, but Belgium went on to reach the European Championship final in Rome, in June 1980. They lost narrowly to West Germany by 2-1, putting the Hampden result in some perspective.

During the same week, Aberdeen manager Alex Ferguson informed Celtic that the Pittodrie pitch was doubtful for the forthcoming Scottish Cup tie, as it was frozen and rutted. Celtic took advantage of indoor facilities at Inverclyde in midweek to keep in shape, although it was clear that the players were becoming dispirited due to continual postponements.

The Pittodrie contest was deemed to be an all ticket affair, and Celtic chairman Desmond White took a stand by refusing to accept tickets for the game from Aberdeen for two reasons.

Firstly, with the freezing weather continuing, the game was unlikely to go ahead, and if the game was to be played, then it was reasonable to make it pay at the gate for the convenience of the spectators.

Secondly, Celtic supporters clubs already held tickets for five postponed games, and this had involved a considerable financial outlay on the part of fans, who may not be able to attend rearranged fixtures. This was especially true for the match in Aberdeen, which involved a considerable distance for supporters to travel. The Celtic Supporters Association applauded White's stance on this matter. They hoped the authorities would show some common sense by limiting all ticket matches until weather conditions improved.

Local referee Billy Knoles attended Pittodrie at 10am on the Friday before the game, and inevitably the match was postponed. Yet another game had been called off and Scotland still shivered in freezing temperatures. There was no light at the end of tunnel for the Celtic players, or for their fans.

The game of the day went ahead at Ibrox, where second placed Rangers faced Dundee United. On a treacherous surface, Rangers had been the better side, but United were well organised and looked like hanging on, until Rangers' substitute Chris Robertson scored with only eight minutes remaining. This victory allowed Rangers to leap frog United to top the league table. Celtic were stranded in seventh place, which sounds worse than it actually was, as the Celts had two games in hand. Incredibly, only twelve points separated leaders Rangers from bottom club Motherwell, in what was fast becoming the most keenly contested league race in Scotland for years.

17 February 1979: Scottish Cup

Celtic v Berwick Rangers (match postponed)

Ever since the draw was made, the press were anticipating a possible cup upset, in what was described as a 'David and Goliath' clash. Berwick still basked in the glory of their sensational 1967 Scottish Cup win over Rangers, on their tiny Shielfield Park ground. This cup tie would be the first time that Celtic had played Berwick at senior level in any competition.

The romance of the cup dictated that neutrals would favour the minnows, and the newspapers rolled out Sammy Reid, Berwick's goal scoring hero from January 1967. He well recalled that famous day when the wee Rangers had defeated the big Rangers by 1-0. The media also recalled that the Rangers star duo of the time, Jim Forrest and George McLean, were unceremoniously dumped by the Ibrox club, following the defeat. Manager Scot Symon showed a ruthless streak, by making both men scapegoats for the sensational defeat. These reports no doubt brought back unpleasant memories for

Rangers' fans, as Celtic supporters amused themselves at the recollection of their greatest rivals' humiliation.

Symon's actions ultimately backfired on Rangers, when they reached the European Cup Winners Cup final in May 1967, and went down narrowly by 1-0 to Bayern Munich. Many observers believed that the retention of Forrest and McLean could have brought Rangers their first European trophy, and a notable victory over Bayern in the process.

The only regret for Berwick was that Celtic had home advantage for the tie. They would obviously have preferred to have the game played at their own small ground, where the fans would be crammed in tightly to create that unique cup tie atmosphere.

There was, therefore, a deep sense of frustration when the Celtic v Berwick match was postponed due to heavy frost, after referee Bobby Kellock made a pitch inspection on the Friday morning before the fixture was due to take place.

A problem arose for the SFA, because, as so many Scottish cup second and third round ties had been postponed, few fourth round ties could actually be played.

An unwanted piece of history in the Scottish game was created when the second round tie between Inverness Thistle and Falkirk was postponed on an incredible twenty nine occasions, between January 6th and February 20th. The game was finally played on 22nd February. Falkirk eventually won 4-0, but only three days later they were required to play Dundee in the next round, when they went down 1-0.

The Scottish football authorities became increasingly concerned that the postponed cup ties would infringe on the forthcoming league matches, and the SFA and Scottish League got together to negotiate possible solutions.

21 February 1979: Scottish Cup

Celtic v Berwick Rangers (match postponed)

The SFA instructed the clubs to play their postponed cup tie the following Wednesday, and the early signs were that the game would go ahead after a considerable thaw in Glasgow. However, as a result of the thaw, the pitch became heavy and at 4pm that day Parkhead was struck by a period of heavy rain. This resulted in flooding of large areas of the pitch, which was said to have resembled 'a duck pond.'

Celtic immediately contacted referee Kellock. He then came to the ground and declared the pitch unplayable. An attempt was made to contact Berwick officials in order to prevent them making an unnecessary journey of some two hundred miles, but to no avail, as they had already set off for Glasgow. Berwick's official party arrived at the ground around 5.30pm, only to be told the disappointing news. The Berwick group then attended the evening cup tie between Rangers and Kilmarnock at Ibrox, which finished in a rather surprising 1-1 draw.

Before travelling the short distance to Ibrox, the Berwick player-manager Dave Smith had to go to the front door at Celtic Park to reason with the one hundred or so angry Berwick fans who had made the wasted trip to Glasgow. After Smith explained the situation to them, the Berwick fans boarded their buses and returned south. The SFA then declared that the game would be played on Monday 26th February.

There was considerable sympathy for the travelling fans of both clubs, and Billy McNeill's frustration with the unpredictable weather was obvious. *'Who can say when it will be played after what happened tonight? If you can't plan hour to hour how can you plan days ahead? The trouble is that the thaw only goes down a couple of inches then there is about six or seven inches of frost under that. When the rain came down it was just pushed back on to the surface. I've never seen so much water on our pitch before. It's a disaster.'*

24 February 1979: Premier Division

Dundee United v Celtic (match postponed)

Forty eight hours before this match, the officials at Tannadice were confident of the game going ahead. The pitch had originally been under snow, but a thaw in the Tayside region had caused some optimism that the game could go ahead. Conditions were said to be improving by the hour, although an 8.30am pitch inspection on the morning of the game was planned as a precaution.

However, a pattern was now beginning to emerge. The high hopes of the clubs to get games played were continually being thwarted by the unpredictability of the weather on nights before games. So it proved on this occasion, when overnight temperatures plummeted again causing severe frost, and the fixture was postponed at the 8.30am inspection. The news was then quickly relayed back to Glasgow to prevent the unnecessary journey for thousands of Celtic fans.

The big news of the day was Hearts' shock 3-2 win over Rangers at Tynecastle. Hearts, second bottom before the game, had shown form which defied their lowly position, and Rangers' defeat had allowed St Mirren to take a shock lead at the top of the table, by one point.

For any Celtic follower, reading the newspapers on Sunday morning made depressing reading. The Celts sat in eighth place in the ten team league, but the more optimistic fans would have taken consolation that Celtic had a considerable amount of games in hand over the teams above them.

Celtic announced over the weekend that their great servant, Jimmy McGrory, was to retire as the club's Public Relations Officer. McGrory was famed as a player and enjoyed some success as a manager before Jock Stein arrived. However, it was his legendary goal scoring exploits for Celtic which would be his legacy, and he scored an incredible 410 goals in 408 games, between 1922 and 1938.

McGrory was approaching seventy five years old and had been connected with Celtic in some shape or form for almost sixty years. He was dearly loved by the Celtic supporters and had earned respect throughout Scottish football for his gentlemanly manner. He was regarded as an elder statesman of the game by all. He said he still planned to attend Celtic's games and the directors said that he would always be warmly welcomed by the club. Jimmy Cairney interviewed McGrory for the Celtic View to ascertain what retirement would bring for the great man.

'One final point was the obvious one. 'What are you going to do with all those hours of leisure that retirement brings?' Jimmy, who must have been pipe man of the year before Harold Wilson had been heard of, lit another match, drew hard on the briar stem, then smiled and replied - 'Enjoy them'.
As a tribute to their great hero, the Celtic Supporters Association invited Jimmy as their guest of honour at their annual rally in the Kelvin Hall. The Association presented him with a huge clock with the Celtic crest emblazoned on it, and the simple engraving - 'To the one and only Jimmy McGrory.'

26 February 1979: Scottish Cup

Celtic   **3-0**   **Berwick Rangers**
Lynch pen 9
Burns 64
McDowall (og) 86

Attendance: 13,000

This game was played on a Monday evening, after Celtic had unsuccessfully attempted to have this game played twenty four hours earlier. The club had called in the Salvage Corps to attempt to remove water from the pitch, which had caused the original postponement. However, Strathclyde Police knocked back the idea, saying that they could not provide adequate Police cover on a Sunday at such short notice.

There was more bad news for Berwick fans, when a football special train to Glasgow was cancelled at short notice, after an industrial dispute by workers at British Rail. The country at this time was gripped by a feeling of strike mania, as unions urged workers to withdraw their labour at short notice, in an industrial struggle with Prime Minister James Callaghan's beleaguered government.

There was considerable relief all round when referee Tom Kellock passed the pitch playable during a morning pitch inspection. Billy McNeill chose this occasion to recall two of his most experienced players. Goalkeeper Peter Latchford, dropped after the October debacle at Tynecastle, was recalled and Danny McGrain continued his phased rehabilitation into the first team, with another appearance in his customary right-back role.

Only 13,000 braved the freezing elements, to stand on the Parkhead terraces and watch the proceedings unfold. Berwick were determined to make a game of it, but they allowed their enthusiasm to run away with them, which resulted in some physical play, and the game deteriorated as a result. Berwick centre-half, Roy McDowall, had a most unfortunate game. In just nine minutes he tripped John Doyle in the area, allowing Andy Lynch to open the scoring from the resultant penalty. Late in the game, he then scored an own goal, when he spectacularly turned a bullet cross from Davie Provan past his own goalkeeper.

Sandwiched between McDowall's calamities was a goal from Tommy Burns, when he fired in a shot from another Provan cross. So happy was Burns with his goal, that he celebrated it with a cartwheel, which the Celtic fans referred to as 'Dixie Deans' style. Berwick's only real opportunity came on the stroke of half-time, when Wheatley smacked a shot off Latchford's crossbar.

The 'wee' Rangers did not make many friends with their physical approach, although player-manager Dave Smith turned back the years with a classy performance, reminding everyone why he was voted Scotland's player of the year in 1972, whilst playing for Glasgow Rangers.

Celtic's star man on the night was their stylish midfielder, Tommy Burns, who was the target of some heavy Berwick tackles, and was said to *'have evaded tackles like a matador avoiding a rampaging bull.'* Observers were not only impressed by Tommy's talented performance but by his growing maturity.

'The temperament of Tommy Burns, which was known to be brittle, was put to its severest test last night. He passed with honours. Against a Berwick side who selected him for a series of offences which would be worth thirty days if they were committed in the street, Burns showed restraint and maturity as he emerged as Celtic's most purposeful player.' Evening Times, 27th February 1979.

The draw for the next round had been made the previous weekend, and Celtic faced a daunting trip north to face Aberdeen at Pittodrie, in what was seen as the tie of the round.

Celtic: Latchford McGrain Lynch Aitken MacDonald Edvaldsson Provan MacLeod McCluskey (McAdam) Burns Doyle Sub: Lennox

Berwick: Frame Rutherford MacLeod D Smith McDowell Jobson Davidson Moyes G Smith Tait Wheatley Subs: Laing McLean

League table at the end of February 1979

	P	W	D	L	F	A	Pts
St Mirren	22	10	5	7	27	21	25
Rangers	21	8	8	5	27	21	24
Dundee Utd	20	8	7	5	26	19	23
Aberdeen	21	6	10	5	33	22	22
Partick Thistle	19	8	6	5	21	18	22
Morton	22	7	8	7	27	31	22
Hibernian	21	5	10	6	24	25	20
Celtic	18	7	5	6	26	21	19
Hearts	21	6	5	10	28	41	17
Motherwell	21	4	4	13	21	41	12

CHAPTER 9 • THE CAPTAIN RETURNS

3 March 1979: Premier Division

Celtic   1-0   Aberdeen
Conn 65

Attendance: 26,000

This was a fixture which almost didn't go ahead. The clubs had actually been scheduled to play each other at Pittodrie on this date, but the huge number of postponed games proved to be a logistical nightmare for the Scottish League.

Aberdeen obviously wanted the match played at Pittodrie as was originally intended. However, Grampian police said they would not be able to provide sufficient manpower, due to a huge man hunt in Aberdeen following the abduction of a child. Added to that, the local ambulance drivers had gone on strike, resulting in the chief constable vetoing any football match going ahead in the city that weekend.

In view of this, Aberdeen were keen to play an outstanding postponed fixture against Rangers at Ibrox. Rangers had a free weekend as their prospective league opponents had postponed Scottish Cup ties to play. On 28th February the League management committee convened, and decided that Aberdeen should play at Parkhead on 3rd March, with Celtic swapping the fixture by travelling to Pittodrie on 21st April. The committee also discussed the possibility of playing the Celtic v Rangers fixture, which had been outstanding since early January, but the logistics of arranging an Old Firm match at such short notice were clearly not practical.

The outcome of the three club tangle left Aberdeen Chairman Dick Donald incensed. *'We have been instructed to play at Parkhead and must comply with the ruling. But we would rather have played one of our outstanding matches and the only one available was Rangers at Ibrox. I think this was who we should have played.'* Donald's attitude was curious, considering the lack of football played over the winter months.

The harsh winter weather of the period relented, for a welcome spell of milder weather, and at five minutes to three, on Saturday 3rd March, the Celtic team finally ran out to a rousing reception from their supporters. The fans were delighted for two reasons. This was Celtic's first league game since 23rd December, and their first league game at Parkhead since 16th December, a long period of ten weeks. Perhaps more importantly, their inspirational captain, Danny McGrain, led his side out for the first time in a league game since 1st October 1977. The supporters feared that they would never see him play at the highest level again, and although this game was seen as a big test for him, the Celtic fans were just grateful to have their skipper back in the fold.

Celtic settled quickly, and could have scored in nine minutes when McGrain's free-kick left Conn with a clear sight of goal, but his shot went narrowly past. Aberdeen seemed taken aback by Celtic's early energy. MacLeod struck a shot over the bar, before a fine McGrain cross went across the face of goal with no Celtic player to take advantage. In twenty seven minutes, Edvaldsson went close, with a spectacular over head kick, but before half-time Aberdeen had settled, and the dangerous Dominic Sullivan saw a powerful shot saved by Latchford.

Celtic came out strongly in the second half and Clark made a fine save after Conn burst through. Just after that, the Aberdeen goalkeeper made another good stop from Lynch's free-kick, and it took a Rougvie clearance to clear the danger from the Dons' goal. Aberdeen were still a danger, and a misunderstanding between McGrain and Provan allowed Scanlon to run clear, but his shot was weak and Latchford saved easily. His miss was costly, as shortly after Celtic made the break through. Provan skipped past McLelland on the right flank, and swung a low cross over for Alfie Conn to sweep the ball into the net from eight yards.

Parkhead exploded as the fans cheered the first goal they had witnessed from open play in the league since 25th November. Celtic managed to hold on until the final whistle was blown. There was much relief at the end that two points were coming to Parkhead, from a game where the players put in a great deal of effort.

The fans noticed something different about McGrain. He now sported the thick black beard which would become his trade mark, and earn him the nickname of 'Barabbas', after the famous Biblical character. He had a superb match on his return to league action, and was the subject of great focus afterwards. *'Danny McGrain is beginning to look like his old self at right-back, and was in fact a better player than the man who replaced him in a Scotland jersey, Stuart Kennedy.'* Daily Record, 5th March 1979.

Manager McNeill was delighted with McGrain's comeback, and intimated that he had feared his captain would never return. *'I honestly didn't think Danny was going to make it. But he is a determined man. He has met every target on the way back, even in training. What he needs now is hard games like the Aberdeen one. He just strolls through friendlies or reserve games.'*

For his part, McGrain wasn't shy at looking ahead and could not be said to be lacking in ambition. *'I am looking forward to things now. Things like the cup final (said with only a hint of a smile) the home internationals and the European Championship match in Norway. There is no other way to look at things. Last year I had nothing to look ahead to. This year I feel entitled to a different attitude.'* Glasgow Herald, 5th March 1979.

Joe Filippi had the difficult job of replacing McGrain during his enforced absence. He remembers the pressures of covering that position, whilst admiring McGrain's dedication in working his way back into the side, after such a long lay off. *'It was something of a burden replacing Danny but he gave me a lot of support even when he was injured. I looked up to him because you have no idea just what a player he was, even behind the scenes, with the way he looked after himself and how he trained to get himself back to what he was before. He was out of the game for over a year and it takes a while to get back to that fitness regime, which was international level, and he pummelled his body just to get back into the team.'*

Celtic - Latchford McGrain Lynch Aitken MacDonald Edvaldsson Provan MacLeod Conn Burns (Filippi) Doyle Sub not used: Lennox

Aberdeen - Clark Kennedy McLelland McMaster Rougvie Miller Sullivan Archibald Jarvie (Harper) Strachan Scanlon

The welcome thaw in the weather allowed Celtic to arrange a friendly at Brockville against Falkirk, in an attempt to get the fringe players in the squad match fit. The players were given a good run out, and the experienced trio of Tom McAdam, Ronnie Glavin and George McCluskey all played well, as they tried to impress before the cup trip to Pittodrie. McAdam scored twice and McCluskey also scored in a 3-1 win.

However, the headlines were being made off the park, when it was announced there would be no televised highlights of the weekend's Scottish Cup quarter-final ties. The football authorities and the television companies had always been uneasy bedfellows, and a row blew up over the usual problem, money. SFA secretary Ernie Walker announced that talks between the SFA, the BBC and STV had ended in deadlock, and no future meetings were planned.

The SFA had requested £2000 per match for the quarter- finals ties to be televised, and £4000 for each of the two semi-finals. The fees represented a rise of 20% on the cost of the same stages the previous season, and the television companies were not prepared to pay.

Scottish and Newcastle Breweries, who were sponsoring the tournament to the tune of £100,000, were said to be deeply unhappy at the lack of TV exposure for their brand. As it was, no further Scottish Cup ties were televised that season, apart from the final in May as prior agreement had already been reached, regarding the showpiece of the Scottish season.

On the transfer front, Celtic's out of favour goalkeeper Roy Baines was sold to Morton for a nominal fee of £10,000. At the same time, Billy McNeill was at pains to point out newspaper claims that Celtic were about to bid £80,000 for Newcastle United's ex-Hibs defender, John Blackley, were wide of the mark.

10 March 1979: Scottish Cup, quarter-final

Aberdeen   1-1   Celtic
Harper 26   Doyle 25

Attendance: 24,000

This was a typical, keenly contested cup tie, in which there were five bookings. Referee Ian Foote struggled to keep control, as matters threatened to get out of hand.

In fourteen minutes Gordon Strachan came to Aberdeen's rescue, when he cleared an Edvaldsson header off the goal line, with his keeper Bobby Clark well beaten in the Dons' goal. The game then sparked to life with two goals within sixty seconds. In twenty five minutes John Doyle gave Celtic the lead, when Edvaldsson headed down a Burns free-kick for Doyle to score with a right foot shot. Seconds later, with the Celtic legions still celebrating, Aberdeen equalised, when Harper raced on to a Kennedy through ball, and tucked a neat shot past Latchford.

In the second half Celtic had the edge, and only a desperate tackle by Miller prevented Doyle from scoring his second goal of the afternoon. In seventy seven minutes Edvaldsson was left cursing the diminutive Strachan for the second time, after the

Dons midfielder cleared another header from the Icelander off the Aberdeen line.

At full-time Celtic were left frustrated, as they had been slightly the better side. Despite all the frantic play, there was one player who stood out from the rest. *'The top Celt in terms of class was Tommy Burns. At times he made the others look as if they had wandered in from a factory kick-around. Maturity seems to be curbing the red headed midfield lad's short temper and he is all the better for it. If he is still rather a luxury in this Parkhead side then that is hardly his fault.'* Glasgow Herald, 12th March 1979.

Aberdeen: Clark Kennedy McLelland MacMaster McLeish Miller Sullivan Archibald Harper Scanlon (Davidson) Sullivan Sub: Cooper

Celtic: Latchford McGrain Lynch Aitken MacDonald Edvaldsson Provan MacLeod Conn Burns Doyle Subs: Filippi Lennox

14 March 1979: Scottish Cup, quarter final replay

Celtic	**1-2**	**Aberdeen**
Lennox 64		Davidson 1
		Archibald 12

Attendance: 37,000

The main criticism of the ten team Premier Division, was that teams played each other four times per season, which was felt to be too often. It meant that players became over familiar with the styles of their direct opponents, and fans became fed up watching the same teams play each other on so many occasions. When cup ties were added to the equation, there was the possibility that teams could face each other many more times in one campaign. And, when Aberdeen came to Parkhead for this midweek floodlit replay, it was actually the third time the teams had faced each other in the short space of eleven days.

However, this mattered not to the fans who packed Celtic Park on the night, and it made for an electric atmosphere. The players may have groaned at the prospect of seeing each other again, but the paying public were clearly anticipating another pulsating fixture between two teams, who, on their day, could be argued to be the two most attacking sides in the country.

There were still thousands of fans queuing outside the Parkhead turnstiles when Aberdeen took the lead, with just over sixty seconds on the clock. The goal was an absolute disaster for Peter Latchford, when he dropped a long punt from Rougvie at the feet of Joe Harper. He gleefully prodded the ball to Duncan Davidson to strike into the empty net.

Celtic were rocked by this, but recovered to storm the Aberdeen goal, only for the Dons to score again in twelve minutes. Once again Latchford did not cover himself in glory. This time a Harper cross found Archibald's head, and as the Celtic 'keeper rashly moved off his line to deal with the cross, he allowed Archibald the opportunity to calmly nod the ball over him, into the space of an empty net.

Celtic went for broke for the rest of the first half, urged on by their huge support, and although they did not create any clear cut chances, they should have had a penalty. Provan's direct cross was handled away by Aberdeen defender Miller, and to Celtic's frustration, neither the referee nor linesman indicated a penalty. This was one of a number of disputed decisions and referee, Ian Foote, who was to feel the wrath of the Celtic support as the game wore on.

In the second half Celtic only improved when Lennox replaced the injured Conn. In sixty four minutes Bobby brought his team back into the game when he fired in a close range shot, after Rougvie's poor clearance struck Miller and fell at the feet of the Celtic substitute. The match had been intense, but the crowd now worked themselves into a frenzy, as Celtic surged forward for an equaliser. The Aberdeen goal had a number of lucky escapes, none more so than when Clark clawed a header from his goal line. As the ball fell to Lennox he struck his shot towards goal only for it to rebound most fortuitously off Rougvie, who knew little about it.

Referee Foote then infuriated the home support further when a shot by Lennox was handled in the area by MacMaster. The official again opted not to blow for a penalty kick. Celtic's constant attacks were becoming more frantic, and a controversial decision by a linesman prompted crowd trouble. Bobby Lennox raced on to a Provan pass and looked marginally onside as the official flagged him down. At that point, several Celtic players raced over to confront the enclosure side linesman, as the tempers of the Celtic fans in the Jungle boiled over. A hail of cans and bottles rained down on the match official, who raced on to the pitch for cover, as Celtic players pleaded with their fans for calm.

Aberdeen managed to hold on until time up, with mayhem going on all around. After the final whistle, John Doyle was booked for venting his frustration at Foote. As the teams went up the tunnel the players' behaviour deteriorated, with individuals from both sides becoming involved in skirmishes as the officials sought in vain to separate them.

'The ugly scenes which climaxed this passionate quarter final replay told their own story. The Celtic players felt that something much less than justice had been done to them and the referee Ian Foote was left in no doubt about their opinions. John Doyle was the first to express his view; then as the players made their way towards the Parkhead tunnel there was pushing, shoving and angry brawling. Frustration had boiled over and although such behaviour cannot be condoned or applauded it can at times be understood. Last night was a case in point.' Evening Times, 15th February 1979.

'Some of the tackling, from players of both sides, had those of us in the press box ducking.' Glasgow Herald, 15th February 1979.

Aberdeen's captain on the night was Willie Miller. A magnificent defender of the highest order, he was a player of considerable experience at home and abroad. He would later lead Aberdeen to their unforgettable European Cup Winner cup success in 1983, against Real Madrid. He also played in two World Cups with distinction for Scotland. In later years Miller wrote his autobiography entitled 'The Don'. He insisted that in his long career he had never played in a more venomous or intimidating atmosphere than he experienced at Celtic Park during that hectic cup replay. He stated that some of the players on the field had actually feared for their safety.

The disappointment for Celtic was that they had put so much in to the Aberdeen cup ties, and had absolutely nothing to show in return for their efforts. Although their wounds had been self-inflicted, there was a lesson to be learned, as the old defensive frailties were on show again. Now that Celtic were out of the cup competitions, Billy McNeill knew that the only source of European qualification was through their League placing and the Celtic boss promised an all out assault on the League to achieve his European objective.

Celtic: Latchford McGrain Lynch Aitken McDonald Edvaldsson Provan MacLeod Conn (Lennox) Burns Doyle Sub: Filippi

Aberdeen Clark Kennedy McLelland MacMaster Rougvie Miller Sullivan (McLeish) Archibald Harper (Scanlon) Jarvie Davidson

17 March 1979: Premier Division

Celtic	**2-1**	**Motherwell**
Lennox 13, 50		Donnelly 63

Attendance: 16,000

Celtic Park on Saint Patrick's Day is always a special place to be. Because of the club's Irish roots, supporters always anticipated the occasion of the feast of Ireland's patron saint with great relish. The obligatory scarf and flag sellers outside the stadium, for one day only, also sold little sprigs of shamrock. Thousands of Celtic fans proudly sported the Irish emblem on the lapels of their jackets, in respect for the club's Irish origins.

How appropriate then, that Celtic's young Irish goalkeeper, Pat Bonner, was chosen to make his Celtic debut in front of the Parkhead faithful, on this most Irish of all days. Across the world the Irish, and people of Irish descent, gathered to celebrate 'Paddy's day', and it was no different at Parkhead. The denizens of the Jungle, normally more renowned for their coarse chanting and raucous behaviour, sang their own version of the famous hymn in praise of the great Irish saint.

'In the war against Rangers
In the fight for the cup
When Jimmy McGrory
Put Celtic one up
We've done it before
And we'll do it again
On Erin's green valleys look down on Parkhead
On Erin's green valleys
On Erin's green valleys
On Erin's green valleys look down on Parkhead'

Unfortunately the weather did not match the happy mood of the fans, as rain fell from a typical dull, leaden Glasgow sky. The Donegal born Bonner was replacing the unfortunate Peter Latchford, after his aberrations against Aberdeen, although Billy McNeill was at pains to point out that he was only being rested and not dropped.

Motherwell were almost certainly bound for relegation, and they brought with them a very young and inexperienced side. Their two biggest assets, Gregor Stevens and Willie Pettigrew were left out of the team, as possible suitors considered bids for two of the most wanted players in Scotland. Billy McNeill was said to covet both players, although Celtic were thought to be reluctant to go anywhere near Motherwell's pricey £350,000 valuation of both men.

The game started with Edvaldsson sending the ball back to Bonner for the young Celtic goalie to get a welcome touch, and a huge cheer from the watching spectators. Celtic attacked keenly and in fourteen minutes they made the breakthrough. Tommy Burns went on a great run through the middle of the park, from inside his own half, towards the 'Well goal. He then slipped a fine pass to Doyle, only for Motherwell 'keeper Rennie to run out to clear. He served only to knock it into the path of Lennox, who scored with ease.

In the second half Lennox made it 2-0, with a powerful rising header from a terrific Provan cross. Minutes later wee Bobby almost made it a hat trick, when he scraped the post with a shot, with Rennie well beaten. Celtic were in total control until sixty four minutes, when Motherwell youngster Donnelly spoiled Bonner's debut, with a cracking shot high past the young Irishman. Celtic almost blew it near the end, when Steve Mungall astonishingly missed an open goal after Bonner had saved a Larnach shot, and diverted the ball into Mungall's path with the goalmouth gaping.

Celtic prevailed, and Saint Patrick's Day 1979 finished on a happy note for a young Pat Bonner and the supporters. However had it not been for that dreadful Mungall miss, the day would have been remembered as an absolute disaster.

Celtic: Bonner McGrain Lynch Aitken MacDonald Edvaldsson Provan MacLeod (McAdam) Lennox Burns Doyle Sub: McCluskey

Motherwell: Rennie Wark Smith Kane Dempsey Kennedy Rafferty (Mungall) Wilson Larnach Clinging Donnelly (Somerville)

21 March 1979: Premier Division

Hearts v Celtic (match postponed)

The Glasgow public, still recovering from the worst winter the city had suffered for many years, looked out in disbelief as snow fell again in the early hours of Tuesday 20th March. Celtic were due to play at Tynecastle the following night, but the main focus of the media was on the huge game at Ibrox, between Rangers and Cologne. They were meeting in the second leg quarter-final of the European Cup. Rangers fought a rear guard action in the first leg, and had been happy to come back from Germany with a 1-0 deficit to make up at home. After their tremendous wins against Juventus and PSV Eindhoven, the Ibrox men were confident of overcoming Cologne. There was a belief amongst the Rangers fans that this was to be their year to do something special in Europe's premier tournament, perhaps even emulating Celtic's victory in the final in Lisbon in 1967.

As a precaution, the SFA sent referee Kenny Hope, a qualified FIFA official, to inspect the pitch on the Tuesday morning and he declared the pitch playable. Sadly, in the early hours of Wednesday morning, heavy snow fell. When the match referee, Angel Martinez from Spain, visited Ibrox for a pitch inspection at 1pm it was still snowing. This meant the official had to return at 2pm, and the inevitable happened when he called the game off, with five inches of snow covering the Ibrox pitch and terraces. Due to the snow covering all of central Scotland, Celtic's match against Hearts in Edinburgh was also duly called off.

UEFA rules dictated that in the event of a postponement, the away club should stay for a further twenty four hours, to allow the home club a chance to rearrange the fixture. Cologne then returned to their base at an Erskine hotel, as Rangers set about clearing the stadium of snow, hoping that the weather would improve.

On the morning of Thursday 22nd March, there was a respite in the weather, and an army of volunteers turned up at Ibrox at

8am in order to clear snow from the pitch and terraces. They were bolstered by a number of school kids, taking advantage of strikes in local schools to come along to assist. Rangers also arranged for bull dozers to come to clear the pitch and when Angel Martinez returned to Ibrox at 10am he declared that the match was on.

A sad result of the postponement was that three hundred Cologne fans had travelled from Germany, and the vast majority of them had return flights on the Thursday morning, the day on which the game was now to be played. Despite their disappointment, the Cologne contingent could be seen handing over their precious match tickets to grateful Glaswegians, in a tremendous gesture of goodwill. Because of this, Cologne would play in the cauldron of Ibrox with virtually no support. Tickets for the match were particularly scarce as Rangers were in the process of building their new Copland Road stand, and this curtailed the attendance to 44,000. Had this game been played twelve months earlier, Rangers would have been confident of attracting a crowd in excess of 70,000.

The TV stations were naturally keen to get in on the act, and Rangers' general manager, Willie Waddell, and STV's Russell Galbraith, were involved in prolonged negotiations over the possibility of live coverage. It was only announced on the day of the game that they had agreed terms, with Rangers receiving £7000 for allowing the cameras in to relay the action nationwide. Live televised matches were few and far between in those days, and so this was a terrific treat for the football loving Scots' public.

A huge TV audience watched the game between Rangers and Cologne, but after the anticipation of the big match it rather proved to be an anticlimax, as the great Rangers European Cup adventure came to an end. The tie was as good as finished in forty eight minutes, when the classy West German striker, Dieter Muller, expertly flicked home a cross from Konopka which had been cleverly dummied by the experienced West German internationalist, Heinz Flohe. This was a hammer blow to Rangers, who were playing in an unusual all blue strip, and it knocked the heart out of them. Although they equalised through Tommy McLean, they never looked like creating the other two goals they required to go through. At full-time the Cologne players gleefully celebrated on the pitch, which was hardly surprising, given that they were on the tremendous incentive of £2500 per man to win through to the semi-finals.

Rangers were dealt a devastating blow before the game when their inspirational captain, Derek Johnstone, failed a fitness test and was named on the bench, with young and inexperienced striker, Billy Urquhart leading the Rangers forward line in his place. There wasn't really much between the teams until Cologne's killer goal, although precociously talented young midfielder, Bernd Schuster, impressed the viewing public greatly.

The STV live coverage is perhaps best remembered for other reasons. Leicester City's ex-Rangers manager, Jock Wallace, had been chosen as the match summariser in the studio, due to his in depth knowledge of the side he previously managed. At full-time Wallace was quizzed as to his thoughts on the main events of the match. He gave brusque one word answers to the clearly rattled anchorman he was sharing a platform with. Wallace was obviously aggrieved at the result, and his reaction made for uncomfortable viewing.

As an aside, half way during the match transmission, viewers were surprised to see a giant crucifixion scene appear on their screens for a few seconds, before the coverage of the game was resumed. It transpired that the STV technicians were preparing to show an advert for the forthcoming TV series 'Jesus of Nazareth', and someone made a blunder by starting it in error during the match. Robert Powell played the Son of God to great acclaim, and the series was shown over the Easter period to huge audiences, receiving rave reviews. This didn't stop certain individuals from complaining strongly to STV that this was somehow a Catholic conspiracy, to embarrass

Rangers on their big night. Celtic supporters, and the public in general, found the whole matter highly amusing.

24 March 1979: Premier Division

Rangers v Celtic (match postponed)

In a season which had already thrown up some controversies, the biggest storm of the season was about to blow up between the country's two major clubs.

Due to the continued reconstruction of Ibrox, this game was to be played at Hampden, courtesy of Queens Park. Because of the recent snowfall, the Scottish League sent match referee Brian McGinlay for an early pitch inspection on the morning before the game. McGinlay was accompanied by officials of both clubs, Billy McNeill and John Clark of Celtic, and John Greig and Willie Waddell from Rangers. McGinlay took the trouble to contact the weather centre and consulted with the Scottish League, before deciding that the pitch was playable, and that the game could go ahead.

At that point things seemed straight forward, but on Friday afternoon Queens Park officials over ruled the referee. They informed the Scottish League that the game was off, as snow on the uncovered terraces had not been cleared, and Queens claimed they could not guarantee the safety of the spectators. On hearing this, Celtic sent a team of ground staff boys to assist with clearing the snow, but they were surprisingly turned away by Queens Park officials.

The Celtic chairman, Desmond White, reacted angrily to Queens Park's decision. *'I believe the game should be on. There is no doubt in my mind that with a little more effort the ground could have been declared safe. But a serious effort by Rangers was not made. Only on Thursday, Ibrox was cleared by an army of volunteers. Yet a day later this game was cancelled.*

We offered to do anything that would make the ground safe. We even sent along a squad to clear the terracings and offered to make salt and grit available but we were turned away.

We are mystified as to why this game is off. In our opinion no serious effort was made to get the game played. I visited Hampden after the game was cancelled and I am sure that fifteen men could have cleared the terracing of snow in two hours.'

Rangers' vice chairman Willie Waddell reacted immediately. *'Queens Park are the licence holders of Hampden, and as such the decision was theirs and theirs alone. Rangers were merely renting the ground for the match.* Under fire Queens Park secretary Frank Campbell stated: *'As the club staging the event I can assure you this decision was not taken lightly. Several parts of the terracing were under snow and although there were volunteers available it would not have been enough. Bearing in mind all the factors we could not guarantee the safety of the spectators at 1pm tomorrow. We were not sitting on our hands but regarding the manpower available we did not feel there was enough to do the job.'*

The feeling amongst Celtic officials and supporters was that it was in Rangers interest to have the game postponed. They would clearly be at a physical and mental disadvantage, having lost to Cologne less than forty eight hours previously, and consequently it was felt they made minimal effort to help the game go ahead. Rangers officials were correct to say that Queens Park had the ultimate decision, as licence holders of Hampden. However it was pointed out that the League Cup final between Aberdeen and Rangers was due to take place seven days later on 31st March, and it was difficult to imagine Queens Park allowing that game to be postponed, given even remotely similar circumstances.

The irony was that the snow covered area of terracing, which had caused so much concern, was at the Celtic end of the ground. Throughout the season, Jack Adams' Saturday

Sportsbag column in the Daily Record had been an amusing place of debate between supporters of rival clubs, especially the regular correspondents, Celtic supporting, 'Paddy the Maddy', and his Rangers counterpart, 'Tam the Bam'. Tam was said to hail from Baillieston and Paddy from Norfolk Court in the Gorbals, and they engaged in lively banter long before the days of the debating chambers of internet forums and Twitter. The bold Paddy was said to write his letters to Adams in green ink, and after the furore of the postponement, the following comment was printed, which rather caustically summed up the feeling of Celtic fans at that time.

'Willie Waddell's concern over the safety of Celtic fans must qualify for the joke of the year award. No doubt this is the reason why the Celtic end at Ibrox has no cover as he is probably afraid the roof would fall on their heads.'

Feelings were running unusually high between officials of the Old Firm clubs, and the press encouraged more conciliatory relations between them, given the traditional tensions between the supporters of their teams. As it was, Rangers arranged a Glasgow Cup semi-final at short notice against Partick Thistle at Ibrox, and Celtic were left with yet another free Saturday afternoon. Astonishingly, this was Celtic's fourteenth postponed game, in a long season, which was obviously going to last a whole lot longer.

Over at Parkhead, Celtic announced that they had arranged a fixture against the Chinese national side at Celtic Park, to be played in August as a pre-season friendly. Celtic toured the Far East in the summer of 1977, playing a number of games in Singapore and Australia. They also received an invite to play in China at that time, but could not manage to fit in a game, due to their tight playing schedule. West Bromwich Albion toured China in the summer of 1978, playing several games to big crowds, receiving a great response from the Chinese public. The Chinese FA then contacted West Bromwich and Celtic to arrange UK summer fixtures, presenting an interesting prospect for the fans.

28 March 1979: Premier Division

Celtic   3-0   Morton
Provan 6
Burns 43
Glavin 80

Attendance: 16,000

Celtic now faced the first of many midweek league fixtures, in order to catch up with their massive backlog of postponed games. Their fans were to become well used to such fixtures in the weeks ahead. The supporters who turned out on a bitterly cold March evening made their feelings known on the postponement of the Old Firm game at Hampden. The Jungle sarcastically sang:

'Oh, the Huns are feart tae play us
The Huns are feart tae play us
The Huns are feart tae play us
And so say all of us!'

Morton came to Parkhead in good form, buoyed by a weekend win over league leaders Dundee United, and played their recent purchase from Celtic, Roy Baines, in goal. Morton's ex-Celtic midfielder, Andy Ritchie, was gaining a tremendous reputation for himself as a dead ball expert, and was a prime candidate for Scottish player of the year. It was ironic, therefore, that Celtic struck twice in the first half, from the type of set pieces that Ritchie was renowned for.

Playing in their change strip of green shirts, white shorts and green socks, Celtic opened the scoring in six minutes, when Davie Provan bent a free-kick round the Morton wall, with Baines looking slow to get down to it. Two minutes before half-time, Tommy Burns scored the second. He took a corner and sent in a swinger from the stand side, swirling high into the air. The ball looped over several Morton defenders, and went in off the post. Rangers' winger, Davie Cooper, had also scored from a corner against Motherwell to a fanfare of publicity, and Burns had now emulated his feat.

But, the main talking point of the match came in thirteen minutes:

'The cruellest blow of all for Morton came when Ritchie sent in a thundering drive from forty yards out on the right touchline. The ball beat Latchford, hit the underside of the bar and bounced into the net. It looked like the goal of the season but as Ritchie turned to salute his former fans in the Parkhead enclosure the far side linesman called over the referee who then disallowed the goal, giving Celtic a free-kick inside the six yard box'
Glasgow Herald, 29th March 1979.

Ritchie had scored one of the all time great goals, and the patrons of the Jungle, who had taunted him with cries of 'Celtic reject', stood open mouthed, clapping in admiration. To this day, it's not known exactly why this goal was disallowed. It long remained a sore point for Andy Ritchie, so much so that he was still recalling his frustrations in his autobiography, which was published in 2012.

In the second half Baines made a great save from a Ronnie Glavin shot, with the Celtic man following up to make it 3-0. The result flattered Celtic, as Morton had not played badly, with Celtic getting the breaks at vital times. The only disappointment for Celtic on the night was that reliable centre-half Roddy MacDonald broke his ankle, and this would keep him out for the rest of the season.

The next day there were newspaper reports that Celtic had made a bid of £100,000 for Motherwell's international striker, Willie Pettigrew. Celtic claimed they had made an official approach for the player, but Motherwell said this included a player swap, and that they would only consider a straight cash deal.

Celtic: Latchford McGrain Lynch Aitken MacDonald (McCluskey) Edvaldsson Provan Glavin Lennox Burns Doyle
Sub: McAdam

Morton: Baines Hayes Holmes Anderson Orr Thomson McNeil Miller Hutchison Tolmie Ritchie Subs: Scott McLaren

31 March 1979: Premier Division

Hibs	**2-1**	**Celtic**
Stewart 3		Glavin pen 82
Rae 16		

Attendance: 17,000

Legend has it, that when the Celtic side ran out at Easter Road, thousands of inebriated Celtic fans thought they were dreaming when they saw a player in the Celtic number nine shorts, who was the spitting image of ex-Celt Vic Davidson. There was tremendous confusion amongst the support, which was only cleared up when the Hibs' stadium announcer declared that it actually was Vic Davidson, and that the fans were not seeing things after all. Vic had been signed late the night before, and most of the newspapers had gone to press, meaning his signing had largely gone unreported. In the days before social media, news of this sort took some time to come through. The Saturday edition of the Glasgow Herald actually reported that Hearts were chasing Davidson's signature, and that he had rejected their approach.

Billy McNeill had been a team mate of Davidson's for many years, and knew all about his attributes. McNeill was desperate for an experienced forward, and having drawn a blank from Motherwell in the pursuit of Willie Pettigrew, Celtic swooped to bring Vic back to Scotland, for a fee of £30,000. Davidson dashed all the way from Oxford late on Friday night, where he was based for Blackpool's' match with Oxford United, to seal the deal.

Roddy MacDonald's absence in the centre of Celtic defence was sorely missed, when the Celts lost two bad goals in the first sixteen minutes. In three minutes Ralph Callachan swung over a corner, and as the Celtic defence watched, George Stewart jumped unchallenged to head home. Hibs then went further in front when Latchford misjudged a high lob from MacLeod, to allow Rae an easy chance to make it 2-0.

New Bhoy Davidson toiled to make an impression, although with eight minutes remaining Ronnie Glavin scored from a penalty, after Arthur Duncan downed John Doyle in the area. Celtic produced a furious finish, but to no avail, and Hibs ran out 2-1 winners. This defeat left Celtic stranded in eighth place in the table, just above the relegation places filled by Hearts and Motherwell.

The mood of Celtic fans on the journey home was not helped by the news that Rangers had defeated Aberdeen 2-1 at Hampden, to win the Scottish League Cup. In a controversial game, Aberdeen defender, Doug Rougvie, was sent off after an altercation with Rangers' striker, Derek Johnstone. With the game finely balanced at 1-1, Rangers scored a winner in injury time against a tiring, ten man Dons side. Rougvie became the first player to be ordered off in a domestic Scottish final since Rangers' Jock Buchanan, in the Scottish Cup final of 1929. Reports stated that it was a harsh decision, considering that vendettas were being fought out all over the pitch in a very tough match.

There continues to be a great deal of bad blood between Rangers and Aberdeen. Aberdonians maintain that they can trace the ill feeling back to this game, and the injustice they felt at Rougvie's harsh sending off and their eventual defeat.

Hibs: McArthur Brazil Duncan McNamara Stewart Bremner MacLeod Higgins Rae Campbell Brown Subs: Kilgour Lambie

Celtic: Latchford McGrain Filippi Aitken Edvaldsson Conroy (Lennox) Provan (McCluskey) Glavin Davidson Burns Doyle

League table at the end of March 1979

	P	W	D	L	F	A	Pts
Dundee Utd	28	14	7	7	43	27	35
Rangers	24	11	8	5	32	22	30
St Mirren	27	12	5	10	37	30	29
Hibernian	27	9	11	7	33	31	29
Morton	28	9	9	10	40	44	27
Aberdeen	25	8	10	7	43	26	26
Celtic	22	10	5	7	33	24	25
Partick Thistle	25	9	7	9	27	27	25
Hearts	24	6	7	11	32	46	19
Motherwell	28	4	5	19	23	66	13

CHAPTER 10 • THE CELTS CLICKS INTO GEAR

4 April 1979: Premier Division

Motherwell 3-4 Celtic
Clinging 20   McGrain 23
Stevens 71   Doyle 32
Larnach 85   Davidson 43
                    Lennox pen 79

Attendance: 8,744

Billy McNeill decided to rest Peter Latchford for this game, and he gave another start to the promising Pat Bonner. This was only Bonner's second appearance, and his debut had ironically been against Motherwell, just three weeks earlier. McNeill was obviously keen to promote his young charges from the reserves, and because of injuries to Glavin and MacLeod, nineteen year old midfielder, John Weir, found a place on the Celtic bench.

New Motherwell manager, Ally MacLeod, had recovered from his trials and tribulations as Scotland manager, and controversially put ten of his most experienced players up for sale, as he set about ringing the changes at Fir Park. 'Well had been bottom of the table since September, and it was only a matter of time before they would be relegated, so MacLeod decided to play his fringe players and youngsters, as he sought to decide who to keep for the following season.

MacLeod had not experienced the best of starts at Fir Park, after taking over from Roger Hynd. His side had suffered the trauma of an 8-0 hiding from Aberdeen at Pittodrie, nine days previously, and this had provoked him into making so many changes to his squad. This scoreline remains Motherwell's record defeat, and was enormously embarrassing for the club and MacLeod.

The crowd was a disappointing 8,744 on the night, with Celtic fans making up the vast majority of spectators. Celtic were shocked when Motherwell opened the scoring in twenty minutes, when young forward, Ian Clinging, gave Bonner no chance with a fine high shot. Celtic were in need of inspiration, and found it four minutes later, when a fine pass by Davidson sent McGrain clear on goal. He blasted the ball past Rennie. Danny and the Celtic fans celebrated wildly, as a McGrain goal was a tremendously rare sight.

Celtic had their tails up, and they notched two more goals before half-time. John Doyle scored before McGrain went on a brilliant run, cleverly beating the 'Well offside trap in the process. He should have scored, but Rennie saved his shot, only for Vic Davidson to slide in and score from the rebound. The move brought back memories of McGrain and Davidson combining in their early 'Quality Street Gang' years, a decade earlier.

At half-time Celtic fans looked forward to more goals and a convincing win, but in seventy one minutes Gregor Stevens headed in from a corner kick, which the young Bonner had failed to collect. Celtic again replied quickly, when Doyle and Lennox combined with a fine one-two. This resulted in Doyle being upended in the area for a penalty. With regular penalty taker Andy Lynch out through injury, the task fell to the experienced Bobby Lennox, who calmly scored from the spot.

As the minutes ticked away, the fans began to head for the exits, but the action was not over yet. What had been a most competitive encounter, developed into an incredible finish. Motherwell scored when Bonner fumbled a Stevens header on his goal line. However, the referee awarded a drop ball in the penalty area, a decision which totally confused everyone inside the ground. Only seconds later and 'Well did score, to make it

4-3, when Larnach struck a ferocious shot against the crossbar, and then managed to convert the rebound low into the net.

The game ended with Celtic defending desperately, as Motherwell hammered away at their goal, and those in green and white were most relieved to hear the final whistle. Young goalkeeper Bonner looked a little raw in his second appearance, but Billy McNeill could take solace from four goals scored, and an old partnership which had been reacquainted.

'New signing Davidson, stronger, more mature in his second spell with the club, produced a tireless, clever performance. His linking with McGrain, particularly in the first 45 minutes, was reminiscent at times of the great partnership the full-back had enjoyed with Kenny Dalglish'. Evening Times, 5th April 1979.

Motherwell: Rennie MacLeod Wark Carberry Dempsey Stevens Smith Pettigrew Clinging Irvine Donnelly (Larnach) Sub: Rafferty

Celtic: Bonner McGrain MacLeod Aitken Edvaldsson Conroy Provan Lennox Davidson Burns Doyle Subs: Weir McCluskey

7 April 1979: Premier Division

Celtic   3-0   Partick Thistle
Conroy 7
Lynch 60

Attendance: 19,000

As the rain lashed down from a leaden sky, it may have reminded the supporters of early winter, rather than early spring. Because of the inclement weather, the pitch was heavy underfoot, and considering the poor conditions both sides combined to put on a fine game. Much to the delight of their fans, Celtic made a fine start when they scored in seven minutes. Provan took a Davidson pass on the left wing, and raced to the bye line to cut the ball back to the onrushing Mike Conroy, who neatly tucked the ball into the net.

Both goalkeepers had excellent games. Latchford made a fine diving save to stop a McAdam header, before Alan Rough bettered that with a flying leap to tip a MacLeod thunderbolt shot round his post. Thistle almost equalised before half-time, when Donald Park struck a free-kick off Latchford's crossbar, with the Celtic defence clearing the danger.

On the hour mark, Tommy Burns made a surging run into the Thistle area and passed to Provan. The Celtic winger flicked the ball forward, and Thistle's O'Hara handled the ball for a definite penalty. There were gasps from the fans when Rough made a fine save from the normally reliable Andy Lynch's kick, but Lynch showed commendable coolness by keeping his head to slot in the rebound.

The scoring ended there, and Celtic fans looking at the league table later that night were encouraged to see their team sitting in joint fifth place, with Aberdeen. Celtic were eight points behind leaders Dundee United, but had an incredible six games in hand.

Renowned Celtic fan Rod Stewart was not at this game and had good cause for missing it. Newspapers reported that Rod had disappointed his many female fans by marrying the American model, Alana Hamilton, in a simple ceremony in Beverley Hills, California.

Celtic: Latchford McGrain Lynch Aitken Edvaldsson MacLeod Provan Conroy Davidson Burns Doyle Subs: McCluskey Lennox

Partick: Rough McKinnon Whittaker Campbell (Houston) Anderson Gibson O'Hara Melrose (Somner) McAdam Love Park

11 April 1979: Premier Division

Dundee United   2-1   Celtic
Holt 38   Davidson 21
Dodds 71

Attendance 14,424

Before this game there was shock news when it was announced that Celtic had put Alfie Conn on the open transfer list. Conn had been a most controversial signing in March 1977, and had been a considerable investment for Celtic, when Jock Stein paid £65,000 to obtain his signature. Alfie's ex-Rangers credentials had never mattered to the Celtic fans and he had been a huge favourite with the supporters. He had shown good form as recently as 3rd March, when he scored a vital winner against Aberdeen at Parkhead.

Conn was a talented, classy player and was arguably Celtic's greatest creative outlet, so it was a huge surprise to learn that his days at Celtic Park were numbered. It was noticeable that McNeill had moved on several of Celtic's more experienced players, as he concentrated on building his squad which now included a large number of younger players. McNeill obviously felt that the younger players were more receptive to his new plans and ideas, and it was clear that Celtic would concentrate on coaching the young talent in their midst.

The team travelled to Tannadice in confident mood and started the game brightly. They opened the scoring when Davidson stooped to head in a perfect Provan free-kick, and Burns went close to making it 2-0. However, United equalised with a carbon copy of the Celtic goal, when Holt headed in a Fleming free-kick. United took full control in the second half, and it was no surprise when they took the lead. A great cross field pass from Holt allowed Sturrock to cross from the left, for Dodds to head into the net. It was a most impressive goal.

Celtic, now sensing that their own title hopes were dying, staged a storming finish. Late in the game they were denied a penalty, when Derek Stark blocked an Edvaldsson header with his arm, but referee Cuthill turned away the Celtic players' furious claims.

Celtic dropped to seventh after this defeat, and were a massive ten points behind leaders Dundee United. The Tannadice team were also six points ahead of second placed Rangers, but Celtic and Rangers had six and five games in hand respectively. This was a vital win for Jim McLean's men, and many observers believed that this could be United's year, and that a title win was not beyond them.

As a footnote it should be noted that the attendance at Tannadice was 14,424. This was only 5,000 more than attended the Scottish Cup semi-final at Hampden, between Hibernian and Aberdeen. This led to a storm of criticism aimed at the SFA for their choice of venue, with Dens Park or Tynecastle thought to have been more suitable options.

Dundee Utd: McAlpine Stewart Stark Fleming Hegarty Narey Addison Sturrock Dodds Holt Kirkwood Subs: Payne Kopel

Celtic: Latchford McGrain Lynch Aitken Edvaldsson MacLeod Provan Conroy (McCluskey) Davidson Burns Lennox (McAdam)

14 April 1979: Premier Division

St Mirren   0-1   Celtic
McCluskey 44

Attendance: 19,721

Supporters attending this game were delighted to be greeted by blue skies and pleasant sunshine in Paisley. It was Easter Saturday and the feeling was that the long endured winter was over, and that spring had finally arrived.

Celtic, however, were unhappy, having being instructed to play a rearranged match against Hearts at Tynecastle on 18th April. This meant the team would have to play four away games in the space of eleven days, which would not only put a strain on the team, but also present financial difficulties for the fans. Celtic were not pleased, as Billy McNeill was quick to point out.

'The fans….are the most important people and we have to play four away games in a row. The league say they are operating strictly by the rule book but that is rather strange considering this season when the rule book has been tossed out of the window on so many occasions…we have a big travelling support but how can one expect them all to meet the cost of four away matches in succession ?' Glasgow Herald, 14th April 1979.

McNeill need not have worried, as the Celtic fans turned out in huge numbers to swell the crowd to a terrific attendance of 19,721. St Mirren were having a fine season, and went into this match two points ahead of Celtic. Thomson, Munro, Fitzpatrick and McGarvey were all showing tremendous form for the Paisley side, and were rumoured to be on the verge of well deserved international call ups, as reward for their good performances. It was clear that this game would be a huge test for the Celts.

This was a hard fought match, which was spoiled by a surface virtually bereft of grass. The winter weather had taken its toll, and damaged every playing surface in the country. The warmer, dry conditions made the pitch fast and fiery, which gave even the best ball players trouble with control and passing.

One moment of real inspiration was to give Celtic both points. On the stroke of half-time, Danny McGrain squared a ball to George McCluskey, fully thirty yards out. There seemed no danger to the Saints defence as McCluskey feinted inside, and let fly with a wonderful shot, which dipped over the desperate hands of Billy Thomson into the Saints' net. The goal was a candidate for goal of the season, and worthy of winning any game. Celtic held the upper hand in the second half, but the lack of a second goal meant there were nervous moments before the final whistle blew.

Then, something notable happened, which was to change the course of the season. News began to filter through that bottom of the table Motherwell had sensationally beaten Rangers 2-0 at Fir Park, with two second half goals. Motherwell, without a win since 20th January, had upset the form book with dramatic effect.

The massed Celtic support behind the Caledonia Street embankment were slowly exiting the ground. Whispers turned to roars as the news spread, and they immediately broke into song.

We're gonnae win the league
We're gonnae win the league
We're gonnae win......
We're gonnae win the league!

This had been a hugely significant day and the league table showed Celtic had moved up to joint third position. Things became clearer, as the clubs gradually caught up with their backlog of rearranged fixtures. Celtic fans did not need a calculator to work out that if their team won the game in hand over Rangers, this would put them above the Ibrox men, and into second place. Also, if Celtic were to win their six games in hand, they would then top the table, although this was admittedly a very tall order.

The pleasant weather coincided with Celtic returning to Championship contention. The winter of discontent Celtic suffered had now passed and there was renewed optimism around the club. However, manager McNeill was quick to play down any title aspirations, stating modestly that his aim was still to achieve a place in Europe, and that the title would perhaps be just beyond his players. The fans, by comparison, were bolder. They knew the league title was theirs for the taking, and with games against Dundee United and Rangers still to play, Celtic were destined to have a huge say in where the title would end up.

St Mirren: Thomson Young Munro Fitzpatrick Dunlop Copland Richardson Stark (Torrance) Bone Abercrombie (Weir) McGarvey

Celtic: Latchford McGrain Lynch Aitken Edvaldsson MacLeod Provan Conroy McAdam Davidson McCluskey Subs: Lennox Mackie

18 April 1979: Premier Division

Hearts	0-3	Celtic
		MacLeod 11
		Conroy 61
		Burns 76

Attendance: 11,000

Hearts were stranded in the relegation zone, and it appeared that only a minor miracle would prevent them being relegated for the second time in three seasons. Hearts fans seem to campaign perennially against the club's owners, and on this occasion they were protesting against Chairman Bobby Parker, and his board of directors. This reduced the attendance to 11,000, the lowest attendance between the sides for many years, and Celtic's travelling support outnumbered the home crowd on the night.

Celtic had an early scare in only two minutes when Willie Gibson hit the post, but after that it was clear there was only going to be one winner. Although Celtic took the points, it was the quality of the goals which pleased their fans and manager most. The first goal came in eleven minutes, when McCluskey made a good run down the right, aiming the ball at McAdam, who cleverly guided the ball to the attacking Murdo MacLeod.

From just inside the area, the Celtic midfielder did not break stride, as he powerfully struck the ball past Thomson Allan.

Celtic's other goals were created by Andy Lynch free-kicks. With his first, Lynch struck a clever low cross, which gave Conroy the chance to hook the ball into the net. But the goal of the game came in seventy six minutes, from substitute Tommy Burns. Lynch's long ball was cleverly headed into Burns' path by Vic Davidson, and the red headed Celt struck a spectacular shot on the drop past Allan, with his weaker right foot. Burns then celebrated joyously, as the remaining Hearts fans deserted the ground in their droves.

Cammy Fraser was later sent off for a crude foul on Burns, and Drew Busby could consider himself a lucky man to remain on the park, having struck Tom McAdam, as Hearts totally lost their discipline.

This win meant that Celtic moved up to second place. The bookmakers declared this a clear three horse race, with Dundee United favourites at 11/10, with the Old Firm duo paired at 9/4. Celtic looked to be the side in form, and were gathering momentum, as some observers were beginning to note.

'Suddenly - and significantly – Celtic's push for the championship has begun in earnest. In the space of one week their ambition has carried them from fourth bottom of the ten club pile to second top, a statistic which reflects the throttling tightness of the Premier League as much as notice that the Parkhead side must now be considered genuine title contenders for the game's major honour.' Evening Times, 19th April 1979.

Hearts: Allan Kidd Brown Tierney Liddell Craig Gibson Fraser Robertson Busby Prentice Subs: Paterson Black

Celtic: Latchford McGrain Lynch Aitken MacDonald MacLeod Provan (Burns) Conroy McAdam Davidson McCluskey Sub: Doyle

21 April 1979: Premier Division

Aberdeen   1-1   Celtic
Strachan 24   Lynch pen 40

Attendance: 19,400

Scottish football fans looked forward to two fantastic fixtures on this day. Celtic were bound to be slightly apprehensive before their trip to Pittodrie, considering the 4-1 hiding they suffered there in October. However, the fixture of the day was at Tannadice, where first place Dundee United hosted third place Rangers.

Both Celtic and Rangers' travelling supports may have been a few hundred lighter, due to events happening that morning. Approximately seven hundred Irish Republican protesters and left-wing activists marched through the city in a 'Troops out of Ulster' march, in protest at the presence of British forces in Northern Ireland. There was a huge Ulster Loyalist counter protest, and the march, which was due to process from Queens Park to the City Halls in Candleriggs, was ended early at Gorbals Cross, on the grounds of public safety.

Glasgow Police strained to keep both sides apart, and sudden heavy rain over the Gorbals had proved a Godsend, as marchers and protestors raced for cover to avoid a soaking. The Gorbals was the ideal place for the march to finish, as it was recognised as being an area with a large Irish community, and there were many Celtic supporters' pubs in the area for the marchers to disperse to. The authorities were said to have been glad that Celtic and Rangers had been playing far away from Glasgow, as this was thought to have significantly reduced the numbers who may otherwise have attended events.

Up at Pittodrie there was an amusing incident, when two referees turned up to officiate at the match. Both Eddie Pringle and Alan Ferguson arrived at the ground following a misunderstanding. Pringle eventually took control of the game, whilst Ferguson took a seat in the stand.

Pringle did not have his greatest game as a match official. In the first half he mistakenly booked George McCluskey, after Mike Conroy had fouled Willie Miller. Admittedly, there was more than a passing resemblance between the two Celtic players, but even after Conroy admitted his guilt, Pringle continued to book McCluskey, much to the frustration of the innocent Celt.

Thankfully, this was a competitive match without the ill tempers that had ruined the Scottish Cup replay at Celtic Park in March. Aberdeen played their young defender Alex McLeish in midfield to give them more strength in that area, and the Dons went ahead in twenty four minutes when Gordon Strachan had time to chest down a Sullivan cross, and fire past Latchford.

Celtic remained admirably calm and played composed football for the rest of the half. They got their reward in forty minutes when Miller sent Conroy sprawling in the area, to give Celtic a penalty. Before the kick could be taken, an irate Aberdeen fan was escorted from the field, whilst Andy Lynch waited to take his penalty. Lynch then showed great self-assurance, sending his shot powerfully past Clark to bring Celtic level.

In the second half, the Celtic midfield dominated, until the last ten minutes when Aberdeen upped their game. Goalkeeper Peter Latchford became the Celtic hero, with two great saves, giving his side a share of the points. He made the save of the game from Sullivan's powerful long range shot, and afterwards did well to touch a Scanlon header on to the post. The genial Latchford, so often maligned during this long season, acknowledged the Parkhead legions at the end, as they sang a familiar song:

Peter Latchford!
Peter Latchford!
Give us a wa-aaave!
Give us a wa-aaave!

At this point the big man waved back to the fans. He had always enjoyed an excellent rapport with them. On seeing this, the fans replied with:

Latchford for England!
Latchford for England!

Peter was much loved by the Celtic fans, but the prospects of him playing for England were extremely unlikely to say the least. It was difficult to imagine him displacing either of the two goalkeeping greats England had at that time, Peter Shilton and Ray Clemence. Latchford did revel in the nickname, 'The Cat', which was a slightly double edged compliment, bestowed on him by the fans.

Celtic officials regarded this result as point gained, especially as Rangers were due to travel to Pittodrie four days later. The only down side on the day was the fact that Rangers won 2-1 against Dundee United at Tannadice, a result which allowed the Ibrox men to leap frog Celtic, to go into second place.

Celtic came through their four consecutive away games unscathed, taking seven points from a possible eight. The team and their supporters were looking forward to the remaining games with great confidence.

Aberdeen - Clark Kennedy Hamilton McLeish Garner Miller Sullivan Archibald McGhee Strachan Scanlon Subs: MacMaster Jarvie

Celtic - Latchford McGrain Lynch Aitken Edvaldsson MacLeod Provan Conroy Davidson (McAdam) Burns (McCluskey)

25 April 1979: Premier Division

Celtic   **2-1**   **St Mirren**
Edvaldsson 75   McGarvey 24
Aitken 88

Attendance: 18,000

Fate can be a funny thing when a team is chasing a league title, and at approximately 9pm on this night Celtic's title hopes looked to be fading fast into the distance. St Mirren were beating Celtic 1-0, and Rangers were drawing 1-1 with Aberdeen at Pittodrie. Fans at both grounds listened intently on their radios for the latest news.

St Mirren were in front at Parkhead due to a farcical goal which the Celtic defence gifted to Frank McGarvey. In the 24th minute, Roy Aitken, with no danger around him, needlessly blasted a clearance into Johannes Edvaldsson's face. The ball fell perfectly to the alert McGarvey, who tucked the ball into the Celtic net, past a bemused Peter Latchford.

Celtic rallied and played some of their best football of the season, but they found Billy Thomson in the St Mirren goal in unbeatable form. His first half save from a point blank Doyle volley was sensational, and he was reckoned by many observers to be the finest goalkeeping talent in Scotland at this time.

Then, fate took a hand in matters. In seventy five minutes Celtic, still frantically attacking the Saints goal, equalised when MacLeod lofted a high free-kick into the six yard box for Edvaldsson. He out jumped Thomson and back headed the ball into the net. It may have looked unorthodox but it was extremely effective. This goal gave Celtic renewed vigour. In eighty three minutes an almighty roar went up from the Jungle enclosure, following the news that Aberdeen had taken the lead against

Rangers. This news had an obvious effect on Celtic's energy levels and sense of purpose.

With just two minutes left on the clock, Tommy Burns took an in swinging corner near the Jungle enclosure, as his side attacked the traditional Celtic end of the ground. A group of players jumped together and the ball broke to Roy Aitken, who fired in a low drive which beat the heroic Thomson. Players and fans celebrated wildly, and when the final whistle was blown, relief was the main emotion, especially for the young defender Aitken, whose aberration had caused St Mirren's goal. He redeemed himself splendidly by scoring the vital, late winner.

Aberdeen managed to hold on at Pittodrie to win 2-1, and this result was a severe setback to Rangers' title hopes. By courtesy of that result, Celtic jumped over Rangers into second place, one point ahead of the Ibrox side but still seven points behind leaders Dundee United. Celtic had five games in hand, which could give them a potential ten point haul, and it was now clear that their destiny lay in their own hands.

The only disappointment of the day was the news that Dundee United had beaten Hearts 2-1 at Tannadice. The stage was now perfectly set for Dundee United's visit to Celtic Park the following Saturday.

Celtic: Latchford McGrain Lynch Aitken Edvaldsson MacLeod Provan Conroy Davidson Burns Doyle Subs: McCluskey Lennox

St Mirren: Thomson Young Munro Fitzpatrick Dunlop Copland Weir Torrance Bone Abercrombie McGarvey Subs: Richardson Stark

28 April 1979: Premier Division

Celtic   **2-1**   **Dundee United**
Doyle 58   Dodds 43
Lynch pen 68

Attendance: 37,000

And to my partial Celtic eyes
There's no more finer sight
A sunny day in Paradise
Ten jerseys green and white

These words were attributed to the former Celtic manager Willie Maley many years before, and they were never more appropriate than on this beautiful spring day, when a huge crowd packed inside Celtic Park. This was one of those occasions which mystified many observers, when the club later announced the official attendance as 37,000. This was an era before clubs had computerised turnstiles, which allowed directors of every club the opportunity to take liberties with attendance figures. As Celtic Park's capacity was then 67,000, it was clearly preposterous to think that another 30,000 spectators could have fitted into the ground that day.

Dundee United brought a large and noisy travelling support from Tayside, estimated to be in the region of 3,000. In 1979 it was most unusual for visiting fans to come to Parkhead, or Ibrox, in such numbers. A small band of away supporters would normally huddle in the lower reaches of the main stand, for reasons of safety, as the terraces were deemed to be extremely dangerous for anyone wearing opposition colours, especially with no segregation in place. The 1970's were notorious for hooliganism in football grounds, and unfortunately Celtic were not immune to large groups of teenagers with the potential to cause trouble and mayhem.

However, on this occasion the vast majority of the United fans congregated in the east terracing, the traditional Rangers end of the ground, and they were colourful, noisy and optimistic about their chances. They sang their own version of the Newcastle United favourite, 'Haway the Lads', to the tune of Blaydon Races and there was a cup final feel to the game. This was not surprising as defeat for either side could ultimately eliminate them from the title race. United fans had every right to be optimistic. This game was their penultimate game of the season, and they held a massive seven point lead. Although Celtic and Rangers had many games in hand, victory for United in this game could see them become champions in all but name.

Jim McLean had been United's manager for eight years, and if they were to win at Parkhead this would bring all his hard work to fruition. In Narey, Hegarty, Stewart and Sturrock, McLean had some of the most coveted players in British football. As evidence of this, on the day before this match, the Derby County assistant manager Frank Blunstone was fined £500 and severely censured, having been found guilty of making an illegal approach to the highly rated Narey.

With so much at stake, the players seemed nervous, and the game descended into a tough and uncompromising encounter, on a hard, dry pitch which made conditions difficult for such talented ball players as Provan, Burns and Sturrock. United had the edge in the first half, and only a great save by Latchford prevented United opening the scoring in thirty nine minutes. A George Fleming cross found the head of Davie Dodds, but from point blank range Celtic keeper Latchford threw himself to divert the header, and then pounced on the ball before it could cross the line.

Celtic did not heed the warning, and four minutes later Dodds was not to be denied again. Sturrock found space on the left, he turned inside Edvaldsson to cross for the unmarked Dodds, who buried a header low into the net at the back post. The United fans celebrated loudly, and at half-time their side deserved their narrow lead.

Celtic, as expected, came out with all guns blazing in the second half. They pressed United back, but could find no weakness in the United defence until the 58th minute, when Andy Lynch sent in a free-kick which Aitken headed on towards goal. United keeper McAlpine came off his line, but missed his punch, and the ball appeared to skim Johnny Doyle's head on the way into the net. It was difficult to see if Doyle had actually made contact and after the game both Aitken and Doyle claimed the goal. It was eventually credited to Doyle, although poor goalkeeping had been the root cause of the goal.

The huge crowd, buoyed by the equaliser, roared Celtic on and United lost their composure as Celtic's midfield took control of the game. Their wide men, Provan and Doyle, became more influential as they enjoyed increased service from midfield. In sixty eight minutes Doyle took on left back Derek Stark, who proceeded to impede the Celtic winger for a clear penalty.

A hush descended around the ground as Andy Lynch approached to take the spot kick, and the tension became unbearable when the wind blew the ball off the penalty spot as he was about to take it. It's no exaggeration to say that Celtic's season now rested on this one kick, and the defender remembers feeling nervous before taking it.

'Apart from the 1977 Scottish Cup final against Rangers that penalty was the most important one I ever took. I had a routine with penalties. When the referee blew for a penalty I would be in the left-back position and I always took my time getting to the other penalty box which gave me time to think, things like what's the conditions, is the wind for or against you, who the goalie is. Hamish McAlpine was a great shot stopper but I had scored against him before.

I did this as quickly as I could and then made my decision. I was very aware that we had to win and then I placed the ball and it blew off the spot and I thought 'Aw naw', and then I had to retrieve the ball. I replaced the ball and in those days the penalty spot was painted on. I didn't want to put the ball down too hard or it would stick but then if I didn't it could blow off again. As I was placing the ball the Dundee United players at the edge of the box had soil on their hands and were flicking it at the ball as I prepared to take it. A United player who I had played with at Hearts, wee George Fleming, was shouting at me also to put me off. The fans were oblivious to this and so was the referee and I must say I was sweating. When I eventually took it I smashed it a lot harder than I normally would and it wasn't that accurate but the power beat Hamish who had guessed correctly. It was a total relief when it went in.'

This goal shook United into action, and McLean threw on his talented play maker, Graeme Payne, in a desperate bid to salvage something from the match. This ploy almost worked, when with just two minutes remaining, Payne cleverly made space for himself, before sending in a powerful shot which Latchford did well to save. In the closing seconds, Celtic's defending was so desperate that McGrain was said to have booted the ball on to the roof of the stand to relieve the pressure on his team. The final whistle blew and Celtic had prevailed.

Despite this defeat, Dundee United found they had won themselves a great deal of admirers and a certain amount of sympathy. This defeat pushed them out to 10/1 outsiders for the championship but they had experienced a magnificent season and had been desperately close to winning at Parkhead. It was felt that if the influential Payne had played from the start, United's chances would have increased significantly.

'Playing for the jersey' has always been a prerequisite for every Celtic team, and the tremendous numbers of fans who flowed happily out of Celtic Park that day could be in no doubt that this 'new' Celtic team had this attribute in abundance.

'In the end it may be guts that count most. And when it comes to resolution, fighting spirit, fire and go then Celtic can't, as Billy McNeill points out, be faulted. All the old tradition, that great pride, came to their rescue at Parkhead when it looked as though they had been worn down and out manoeuvred by Dundee United.' Evening Times, 30 April 1979.

Willie Maley would have been extremely proud of the Celtic players' efforts on the day.

This result meant it was essentially a two horse race between Glasgow's big two. Both teams had six remaining fixtures which had been cleared by the league. They were as follows:

Celtic – Hibs (h) 2nd May, Rangers (a) 5th May, Partick (a) 7th May, St Mirren (a) 11th May, Hearts (h) 14th May, Rangers (h) 16th May.

Rangers – Motherwell (a) 2nd May, Celtic (h) 5th May, Aberdeen (h) 7th May, Celtic (a) 16th May, Partick (h) 19th May, Hibs (a) 23rd May.

It was noted that the sides were still to play each other twice and these would be tremendous affairs for the clubs, the fans and the media to look forward to.

Celtic - Latchford McGrain Lynch Aitken Edvaldsson MacLeod Provan Conroy Provan McCluskey Burns Doyle Subs: Lennox. McAdam

Dundee Utd - McAlpine Stewart Stark Fleming Hegarty Narey Addison Holt Kirkwood (Payne) Sturrock (Kopel) Dodds

League table at the end of April 1979

	P	W	D	L	F	A	Pts
Dundee Utd	35	18	7	10	54	35	43
Celtic	30	16	6	8	49	32	38
Rangers	30	14	9	7	37	30	37
Aberdeen	32	11	13	8	50	31	35
St Mirren	34	15	5	14	44	38	35
Hibernian	34	11	13	10	41	44	35
Morton	35	11	12	12	51	53	34
Partick Thistle	31	12	7	12	37	33	31
Hearts	32	8	7	17	39	62	23
Motherwell	35	5	7	23	32	84	17

CHAPTER 11 • EXPECTATION GROWS

2 May 1979: Premier Division

Celtic	**3-1**	**Hibernian**
Conroy 32		Callachan 86
Provan 67		
McGrain 69		

Attendance: 23,000

Billy McNeill had long been modest about his side's title chances, but after such impressive results he began to put on a bold front:

'When I took over as manager of Celtic I said that my main priority was to get the club back into Europe. I will be satisfied with that...but the League Championship would be a tremendous bonus. People have said that we are not good enough nor ready to win the title but this game is all about grabbing the opportunities when they come along. When I was offered the managerial job at Aberdeen I didn't think I was ready but I had to take the opportunity and looking back it was a good thing.'

Then pointing to a picture of the Celtic Scottish Cup winning team of 1965, which he captained, he said 'At that time no one had any idea what was ahead then for the players of that side but it was the start of a great run which included nine successive championships and a European Cup win. Who is to say the present squad at Parkhead won't go on to succeed?'
Glasgow Herald, 30 April 1979.

Part of the reason for McNeill's optimism would have been the tremendous bond which had been forged between the players and the fans. The fans backed the players without reserve during the poor results of autumn and winter, and the players had responded magnificently. There were many characters within the team and they established a tremendous rapport with the fans.

There was the popular English goalie, Peter Latchford, who had his name chanted by the fans before every game, and after every decent save he made. Latchford would affectionately salute the fans in return.

There was the big Icelandic centre back, Johannes Edvaldsson, known to the fans endearingly as 'Big Shuggie'. He was a whole hearted, committed defender, prone to occasional error, but the fans loved him despite his failings. He was said to, *'plough through strikers like an Icelandic battleship, steaming through the North Sea during the Cod War.'*

In midfield was the young Roy Aitken, who switched between marauding around the centre of the park and filling in at the back, so much so that the fans were divided as to which position Roy was best suited.

Also in midfield was new Bhoy Murdo MacLeod, christened 'The Rhino' by the fans, due to his combative playing style and powerful shooting.

Tommy Burns was fast becoming an icon amongst the supporters. Whilst warming up in front of the Jungle enclosure, the fans would chant his name, and he would respond with a clenched fist salute, to their loud acclaim.

Playing on the wings were curly haired twins, Davie Provan and Johnny Doyle. They had similar haircuts and playing styles, which often confused the spectators. Provan had established himself as Celtic's main creative outlet on the right-wing, with his terrific delivery of crosses and set pieces. Doyle was more temperamental and wore his heart on his sleeve, but he had a real competitive nature and the fans held him in high affection. There was a real feeling of players and fans pulling together in the same direction, and there was now a belief that something special could be achieved.

In the days before this game McNeill sprang a huge surprise, when he announced that Alfie Conn had been given a free transfer with immediate effect. Conn, who was already on the transfer list, was to be released without the club seeking a fee. He had made a fine contribution to this campaign, with ten goals for the season, and as recently as March he had been first choice striker in the Celtic attack.

Several Celtic players of the period recall a vociferous bust up between Conn and Billy McNeill. There appears little doubt that the manager decided to make an example of Conn to assert his authority amongst the rest of the squad, which may explain the abrupt haste in which Alfie was released. Conn still feels aggrieved at the way he was treated and declined to comment when asked to discuss the matter, saying only that his Parkhead exit was the biggest disappointment of his career. His departure would be a sad parting for club and Conn, as he had been an influential player, especially in the early months of the season.

McNeill also announced that John Dowie, Brian Coyne, Robert Ward, Bernie Godzik, Billy Russell and Jim Marr were on the club's end of season free transfer list. As McNeill continued his policy of change, there was a further surprise. Ronnie Glavin was made available for transfer. Bobby Lennox was also set to depart at the end of the season.

Hibs came to Celtic Park in buoyant mood, having won a place in the Scottish Cup final against Rangers, to be played ten days later. The Edinburgh side defeated the highly rated Aberdeen in the semi-final, and were hoping to land the cup for the first time since 1902, when they had beaten Celtic in the final at Celtic Park.

McNeill had become greatly concerned about Celtic's tendency to lose the first goal. He need not have worried on this occasion, as his side raced into an impressive 3-0 lead by the 69th minute. This was an academic win for the Celts, who attacked from the start. The opening goal from Conroy in thirty two minutes was much deserved, when he ran on to a Provan cutback to shoot past McArthur in the Hibs goal.

In the second half the game was over when Celtic scored twice within two minutes. In sixty seven minutes Provan scored when he converted a Doyle cross into the net, and two minutes later came the moment of the night.

'A Tommy Burns corner from the right was scrambled clear but only as far as Danny McGrain who, from fully thirty five yards, hit a magnificent low shot into the net...McGrain doesn't score many goals and, for sure he won't score any better than last night's'. Evening Times, 3rd May 1979.

Until that point, Danny McGrain had only scored five goals in his nine years with Celtic. Now he had scored twice within four weeks, and by these standards, was becoming rather prolific.

The fans showed approval of the team's performance, with an unlikely tribute to Doris Day:

*Que sera sera
Wherever you'll be we'll be
We'll follow the boys in green
Que sera sera*

*Que sera sera
Wherever you'll be we'll be
We're gonnae win the league
Que sera sera*

Hibs put in a disappointing performance, and it seemed as if their players were focusing on their forthcoming big day at Hampden. Ralph Callachan scored a fine consolation goal from twenty five yards, but the newspapers were quick to point out that this had been Hibs' first shot at goal, coming in the 86th minute.

Over at Fir Park, Motherwell put up another terrific performance against Rangers, before succumbing to a late goal. Leading 1-0 at half-time, Motherwell had defended stoutly and they were unfortunate when Smith scored Rangers' equaliser, but only after 'keeper Rennie saved a Jardine penalty. With only one minute left, the experienced centre-half Colin Jackson spared Rangers' blushes with the winning goal, much to the despair of Celtic fans. As both Glasgow teams emerged victorious, this meant that not much had changed at the top of the table.

	P	Pts	GD
Dundee United	35	43	+19
Celtic	31	40	+19
Rangers	31	39	+16

The media then turned their attention to the next game, when Celtic would travel to Hampden to face Rangers in a vital match. In this exciting climax to the season, the press were running out of superlatives, with late goals and twists and turns happening regularly. The upcoming game was vital to both halves of the Old Firm, and the victorious team would undoubtedly have an enormous psychological advantage in the run in.

Celtic: Latchford McGrain MacLeod Aitken Edvaldsson Conroy Provan Davidson McCluskey Burns Doyle Subs: McAdam Lennox

Hibs: McArthur Brazil Duncan Bremner Stewart McNamara Rae MacLeod Campbell Callachan Brown Subs: Hutchison Farmer

5 May 1979: Premier Division

Rangers   1-0   Celtic
MacDonald 57

Attendance: 52,841

Since their European Cup exit against Cologne in March, Rangers responded well, winning the League Cup and making it to the Scottish Cup final, which would take place seven days later. However, they had struggled along the way, with a few replays required. These extra games, together with a backlog of league fixtures conspired to make it an exhausting period for the Ibrox club.

There was a feeling in many circles that this was an ageing Rangers side, which was on the wane. The old guard of McCloy, Jardine, Johnstone, MacDonald and McLean still remained from the victorious side which had won the European Cup Winners Cup in 1972. Other players, such as Tom Forsyth, Derek Parlane and Alex Miller were tremendously experienced and had also been at Ibrox for a considerable period. The advantage Rangers had was clearly in experience, but Celtic's team, being much younger, were perceived as having a slight edge, due to their fitness and youthful enthusiasm.

On the morning before the match, Britain awoke to the news that Conservative leader, Margaret Thatcher, had been elected as the country's first female Prime Minister, defeating the Labour party and their besieged leader James Callaghan in the process. On approaching the entrance of number 10 Downing Street, Thatcher had quoted Saint Francis of Assisi, with the following verse.

Where there is discord, may we bring harmony.
Where there is error, may we bring truth.
Where there is doubt, may we bring faith.
And where there is despair, may we bring hope
These were impressive words and a great many people were hopeful that she would remain true to them. The majority of the 52,841 fans who turned up at Hampden, from both sides of the Old Firm divide, were blue collar workers. They would have worked in mining, car manufacturing, shipbuilding and other heavy industries. They were not to know it at the time, but the country would be utterly changed under Thatcher's period as Prime Minister, many of them suffering directly as a result of her

government's policies. In political terms, times were definitely changing.

Two young midfielders made a tremendous impression on the Scottish game during the course of the season, Tommy Burns of Celtic and Bobby Russell of Rangers. Media pundits found it almost impossible to separate their teams, and it was felt that Burns and Russell were the two biggest influences on their respective sides. They were in direct opposition in midfield, and the winner of this personal dual could very well hold the key to winning the game.

Burns could be infuriatingly inconsistent, but had a wonderful talent for carrying a ball from midfield and running directly at the opposition. Russell was more of a ball player, and his main asset was his subtle touches and slick distribution. The media had given him the tremendous compliment of comparing him to the late, great, John White of Spurs and Scotland fame. Both Burns and Russell were elegant movers and the purists loved watching them when they were on their game.

Both sides were affected by injuries before kick-off. Rangers were missing influential defender Tom Forsyth, and Derek Johnstone had been moved to centre-back to provide suitable cover. For Celtic, Andy Lynch had failed a fitness test on a shoulder injury, and was only deemed fit enough to be named on the bench, with midfield man Murdo MacLeod stepping in to replace him at left-back.

The game's first flashpoint came in the 18th minute, when Derek Parlane was booked for a shocking late challenge on Celtic defender, Johannes Edvaldsson. Celtic officials were irate and felt that Parlane's challenge merited a straight red card. There was some concern that the game would deteriorate into the bad tempered affair that marred the League Cup semi-final in December, but both sides managed to retain their discipline on this occasion.

Celtic never really looked comfortable on the day, whilst Rangers always carried a threat to the Celtic goal. In the first half an intricate Rangers passing move ended with Davie Cooper smacking a shot against the Celtic crossbar. After that, Latchford came to Celtic's rescue when he saved from Russell, when the Rangers man was clean through on goal. Shortly afterwards the Celtic 'keeper did well to turn a free-kick from Cooper over the bar. Celtic's sole first half opportunity was when Doyle failed to connect with the ball in a goalmouth scramble in the Rangers area.

In the second half, Rangers continued to carry the game to Celtic, and in fifty seven minutes they made a vital breakthrough. McLean's cross from the left was missed by Russell, and Alex MacDonald, falling off balance, could only 'sclaff' a shot at goal. The ball frustratingly passed Latchford and Edvaldsson, who was standing guard on the Celtic goal line. Had MacDonald struck his shot properly, Edvaldsson would likely have cleared it, but the shot deceived the big Icelander and the ball bobbled in to the Celtic net. It was the decisive moment of the game, and a poor goal for Celtic to lose, but one that Rangers fully merited on the balance of play.

MacDonald had actually started the move which led to his goal, with a great pass to McLean on the left-wing, and the Rangers man proved yet again that he was the man for the big occasion. He was not a prolific scorer from midfield, but he was in the habit of scoring against Celtic in big games, and had already scored vitally important goals against Juventus in the European Cup, and Aberdeen in the League Cup final.

Billy McNeill then threw on substitute Lynch for the ineffective Burns. He pushed MacLeod into midfield for some much needed urgency, in an effort to salvage something from the game. Celtic, at last responded, when John Doyle ran at the Rangers defence and cracked a low shot off the Rangers post. This proved to be a fleeting moment of respite as Rangers again took control. In the dying minutes, a Russell shot came off

Latchford's right hand post, and Smith then wastefully fired the rebound high over the bar.

Rangers had won and been worthy winners and the feeling was that Celtic had been let off lightly. The Celtic fans, standing in Hampden in the bright sunshine, were disappointed that their side had gone down tamely on the day. They knew that Rangers had grabbed the initiative, and were now a point in front with only four games remaining. The only consolation was, as Billy McNeill was quick to point out, that Rangers still had to visit Parkhead, and Celtic would then have the perfect opportunity of having their revenge.

After the match Celtic announced that Edvaldsson, who had bravely played on after Parlane's shocking tackle, had been taken to hospital for x-rays on a suspected broken ankle. It was a relief to discover that there was no serious injury. There was some small consolation for the big man when the whisky firm, McKinlay's, announced that he had been chosen as their personality of the month for April.

It was also discovered that the police had a busy day of their own.

'Five turnstile operators from Hampden were being questioned by police at Craigie Street police office this afternoon after the Rangers - Celtic game. The men were talking to police after alleged irregularities with gate receipts. Fifty fans were arrested at Hampden and trouble flared in Toryglen, Glasgow, after the game when groups of fans rampaged through the scheme and wrecked buses.' Evening Times 5th May 1979.

Rangers: McCloy Jardine Dawson Johnstone Jackson MacDonald McLean Russell Parlane Smith Cooper Subs: Denny Urquhart

Celtic: Latchford McGrain MacLeod Aitken Edvaldsson Conroy Provan Davidson (McAdam) McCluskey Burns (Lynch) Doyle

7 May 1979: Premier Division

Partick Thistle   **1-2**   **Celtic**
Somner 3   Provan 14
                           McCluskey 71

Attendance 17,000

Less than forty eight hours after the Old Firm clash, both sides were back in action, with Rangers playing Aberdeen at Ibrox, and Celtic travelling to face Partick Thistle at Firhill. Both games were played on a Monday afternoon, courtesy of the traditional May Day bank holiday. With such a backlog of matches from the winter, it had been a clever decision by the authorities to utilise the holiday Monday to play outstanding fixtures.

Roddy MacDonald and Johannes Edvaldsson, Celtic's first choice centre-backs, were both missing, leaving manager McNeill with an enormous defensive headache. Fate can be a strange thing and Tom McAdam, who was Celtic's top scorer with fifteen goals, had recently found himself out of favour in attack. Due to an injury crisis in the reserves, he had been deployed as a centre-half for a number of games. The position was totally new to McAdam, but McNeill felt he had done sufficiently well to gamble on playing him at centre-half at Firhill.

McNeill had given his players time off before the match to recover from a hectic schedule, and from the Rangers defeat, which was clearly a bitter disappointment to them. It was also felt that some rest was long overdue, before the stresses and strains of the final fixtures. This may have explained Celtic's rusty start as Thistle took the lead in only three minutes. Thistle goalie Alan Rough launched a long ball over the Celtic defence for Melrose to chase. The Thistle forward collided with Celtic keeper Latchford, and the ball broke to Doug Somner, who drilled the ball into the net. Celtic were now frustratingly back in the bad old habit of losing the opening goal. Latchford was injured in the clash with Melrose, and although he bravely played on, he was unable to take goal kicks for the rest of the match.

Celtic responded well with a series of efforts on the Thistle goal, and the equaliser was a welcome sight. It came in fourteen minutes, when Provan turned and fired a glorious shot past Rough from fourteen yards, after good work from Davidson and MacLeod set him up for the shot.

In the second half Celtic camped in the Thistle area, with Rough choosing to have one of his exceptional displays. He first defied MacLeod from close range, and then Doyle, with magnificent saves. With McAdam looking settled in his new role in defence, Celtic continued their onslaught on the Thistle goal, whilst remaining alert to the fact that the injured Latchford had to be protected.

With twenty minutes left, the nerves of the Celtic fans were at breaking point and their patience was tested to the full when a Davidson goal was disallowed by a very narrow offside decision, made by referee Brian McGinlay. This infuriated the green and white clad spectators. However, it was only a matter of minutes later when Celtic gained their vital breakthrough. Provan's corner was headed on by Aitken, and McAdam headed the ball down for McCluskey to score with a firm shot, the valiant Rough being beaten at long last.

There was relief at the final whistle, as the Celtic fans departed in a mood fitting for the May Day holiday. This sense of relief in gaining two invaluable points intensified, when news broke that Rangers had also won, beating Aberdeen 2-0 at Ibrox. This result meant Rangers were still ahead, but by a narrow one point margin.

After the match it was confirmed that Celtic had qualified for the following season's UEFA cup, by virtue of their victory at Firhill. They had accumulated forty two points and their European place was guaranteed. A place in Europe had been Billy McNeill's main target since day one. He was delighted at his new charges' achievement in their first season: *'They deserve that European place. They've worked very hard for it. Now we can start looking forward to even bigger things like the championship itself. If we win the remaining three games then we take the title. There is everything to play for.'*

Partick: Rough McKinnon Whittaker McAdam Campbell Marr O'Hara Gibson Somner Melrose Park Subs: Love Houston

Celtic: Latchford McGrain Lynch Aitken McAdam MacLeod Provan Conroy McCluskey Davidson Doyle Subs: Lennox Burns

11 May 1979: Premier Division

St Mirren 0-2 Celtic
McCluskey 68
Lennox 80

Attendance 23,000
In midweek the Scottish League decided that Celtic and Rangers would play their last remaining postponed fixtures as follows:

Celtic: Hearts (h) Monday 14th May, Rangers (h) Wednesday 16th May.

Rangers: Hibs (a) Monday 14th May; Celtic (a) Wednesday 16th May, Partick (h) Friday 18th May.
The reason for the urgency in issuing new dates was that Scotland were required to play three games in the Home Championship tournament, against Wales in Cardiff on Saturday 19th May, Northern Ireland at Hampden on Wednesday 23rd May and the big one at Wembley against England on 26th May. The SFA also announced they had received an incredible 200,000 applications from Scots fans for tickets, which was double the capacity of Wembley at that time.

The media were quick to observe that a Celtic victory against Rangers at Parkhead on16th May could win them the title, but only if they managed to negotiate full points against St Mirren and Hearts in their preceding games. In theory, the Rangers fixture at Celtic Park could be a league decider and was a hugely exciting prospect after such a long hard season.

Johannes Edvaldsson received mixed news before this match. Firstly, he failed a fitness test on his injured ankle, but was then was named as whisky firm Mackinlay's personality of the month for April. Big 'Shuggie' was the first Celtic man to win the award that season. He was rewarded for his sterling efforts with a cheque for £100 and a giant bottle of whisky.

The game against St Mirren was to be played at Ibrox. St Mirren were given permission by the Scottish League to move the fixture because of urgent renovation work at their Love Street ground. The irony was that Ibrox was also undergoing restructuring, and the spectators inside Ibrox on the night looked on in fascination, as the skeleton of the giant new Copland Road stand took shape. This building work cut the capacity considerably, and Celtic's fans in the main stand, west enclosure, Centenary stand and west terracing vastly outnumbered the small band of Saints fans, who were huddled in the confines of the east enclosure and the main stand.

The authorities only agreed to Ibrox being used on the condition that the game was played on the Friday evening. The Police were keen to avoid two major games in the city on Saturday 12th May, when a large crowd was expected at Hampden for the Scottish Cup final, between Rangers and Hibs. This led to statisticians scurrying to their record books to find when Celtic had last played a match on a Friday. It was discovered that the last occasion was on Friday 11th April 1969, when Celtic lost 4-3 to Rangers in a Glasgow Cup semi-final at Celtic Park.

Johannes Edvaldsson is Mackinlay's personality of the month for April 1979.

The prospect of a St Mirren versus Celtic tussle at Ibrox would have brought back contrasting memories for the respective team managers, Jim Clunie and Billy McNeill. The clubs had fought it out at Ibrox once before, in March 1962, when both men had been fielded at centre-half, and were also the respective captains in a Scottish Cup semi-final. On a day of great controversy, Saints, inspired by the ex-Celt Willie Fernie, sensationally ran up a three goal lead, well before half-time.

In seventy minutes, sporadic fighting broke out on the terraces, fuelled by alcohol, and a pitch invasion ensued. Youthful Celtic fans stopped the match as mounted police fought to clear the field of play and it was feared that the match would have to be abandoned. It is claimed that Celtic chairman Bob Kelly actually conceded the tie to his St Mirren counterpart in the directors' box, such was his disgust at the behaviour of his club's own supporters. As it was, the game was restarted, with Saints eventually triumphing by 3-1. Celtic representatives were obviously hoping that there would be no repeat of this debacle.

Celtic suffered a blow shortly before the game, when midfield man Mike Conroy was sent home from Ibrox, having taken ill. Saints were disappointed to see their star man Frank McGarvey leave a few days earlier for Liverpool, for a huge fee of £300,000. However, they were buoyed by the news that their left-back Iain Munro, who had enjoyed an excellent season, had been named in the Scotland squad for the home internationals by Jock Stein

Despite the loss of Edvaldsson and Conroy, Celtic did not let this affect them, and they took the game to St Mirren from the start. The first half was a tale of two penalty claims, one for either side. Neither was given by the match official David Syme. A shot by Tommy Burns struck a Saints defender on the arm, before Andy Lynch appeared to handle the ball, as Lex Richardson broke into the Celtic area, during an isolated St Mirren attack.

At half-time, a group of young Celtic fans in the west terracing tore down corrugated fencing in order to gain entry into the Centenary stand. This was a more expensive area of the stadium and afforded a better view. Their fellow supporters on the terracing loudly roared in encouragement.

Celtic attacked relentlessly in the second half, but lacked the sharpness to pierce the St Mirren defence, which was marshalled brilliantly by their reliable captain, Jackie Copland. Billy McNeill threw on the evergreen Bobby Lennox for the ineffective Vic Davidson, in an attempt to add some much needed spark to his attack and in sixty eight minutes the breakthrough came. Copland conceded a corner under pressure, and Davie Provan took a swerving in swinger for George McCluskey to leap and glance a header past Billy Thomson. This gave Celtic a vital lead. They continued to press, and when Copland gave away another corner in an identical position, Provan sent in a similar in swinger, enabling the veteran Bobby Lennox to head home a vital second goal, which all but killed the game.

This Celtic team, which McNeill had crafted, had an endearing trait of never giving up. When the going got tough they refused to become frustrated. They kept at their task and were justly rewarded for it, and now had a growing army of admirers.

'Celtic again showed tremendous resource and cool courage. They take credit for refusing to lose their heads or their concentration when the match appeared to be slipping away from them....even if Celtic aren't yet one of the great Parkhead teams this young side are certainly amongst the most spirited, determined - and patient.' Evening Times, 12 May 1979.

The Celtic support left Ibrox in full voice as they departed the steep stairways behind the west terracing. Some of the younger, bolder element hurtled down the grassy embankments between the exits for a quick getaway. This game was poignant for the fans, as it was the last time the Celtic support would mass together on the huge Ibrox west terracing, traditionally known as the 'Celtic end' of the ground. The next time Celtic would visit Ibrox, in August 1979, the west terracing would be levelled to the ground, making way for Rangers' modern new Broomloan Road stand.

Bobby Lennox scores against St Mirren at Ibrox on a Friday evening in May 1979.

Many of the Celtic fans attending this game would have tremendous memories of watching some of Celtic's finest moments, on the very same Ibrox terracing they were standing on. In 1938 Celtic had memorably defeated Everton in the Exhibition Cup final, earning themselves the title of Britain's finest team. Captain Willie Lyon proudly lifted the unique and splendid trophy of the distinctive Tait Tower. This was a great moment in Celtic's glorious past and Ibrox Park had actually changed very little since then, when Johnny Crum scored Celtic's winning goal during extra time.

In 1967, Celtic won the Scottish League title at Ibrox, in a game best remembered for Jimmy Johnstone's outstanding long range shot. A day of miserable, wet weather had reduced the pitch to a mud bath. Sean Connery and Inter Milan manager Helenio Herrera, looked on, only a matter of weeks before the Lisbon triumph in the European Cup final. This was also a great moment in the club's history, but tends to be forgotten as it was dwarfed by the magnitude of the European Cup achievement shortly afterwards.

During August and September of 1971, Celtic visited Ibrox three times within a four week period, and memorably won all three matches. The first game is probably best remembered, due to the first goal in Celtic colours by a young Kenny Dalglish. He casually stooped to tie his boot laces, before coolly firing a penalty past Peter McCloy in the Rangers goal. Scotland's greatest ever footballer was on his way and there would be no stopping him.

But, some of the supporters would also recall more distressing moments whilst watching from the Ibrox slopes, which didn't actually have a bearing on any result. Celtic's legendary goalkeeper John Thomson died in September 1931, after an accidental clash with Rangers player Sam English, on what was undoubtedly Celtic's darkest day. Thomson lives forever more in the hearts of all Celtic fans.

On 2nd January 1971, sixty six football fans perished whilst exiting Ibrox after an Old Firm game. No one in attendance would ever forget the tragic events which unfolded after the game, on an occasion when Jock Stein and his Celtic backroom team helped attend to the dead and injured all around them.

Scottish football grounds had not changed much since pre war times and Rangers were to be commended for leading Scottish football out of the dark ages, giving the fans conditions and facilities more in keeping with the latter years of the twentieth century. The days of fans standing out in the elements on open terraces, with precious few comforts, were coming to an end.

However, it would take another disaster, south of the border, at Hillsborough in 1989, before the rest of British football would be dragged kicking and screaming into the modern age.

St Mirren - Thomson Young Munro Fitzpatrick Dunlop Copland Stark Richardson Torrance Abercrombie Docherty Subs: Weir Fulton

Celtic - Latchford McGrain Lynch Aitken McAdam MacLeod Provan Davidson (Lennox) McCluskey Burns Doyle Sub: Mackie

14 May 1979: Premier Division

Celtic 1-0 Hearts
Conroy 55

Attendance: 18,000

Forty eight hours before this match, Scottish football witnessed its showpiece game of the season, in the national stadium, where Rangers and Hibs faced each other in the Scottish Cup final. The game was a total anti climax and the crowd within Hampden, and those watching at home, must surely have been disappointed.

The final finished scoreless and on ninety minutes, the referee, Brian McGinlay, brought matters to a close, meaning that a replay would be required to decide the winners. The media and football public were equally united in their outrage that a period of extra time had not been played. The paying customers were cheated out of a potential outcome and would have to fork out more hard earned cash in order to watch the replay. As always, finance dictated, and the authorities were perceived as being greedy. Ian Paul perfectly summed up the mood of the moment in his Glasgow Herald column.

'Like Tennyson's brook the domestic season in Scotland seems to be going on forever...another game means another gate and

more cash. Football is a big business and business is all about making as much money as possible. But on this occasion it would have been more sensible to play extra time in an attempt to ease the fixture congestion. Personally I would like to see the rule changed whereby extra time would be played at every final in the event of a draw after ninety minutes. It is a gala occasion and the paying customer is entitled to see the cup being won on the day.'

In the months that followed, the SFA eventually listened to such concerns and in the next Scottish Cup campaign extra time was at last permitted in the final. Celtic were actually to become the first beneficiaries of this new rule in the 1980 final. Celtic followers still fondly recall George McCluskey's winning goal in the 108th minute, which allowed the Celts to carry off the trophy for the 26th time.

Unfortunately, the 1979 final was a letdown in terms of the quality on show and had not been the spectacle that many hoped for. This was in sharp contrast to the exciting, high scoring affair in the English FA cup final at Wembley. Manchester United stormed back from behind with two goals to level the game, only for Alan Sunderland to score a dramatic winning goal in the dying seconds, with Arsenal winning by 3-2.

With the backlog of league fixtures remaining, the last thing anyone wanted was a cup final replay to contend with, but the replay took precedence and was scheduled to be played on Wednesday 16th May. This meant the Scottish League management committee had to reconvene for the umpteenth time, to work out dates for the remaining league fixtures. Just hours before their match against Hearts, Celtic were notified that their final league game against Rangers would be played on Monday 21st May.

At last Celtic knew the dates of their two remaining league fixtures, games which stood between them and the league title. Optimism began to spread like wildfire amongst Celtic followers. Television coverage of the final had shown Rangers to look a very tired and jaded team, and the feeling now was that Rangers were definitely there for the beating.

Hearts arrived in Glasgow in despondent mood, which was to be expected from a team recently relegated. They were on an astonishingly bad run, in which they had lost all of their previous nine league games, scoring only twice in the process. A Celtic win was not only expected, but a comprehensive one at that.

Things don't always work out as expected and Celtic had a very frustrating evening. Perhaps nerves overcame them slightly. The weight of having a League Championship within touching distance seemed to throw the players off their stride, although Hearts were to be commended for putting up such a spirited show, when they had absolutely nothing to play for.

As always, the commitment of McNeill's players couldn't be questioned, but they lacked the necessary composure, especially in the Hearts penalty area. Hearts' keeper, Thomson Allan, made two great first half saves from Provan and Conroy. This served to add to the frustration of the supporters, who were willing their team to score. A succession of penalty claims were refused, which only served to add to the ire of the fans.

Thankfully, there was one player who showed the class required on the night. Wide man Davie Provan was on form and sent in a number of inviting crosses. His efforts were to no avail, as Celtic players could not capitalise on the good service he was providing. That all changed in fifty five minutes, when Provan made space and chipped the ball across goal for Doyle. He headed it on and midfield man Mike Conroy was ideally placed to send a firm header past the gallant Thomson Allan, and into the net.

The relief was noticeable amongst players and fans, although the team still appeared nervous. Late on, Provan missed an absolute sitter, when a McCluskey shot was well saved by Allan, only for Provan to slice his shot past an open goal. This led to an edgy last few minutes, but Hearts had neither the quality nor confidence to pierce the Celtic defence, and Celtic ran out narrow but worthy winners at the end.

Mike Conroy scores the vital winning goal against Hearts.

Davie Provan has good reason to recall two particular moments from this game.

'Firstly, I missed a sitter at 1-0. Mick Conroy had got to the bye line and cut the ball back and I opened my foot too much and put it past the post by a yard and I remember thinking that night if Hearts equalise here then I've just cost us the league with that miss. I was never so glad to hear the final whistle than I was that night. Secondly, after the game was over it was only then that I truly thought we could win the league. Up until then I always believed that Rangers were in pole position but then it crystallised the whole thing and it was now down to the last game, ninety minutes winner takes all.'

After eight long months and thirty five league games, Celtic's title destiny would be decided against their greatest rivals. Rangers awaited them on 21st May.

Celtic: Latchford McGrain Lynch (Lennox) Aitken McAdam Edvaldsson Provan Conroy McCluskey MacLeod Doyle Sub: Davidson

Hearts: Allan Kidd Black More Liddell Brown O'Sullivan (Jefferies) Fraser Gibson Stewart MacLeod (Scott)

CHAPTER 12 • THE SHOWDOWN

21 May 1979: Premier Division

Celtic	**4-2**	**Rangers**
Aitken 66		MacDonald 9
McCluskey 74		Russell 76
Jackson (og) 85		
MacLeod 90		

Attendance: 52,000

In the build up to the game, Billy McNeill tried to keep things deliberately low key, and Celtic spent a great deal of time relaxing. The players were happy to spend some time on local golf courses, getting away from the pressures of the approaching showdown.

There were still concerns over the fitness of Tommy Burns and Johannes Edvaldsson. Burns was doubtful with an ankle injury, but McNeill was keen to point out that his situation was improving daily, and he was responding well to the treatment given by the Celtic medical team. Burns was crucial to Celtic's chances, and he would be given every opportunity to get fit, right up until the last minute.

In the meantime Rangers played in the Scottish Cup replay against Hibs on 16th May. Yet again the teams could not muster a goal between them, even after extra time, the game finishing in another 0-0 draw. Another replay would be required, in this longest of seasons, although Rangers would be grateful for a five day break before the potential league decider at Celtic Park. The second replay between Rangers and Hibs was scheduled for 28th May, in between Rangers' final two league games. The replayed final had been a more exciting affair than the original match, but the lack of goals over two games was disappointing. John Greig was forced to admit that another game, in an already hectic schedule, was far from ideal.

On the same night as Rangers played Hibs in the replayed final, another Rangers eleven faced Celtic in the Glasgow Cup final at Ibrox. This fixture had attracted a 55,000 crowd to Parkhead as recently as August 1976, although the tournament had been in decline for some time due to the advent of European football. In such a crowded schedule at the end of the season, the Glasgow FA had no option but to ask the clubs to play out the final with what basically amounted to reserve teams.

Celtic fielded the transfer listed Glavin at centre forward, with the experienced pair of Filippi and Lennox, whilst Rangers had Stewart Kennedy, Alex Forsyth and Kenny Watson adding some maturity to their young team. Rangers ran out winners by 3-1 on the night. It was interesting that the small crowd of a couple of thousand spectators saw Celtic fans in the majority, at the home of their greatest rivals. This was understandable, given that tens of thousands of Rangers fans were in attendance at Hampden to watch the Scottish Cup final replay.

The main focus of the media at this time was on Scotland's preparation for the Home International Championship. Their first game was to be played on Saturday 19th May at Ninian Park, Cardiff. Rangers were forced to withdraw Sandy Jardine and Bobby Russell from the Scottish squad, due to fixture congestion. Jock Stein had not deemed any Celtic player worthy of selection in his twenty two man squad, so Celtic were not affected. Russell had been assured of his first cap, having had such a fine season for Rangers, but after having to withdraw from the squad because of club commitments, he was never to get another opportunity to play for his country, which was a tremendous shame for such a fine player.

Hopes were high in the Scottish camp that the team would perform well in the three game tournament. Stein built his team around the hugely talented Liverpool trio of Kenny Dalglish, Graeme Souness and Alan Hansen, who had all had tremendous seasons with the English league champions. Young Anglo-Scots George Burley, Frank Gray and Ian Wallace were also given their chance to impress, but things were to go disastrously wrong for the Scots in Cardiff.

Wales were worthy winners by a 3-0 scoreline, with the veteran Welsh striker John Toshack hammering home a spectacular hat trick, overshadowing his ex-Anfield team mates in the process. The Swansea player manager easily took advantage of an inexperienced Scottish defence. The Scots' press were scathing in their criticism of the team's performance, and Stein's team selection in particular.

After the Cardiff debacle, the media settled down to concentrate on the league decider at Celtic Park. The hype that surrounds Old Firm games as they approach can generally be said to be over the top, but this time there could be no doubting the magnitude of this game, with so much at stake.

'Monday night at Parkhead will neither be the time nor the place for those of a nervous disposition. Because, although every Old Firm game is special, this latest game in the ninety year series is absolutely unique. Monday is different and that's a fact recognised by both managers, sets of players and supports.' Evening Times, 19th May 1979.

Rangers were seen as slight favourites after their win over Celtic on 5th May, and were in hot pursuit of their second successive domestic treble. Their manager John Greig was in a fighting mood and in a pre-match interview he boldly declared, *'We are the champions and what I will say is this - if anyone wants to take the title from us then they will really have to play. Nothing will be given away easily.'*

Television coverage of football matches had been a bone of contention all season, and matters where not about to improve. Celtic chairman Desmond White publicly lambasted STV on the morning of the match, after weekend newspaper reports indicated that television companies were in discussion with

Celtic, with regard to the game being shown live on television. White stated that the game was not a sell out, and that tickets were still available from the usual outlets. White claimed to have been inundated with people calling the ground to enquire about live coverage. He maintained his stance that Celtic's priority was to look after the paying customer, and not armchair fans. He stated that there was never any chance of live coverage, but did confirm that STV would be allowed to show a highlights package on 'Scotsport Special', after the match had finished, starting at 10.35pm.

The fans were required to look out tickets purchased for the original game, and the date on the ticket, 6th January 1979, was a sharp reminder of how long the season had been. Celtic placed an advert in the press on the morning of the game stating that entry would be by ticket only, but some eye witnesses from the time confirm that there were actually cash turnstiles open at the ground, certainly at the Celtic end.

There was concern for fans hoping to travel to the game by public transport, when bus drivers at Gartcraig and Parkhead depots refused to operate their buses in the area around Celtic Park, after a 6pm curfew was drawn up. Unions were quick to point out that there was no block withdrawal of buses in the city, as had happened on several occasions earlier in the season. This time the local drivers from those depots had taken the decision voluntarily, after a series of attacks on them after big games at Celtic Park. Police then advised fans to take note of the bus withdrawals when making plans to travel.

Some of the bus drivers had an ulterior motive for walking out. Celtic fan, John Flynn, was a bus driver with Glasgow Corporation at the time, and he recalls the show of hands at a bus drivers' union meeting to decide whether or not to withdraw their labour. *'I voted to walk out not because I particularly believed in what we were doing but because I had a ticket for the game and had a shift I couldn't get out of. This gave me and a lot of other fans of both teams the ideal opportunity to get to the game. To this day I'm glad I walked out or I'd have missed it.'*

Celtic were dealt a severe pre-match blow when Tommy Burns failed a late fitness test. Billy McNeill then elected to push Roy Aitken into midfield, with Johannes Edvaldsson, now fully recovered from injury, taking his customary place in defence, alongside Tom McAdam. This game was sure to be a huge test for McAdam, who was playing only his fourth game at centre-half, after his conversion to defence from centre-forward.

John Greig was able to name a full strength Rangers side, with the exception of influential defender Tom Forsyth, who had been missing since Cologne eliminated Rangers from the European Cup in late March. The versatile Rangers' skipper Derek Johnstone was named in the number four shirt as Forsyth's defensive replacement, with Derek Parlane being fielded in Johnstone's place in attack, giving the Ibrox men a strong looking side.

Many a Celtic fan would have suffered a dark night of the soul on the night before this match. Naturally, there was a tremendous amount of excitement, and there was no doubt that this was a wonderful opportunity for this young Celtic team. Nevertheless, there was also the distinct possibility that they could falter when so close to the finishing line. The prospect of failing against Rangers, and another treble going across the city to Ibrox, was not one that Celtic fans would relish. However, there was now no turning back.

Celtic knew that only a win would guarantee them the League title, with Rangers having the slight advantage of being able to accept a draw. This would leave them with two remaining fixtures in which to accumulate the four points they would need to assure them the championship.

	P	W	D	L	F	A	Pts
Celtic	35	20	6	9	57	35	46
Dundee Utd	36	18	8	10	56	37	44
Rangers	33	17	9	7	48	29	43
Aberdeen	36	13	14	9	59	36	40

Parkhead was bathed in sunshine on a pleasant spring night. There was a slight breeze and the pitch was fiery and slightly bare in patches. The players would be sure to find it difficult to control the ball in these conditions. This would ensure that the game be played at the usual frantic pace associated with Old Firm games. The fans took their places at either end of the ground and sang their battle hymns loudly, even before the teams had entered the arena. Celtic supporters sang their traditional rendition of 'You'll Never Walk Alone', with their scarves and flags raised in a sea of green and white. The Rangers fans, in return, showed their colours in a similar way, whilst chanting a less appropriate song for a football match.

This was still a time when clubs gave each other a large percentage of tickets for visiting supporters, and Rangers had an estimated 20,000 fans massed in the ground that night, amongst the official attendance of 52,000. Rangers fans had the entire away end of the ground, and a good section of the main stand, which wasn't segregated, with rival fans sitting together in certain areas. This made for a tremendous atmosphere, far better than in later years, when Ibrox and Celtic Park became all seated, and the clubs slashed away allocations to a paltry 7,500. Although the crowd was recorded afterwards as 52,000, it's worth remembering that this was a time when youngsters could still gain entrance to the ground unofficially by being lifted over the turnstiles. Their numbers would not have been included in the official figures, and would have increased the attendance significantly.

Celtic players of the time recall that Billy McNeill was remarkably calm before the game. and Davie Provan remembers that, *'Billy's team talk was short and took about two minutes. Davie Cooper and Derek Johnstone were the only two players to rate a mention.'*

Celtic settled immediately, and hoped to strike in the early stages, as they had done in the corresponding fixture in September. Doyle and Provan carried the fight to Rangers from the start, with their darting runs on the flanks. However, first blood on the night was to go to those wearing blue, in the ninth minute. Davie Cooper, unusually on the right wing, skipped passed MacLeod and Lynch and sent over a perfect cross for Alex MacDonald to dart in, and prod the ball past Latchford. 'Wee Doddie', much loved by the Rangers fans, had proved himself once again as the man for the big occasion.

The Rangers players celebrated their lead, but for the rest of the half Celtic had the better of the play. Aitken was tremendously unlucky when his powerful header from a Provan cross came crashing off the junction of the post and crossbar. Peter McCloy was helpless in the Rangers goal, the goalkeeper being required to wear a cap to help him contend with the setting sun, which was now shining directly in his line of vision. The game then became scrappy towards half-time, with Rangers sitting in and coping well with Celtic's increasingly frenetic attacks. The break arrived with Rangers in the lead, and seemingly in control, as the Celtic masses made a uniform plea to their team by singing the John Lennon song with the slightly changed words - *'All we are saying... is give us a goal!'*.

During the half-time interval a spectator collapsed in the Celtic end of the ground, and the fans in that area made a channel for the St Andrew's ambulance men to attend to him. He was then stretchered around the track to loud roars of derision from the Rangers fans at the opposite end of the stadium.

Celtic had not played badly in the first half, and during the interval Billy McNeill encouraged his players to continue in the same vein, assuring them the goals would come. McNeill, though, could not have accounted for what happened in the

55th minute, when Alex MacDonald went down in midfield after a heavy challenge by Mike Conroy.

Those most partisan of Celtic fans in the Jungle enclosure clearly had no sympathy for the injured Ranger. As he lay on the ground they chanted:

Dig a hole and bury him! (clap-clap....clap-clap-clap-clap)
Dig a hole and bury him! (clap-clap....clap-clap-clap-clap)

Die, die, die, die yah Hun
Die, die, die, die
Die, die, die, die yah Hun!

As MacDonald lay prostrate on the turf, Celtic winger John Doyle took MacDonald's hand to help him up, which the Rangers' man angrily withdrew. This incensed Doyle, who seemed to think the Rangers man was exaggerating his injury. In his frustration he proceeded to give MacDonald a sly kick in the ribs, which he thought was discreet, but was actually in full view of the Jungle side linesman. After the Rangers players had remonstrated with the referee Eddie Pringle, the match official ran across to consult his colleague, and following a very short discussion produced his red card and correctly sent off the Celtic player for his indiscretion.

Doyle and MacDonald had a history of antagonising each other during Old Firm encounters. They were both ardent supporters of their respective clubs, as well as fine players. They were also huge favourites with their own supports, but on this occasion Doyle had let the Celtic fans down badly, and as he ran off the field to contemplate his actions most observers believed that Celtic's title hopes were now disappearing up the tunnel with him. As he passed the Celtic dugout Billy McNeill chastised his distraught player with the comment, *'Doylie, I hope to hell we win because if we don't you're in right trouble.'*

Amazingly, Celtic began to play with renewed vigour even though they were a man down. After a short period of pressure,

Parkhead exploded in sixty six minutes when Celtic mustered an equaliser. McCluskey superbly controlled a Latchford kick out and lobbed a pass to Provan on the left side of the area. The Celtic winger raced past Russell and cut the ball back with his left foot for Roy Aitken to steady himself, before firing a low shot past McCloy.

Fortified by their equaliser, the Celtic fans roared their heroes forward as Rangers struggled to deal with Celtic's enthusiasm. Both managers made their tactical moves. Billy McNeill sent on his veteran Lisbon colleague Bobby Lennox for Mike Conroy, whilst John Greig replaced Tommy McLean with Alex Miller. These substitutions were to have a major bearing on the game, with Celtic bringing on an attacker, whereas Rangers chose a defender. The appearance of Lennox was a master stroke as he served to increase Celtic's attacking options, whereas the resolute Miller only assisted in helping Rangers sit in, despite having a numerical advantage on the field.

At this stage in the game Davie Provan recalls a moment where he thought Celtic's bid had hit the rocks. *'Gordon Smith found space in the inside right position and was racing goalwards into the area and a Celtic defender, maybe big Shuggie, brought him down for a clear cut penalty. Eddie Pringle was referee and he waved play on. It was a huge relief.'*

Research for this book required extensive reading of many reports of this game. No record of this incident was found in any of them. It may actually be that so much was to happen in this extraordinary game that the incident wasn't deemed worthy of comment in match reports afterwards.

Alex Miller came close with a rare Rangers effort before Celtic were back on the attack, with Rangers having to defend deep inside their own penalty area. Provan, a constant thorn in Rangers' side, jinked his way into the area and set up Aitken for a shot. His effort was blocked by a defender, but the ball fell perfectly to McCluskey, who instinctively swivelled and sent a glorious shot high into the Rangers net. The Celtic fans celebrated as the players rushed to hail McCluskey's fine effort. The League Championship was now within their grasp, and they only had to defend their hard earned lead for another sixteen minutes.

It is said that a team is at its most vulnerable just after they score, and so it proved on this occasion. Celtic's lead lasted a mere two minutes. A corner from Davie Cooper from the left flank was floated across and was then cleared to the right side of the area. Bobby Russell sent a low shot through a forest of Celtic legs, for the ball to creep in at the far post. This was a gut wrenching blow to Celtic hopes. The contrast between the players was huge. Rangers players celebrated gleefully as their Celtic counterparts looked devastated by comparison.

Rangers fans were now understandably in full voice:

'Sing in the chapel, you only sing in the chapel
Sing in the cha-pel, you only sing in the chapel!

Then something happened that was perhaps to change the entire course of the game. The Celtic fans began chanting for their team, at first softly and slowly, but as the singing spread it became louder and faster, building into a deafening crescendo of noise, almost frightening in its intensity, for those who stood amongst the din.

'Cel-tic....Cel-tic....Cel-tic....CELTIC! CELTIC! CELTIC!'

This had been a long season and the fans were not about to let their team down, with a mere fourteen minutes of the campaign remaining. Celtic's ten men had scored twice already, and there was an absolute belief amongst the fans that they could do it again. As the fans gave their all on the terraces, the players, spurred on by this fanatical backing, were to respond in turn.

Perhaps subconsciously Rangers had settled for the draw. This outcome would suit them, and allow them the opportunity of claiming the title in their two remaining fixtures. Rangers had perfected a controlled defensive system under John Greig which had served them well, particularly in their high profile European ties. They now sat back and let Celtic come on to them. The only thing to be decided was could Celtic break the Rangers rearguard and score another goal?

Danny McGrain was a player of the highest calibre, having played many tremendous games for Celtic. On this night Danny was more vitally important to his team than ever, as he rallied his young troops for one final assault, when time was against them and fatigue must have been setting in. The average age of the Celtic team on the night was only twenty four years old whereas Rangers average age was twenty seven. Rangers' experience was obviously a tremendous advantage for them and they also had a numerical advantage on the field of play. Playing a true captain's role, McGrain could be seen cajoling and urging his young charges to greater effort, and ensuring that their heads did not drop after such a hammer blow.

When the game restarted Celtic attacked at frantic pace with the clock rapidly running down. In eighty five minutes the energetic MacLeod intercepted a pass in midfield, and laid the ball off to McCluskey. The Celtic striker, who had ran tirelessly all night, burst past two Rangers defenders on the right side of the area. He fired a hard shot across the face of goal, which the Rangers goalkeeper, Peter McCloy, only managed to palm away. The ball immediately rebounded off the body of hapless Rangers defender, Colin Jackson, a stalwart throughout the match in the Gers' overworked defence. It then rolled towards the empty goal, taking what seemed like an eternity to do so. Jackson could only look on helplessly as Aitken and Dawson raced in pursuit of the ball, and although the Celtic man won the chase the ball had already crossed the line. Celtic had taken the lead in the most dramatic circumstances, with only five minutes remaining. The Celtic supporters were now in a nervous fervour, as having already lost a lead, the prospect of it happening again was absolutely unbearable.

The noise cascaded from the Celtic supporters towards their rivals' end of the ground as the fans sang:

'Oh it's all gone quiet over there
Oh it's all gone quiet over there
Oh it's all gone quiet, all gone quiet
It's all gone quiet over there'

'Show them the way to go home
They're tired and they want to go to bed
Oh they've only half of a football team
And the other half is dead
Ohhh!'

Rangers where now akin to the ageing heavyweight boxing champion, who was required to come off the ropes and desperately fight for his title. However, it was Celtic, the young contenders, who were to deal the devastating knockout blow. With only seconds remaining, Celtic broke forward through George McCluskey, with MacLeod and Provan racing up alongside him in support. The instinct of the fans was to roar to the players to manoeuvre the ball towards the corner flag, in order to waste time and run down the clock, but McCluskey elected to pass to McLeod. The young Celtic midfielder instinctively fired a bullet of a shot high past McCloy, for a spectacular killer goal. The Celtic fans erupted with joy, safe in the knowledge that the game was now as good as over, as MacLeod was swamped by happy team mates, many of whom collapsed on their knees through sheer exhaustion.

The Jungle fans who had been chanting *'We're gonnae win the league, we're gonnae win, we're gonnae win the league'*, (*to the tune of Mary Hopkins' popular hit song, Those Were the Days*), now changed their lyrics in mid chorus to *'We are the champions, we are the champ, we are the champions!'* as the realisation dawned on them that their heroes were now most certainly destined for victory.

Rangers took centre, and Miller sent a high looping cross towards Latchford, and as the Celtic keeper caught the ball, referee Pringle blew for time up. Celtic had triumphed and against all the odds. To use a Chuchillian phrase in Celtic terms - *never had so few given so much for so many.*

Provan drops to his knees, as MacLeod (10) celebrates Celtic's fourth goal against Rangers, with Andy Lynch racing up in delight.

McGrain collapsed on the turf as Latchford sat astride him and hugged him in disbelief. Pockets of Celtic players were hugging and dancing all over the pitch, in scenes reminiscent of Lisbon 1967. Many of the Celtic fans were still happily celebrating MacLeod's goal, unaware that the final whistle had gone, as mass hysteria broke out around the stand and terraces of Celtic Park. The old ground had witnessed many fine occasions and dramatic moments through the decades, but perhaps none as tremendous as this one. Rangers' fans, devastated by their team's late collapse, visibly raced for the exits, in order to avoid the sight of the happy sea of green and white all around them. For many of the Celtic supporters, the last few minutes were a total blur, as they experienced a huge contrast of emotions - from the unbearable tension of possible victory, to the trepidation of the disaster of a potential Rangers equaliser, but MacLeod's goal had put an end to all of that.

A few dozen Celtic fans, good natured, inebriated and euphoric, invaded the park to salute their tired heroes as the crestfallen Rangers players left the pitch. Thankfully, a full pitch invasion did not materialise, due to the immediate action of Strathclyde's finest. The players were allowed the satisfaction of coming back out for a lap of honour, to take the acclaim of the fans and to salute them for their backing, not only in this game but during the course of the entire season. Captain Danny McGrain was hoisted high on the shoulders of the players as Parkhead reverberated to the sound of *You'll Never Walk Alone,* surrounded by a sea of green and white scarves. This was a truly magnificent sight.

The injured Tommy Burns came out on to the field to join in the celebrations, looking resplendent in his suit and green and white club tie. Tom McAdam was barefoot after throwing his boots and socks into the Jungle, giving some lucky fans memorable souvenirs of the occasion. Roy Aitken, covered in sweat after his exertions on the field, was wearing a green and white woollen tammy, and as the players went indoors to celebrate further, they were photographed drinking from bottles of Solripe soft drinks. Several players recall that none of the directors had the presence of mind to order champagne in case of victory. Not for the first time, that legendary Celtic servant Jimmy Steel, came to the rescue with a few bottles of bubbly for the happy band of players, who thoroughly deserved the taste of champagne. It wasn't the fact that Steel paid for this from his own pocket, it was the measure of the man that he had taken the time to purchase it, knowing that it would be a special moment for the players.

The fans wandered off deliriously into the night, back to their pubs, clubs and homes. They would have their own stories to tell about the legend of the night of 21st May 1979. They were still stunned after watching such a remarkable triumph, and in later years, Pat Nevin, who attended the game, was moved to say that watching the 4-2 game was the closest he had come to *'having a religious experience.'*

It's easy to exaggerate the events during the match, and in view of this it's important to take into account the reports of more impartial observers, of the happenings on the field of play that night.

Celtic are the champions and they did it in champion style, coming off the ropes not once, not twice, but three times to a victory every bit as memorable as anything achieved on the domestic scene by the Lisbon Lions. The bottomless courage, dynamic determination and resolute reserves of stamina which have carried this Parkhead team from virtually nowhere to the title were displayed in glorious Technicolor. No wonder thousands of Celtic fans stayed behind to salute their bedraggled but triumphant favourites. They barely had the breath to do so… and there was also a performance from Roy Aitken which must rank amongst the finest by any Celtic player in any ninety minutes. Ian Paul, Glasgow Herald, 22nd May 1979.

Celtic are Scottish league champions for the 31st time and the title came on a night as dramatic, as memorable and as downright unbelievable as any in all their history. They clinched it in just a half hour of the kind of mayhem football you see just once in a lifetime. Ian Archer, Scottish Daily Express, 22nd May 1979.

This match sizzled for ninety minutes. The Celts attacked Rangers as if their lives depended on it. The Ibrox team were kept in their own half for two thirds of the match. Rangers seemed like a side who would settle for a draw - even when they were leading 1-0. Every Celtic player was outstanding but I would single out Aitken, McCluskey, MacLeod, McAdam and Provan as the miracle men on this history making night for a Celtic team who three months ago could never have forecast themselves as champions. Alex Cameron, Daily Record, 22nd May 1979.

George McCluskey is mobbed by happy fans after the final whistle in the league decider against Rangers.

Celtic are champions - really great champions. They proved that with a display of fantastic football unsurpassed by any of the heroes of the Parkhead past. A torrid, heart stopping, courageous display that had everything that is superb in Scottish football. It wasn't soccer in the silken, languid style. It wasn't soccer which bore the hall mark of elegance, of grace. It wasn't soccer that the purists dream about. But by heaven it was the most exciting soccer we have seen here in a decade. Hugh Taylor, Evening Times, 22nd May 1979.

To use a musical analogy, the Celtic team of the Lisbon era could be compared to the popular music of that period - timeless, classy and refined.

This new Celtic side was more akin to the sounds of their own era. The punk rockers of the late 70's, the young upstarts who were vibrant, played at one hundred miles per hour, were full of energy and stood on ceremony for no one. Stein's team played a pure brand of football, whereas McNeill's young Celts had vigorously run Rangers into the ground on the night.

And what a glorious night it had been.

Celtic: Latchford McGrain Lynch Aitken McAdam Edvaldsson Provan Conroy (Lennox) McCluskey MacLeod Doyle Sub: Davidson

Rangers: McCloy Jardine Dawson Johnstone Jackson A MacDonald McLean (Miller) Russell Parlane Smith Cooper Sub: J MacDonald

Celtic players frolic in the bath after their memorable victory over Rangers.

End of season Premier Division table 1978/79

	P	W	D	L	F	A	Pts
Celtic	36	21	6	9	61	37	48
Rangers	36	18	9	9	52	35	45
Dundee Utd	36	18	8	10	56	37	44
Aberdeen	36	13	14	9	59	36	40
Hibernian	36	12	13	11	44	38	37
St Mirren	36	15	6	15	45	41	36
Morton	36	12	12	12	52	53	36
Partick Thistle	36	13	8	15	42	39	34
Hearts	36	8	7	21	39	71	23
Motherwell	36	5	7	24	33	86	17

Note: This table includes Rangers last two league games which ended as follows:
23rd May Rangers 1-0 Partick Thistle
31st May Hibernian 2-1 Rangers

CHAPTER 13 • THE AFTERMATH

One of the most remarkable matches in Scottish football history had just concluded, and the supporters rushed home to watch the televised highlights of the game on STV, as had been previously advertised. For those who had not been at the game, and were relying on news announcements, the BBC's flagship 9pm news programme reported the scoreline. However those not at the match could not have appreciated the full level of drama which had unfolded earlier that evening. They would have been looking forward with relish to the TV highlights.

Despite all the hype surrounding the game, none of the radio stations elected to cover the match. Radio Clyde had the Tiger Tim show on air and the bold Tiger kept his audience up to speed, with regular updates from Celtic Park, in between reviewing Abba's *Voulez Vous* LP as his album of the week. He struggled to maintain some sense of neutrality, given the fact that he was well known as a huge Celtic fan. For their part, Radio Scotland had decided to broadcast, 'The Monday Play', which was regarded as poor show from the national broadcaster. For those listening on radio, the first chance they would have had to learn more, would have been through the traditional nightly Sports Desk, on BBC Radio 2 at 9.55pm. This was the forerunner of the current BBC Radio 5 Live channel.

If the 4-2 game is remembered for the events on the field, then it will also be remembered for another matter entirely. As TV viewers from all over the country looked forward to watching the highlights in keen anticipation, it emerged that the game had not actually been filmed, due to a wildcat strike by STV programme directors. This was a huge blow to all football fans, and this was the only disappointment of the night. It was sad that so many had been deprived of the enjoyment of watching the game unfold on in their own homes. The abrupt short notice of this industrial action only served to fuel the paranoia of Celtic fans, some of whom still recalled that the last truly momentous victory over Rangers, the 7-1 League Cup final triumph in 1957, had

At 2-1 for us I remember very clearly Rangers getting a corner on our left side. I was on the left-hand post and Danny on the right one. The corner got cleared to the edge of the area and Bobby Russell had that wee shuffle, he was a good player, and he made out he was going to hit with his left, then feinted and rifled it with his right foot. It went through a number of players and in those days, the goalposts were made of metal, and when the ball struck it there was a 'zinging' noise. I heard the 'zing' and I thought it came back out, but when I looked round the ball was nestling in the net and all of the Rangers' players were all over Bobby Russell.

We fought back to 3-2, and then I remember they threw everything at us. We then broke up the park on the left and I was racing up in support. They were totally caught out and Murdo MacLeod had it, and I was screaming for him to hold it until we caught up, and then he fired a most magnificent shot right into the postage stamp corner. I thought Murdo shouldn't have tried a shot but there you are, it worked out well. You couldn't have written the script that night.

The dressing room was absolute pandemonium afterwards. There was a feeling of euphoria and protocol went out and anything went. Doylie was so grateful to all the boys and he was celebrating like mad because he was a fan at heart anyway. I suppose we saved his bacon because had we lost he would have been in deep trouble. Johnny had a big heart. He was fast and was great at knocking it past big defenders and running into them and he got a lot of penalties which I scored from. He was frightened of no one.

Jock Stein used to have a phrase 'Celtic fit'. I used to wonder what he meant by that, and I later found out that Celtic players would come back in the afternoons after normal morning training, twice a week, and the training regime was much harder. For example, at Hearts, I was trained by Jock Wallace, but he had nothing on what we got at Parkhead. On those afternoons we would do the terracing steps, up and down nonstop for 40 minutes. Our fitness levels were terrific and I'm not been shown on television either. On that occasion a cameraman's error was said to be the reason, although footage was to mysteriously appear in the late 1980's.

When the strike was announced shortly before kick-off, only some quick thinking by the members of the Celtic Film Club helped to save the day. The late John McFadyen, secretary and a founder member of the film club, explained what went on behind the scenes. *'A few minutes before the teams came out an industrial dispute meant that the STV crew walked out of the ground. We had intended to purchase the film of the game from them. However by good luck we also had a small video camera at the ground. We went into action and recorded that great game and eventually transferred it to 16mm film. That's quite a difficult job and in fact took us several months to get that job competed. The reason for that was a strike of technicians which affected the labs of the firm who agreed to undertake the commission. However it was well worth the wait. We have the film of the game and it's the only record there is of it. I'm sure it will be shown for many years to come'.*

McFadyen's words were quite prophetic. Because of the absence of TV coverage, their 4-2 film footage was most sought after, and the film club took it around Scotland for the benefit of the fans. It's no exaggeration to claim that the film helped to raise tens of thousands of pounds over the years, for charities and other good causes, as fans filled church halls, schools and community centres all over the country. Film club members also travelled further afield to England, Ireland, Canada and the United States to satisfy the terrific demand from happy Celtic fans, who desperately wanted to view the game, which had earned legendary status.

The Celtic Cine Club was formed in 1969 to record important Celtic games, showing them for supporters clubs, charities and schools to assist them with fund raising. Later renamed as 'The Celtic Film Club', it had proved to be an enormously popular concept with Celtic supporters. Club records show that that from September 1979 to May 1980, John McFadyen and his colleagues gave sixty four shows in various venues, to over ten thousand people. It is interesting to note that the film club had a very cordial relationship with Rangers and their supporters. The Ibrox club were always most cooperative in assisting the club with filming Old Firm games on Glasgow's south side, and the film club attended Church of Scotland and Boys Brigade fund raisers, showing Rangers victories, again for the good cause of raising funds for charity.

Sadly the quality of the 4-2 game footage wasn't up to usual standards, but everyone appreciated the huge effort made by film club members in order to have some record of the match for posterity. Nowadays fans watch short grainy excerpts of the match on the new medium of YouTube. However, for the fans who attended on the night, no amount of TV coverage could replace the wonderful experience of being inside Celtic Park on that historic occasion.

As the dust settled at Celtic Park, Billy McNeill struggled to take in the magnitude of his team's success, as congratulations flooded into the club. The Celtic View delayed print until Friday May 25th, a date that was not lost on Celtic fans, as it was the 12th anniversary of Lisbon 1967. The banner headline read, 'WORLD HAILS THE CHAMPIONS', and reported that the first team squad were about to go off on a well deserved end of season trip to Majorca, as just reward for their tremendous efforts in winning the league title.

'It has been quite unbelievable the number of telephone calls, letters and telegrams we received. They've come from the USA, Canada, Australia, South Africa and all over Britain. With the best will in the world it's impossible to answer them all individually but the senders can be assured they were greatly appreciated. Paul Wilson, Jimmy Johnstone, Bobby Murdoch, Jim Brogan and Pat McCluskey were in there after the match in person to say well done and the first telephone call I received after the game was from Kenny Dalglish who is absolutely delighted with our success and there were also calls from

The Celtic View salutes the new league champions.

Tommy Gemmell and Denis Connaghan'. Billy McNeill, Celtic View 25th May 1979.

'It has been quite unbelievable the number of telephone calls, letters and telegrams we received. They've come from the USA, Canada, Australia, South Africa and all over Britain. With the best will in the world it's impossible to answer them all individually but the senders can be assured they were greatly appreciated. Paul Wilson, Jimmy Johnstone, Bobby Murdoch, Jim Brogan and Pat McCluskey were in there after the match in person to say well done and the first telephone call I received after the game was from Kenny Dalglish who is absolutely delighted with our success and there were also calls from Tommy Gemmell and Denis Connaghan'. Billy McNeill, Celtic View 25th May 1979.

McNeill revealed that John Greig, despite the great disappointment he must have suffered, had been the first person to congratulate the victorious Celts after the final whistle. McNeill remarked, *'I thought this was a splendid gesture and I would like to think I would have done the same thing had we lost.'*

In the media, the Celtic manager was full of praise for his players. He observed that there was a period in the game where Celtic players had given up their set positions, and were running around the field giving their all, wherever they were needed.

'You know the thing that struck me so forcibly as we moved into the last few minutes was that by going 2-1 ahead we had got a helluva lift but equally the impact of them scoring an equaliser could have been too much of a drop for us. But our team could have taken anything and come back that night. I remember they had an attack down their right side, our left and Bobby Russell had got free and was boring into the box'.

'And I saw this figure flying across the pitch and slamming into the tackle. I couldn't believe my eyes - it was Davie Provan.

Now how the hell he got there, I don't know. Nobody has been able to tell me because he was playing on the right-hand side of the pitch for us and he came racing right across the park and put in this perfect saving tackle.'

The next day John Doyle was full of remorse in the press as he recalled his aberration. He explained what had gone on afterwards when he had been conspicuous by his absence in most of the celebratory pictures. He revealed that only after much coaxing from his manager and team mates, had he eventually decided to come back out to join the celebrations.

'I couldn't argue against the ordering off. But the worst possible result would have been a Rangers victory. I put the rest of the lads in a hole and they pulled me out of one by winning the game and the championship. I'm really chuffed for them in fact I can't thank them enough. I honestly didn't think I deserved to be in the photos. Even when I did come out it wasn't the way it should have been because I was sick at being sent off and letting everyone down. Even now I find it hard to take.' Daily Record, 22nd May 1979.

Press reports also reported that Celtic would fine Doyle for being ordered off. This would be seen as sufficient punishment for his misdemeanour, and the truth is Doyle suffered enormously as he sat in the Celtic dressing room, listening to the roars of the crowd. The Celtic winger must have felt utter anguish as he sat contemplating his actions, and one can only imagine his delight when he was informed that his ten team mates fought on so bravely and had prevailed in the end.

It seems that Doyle was something of a wayward soul, and he appeared to have been intent on causing further havoc, as Joe Filippi recalls. *'As a reward for winning the title the club took the first team squad to Majorca for a week's holiday. I was sharing a room with Johnny and he found some eggs. We were three storeys up and on our veranda he saw Billy McNeill and John Clark walking below and he started hurling these eggs at them. Billy and John ran inside and couldn't understand why any locals would want to do this to them. They never did find out it was Johnny.'*

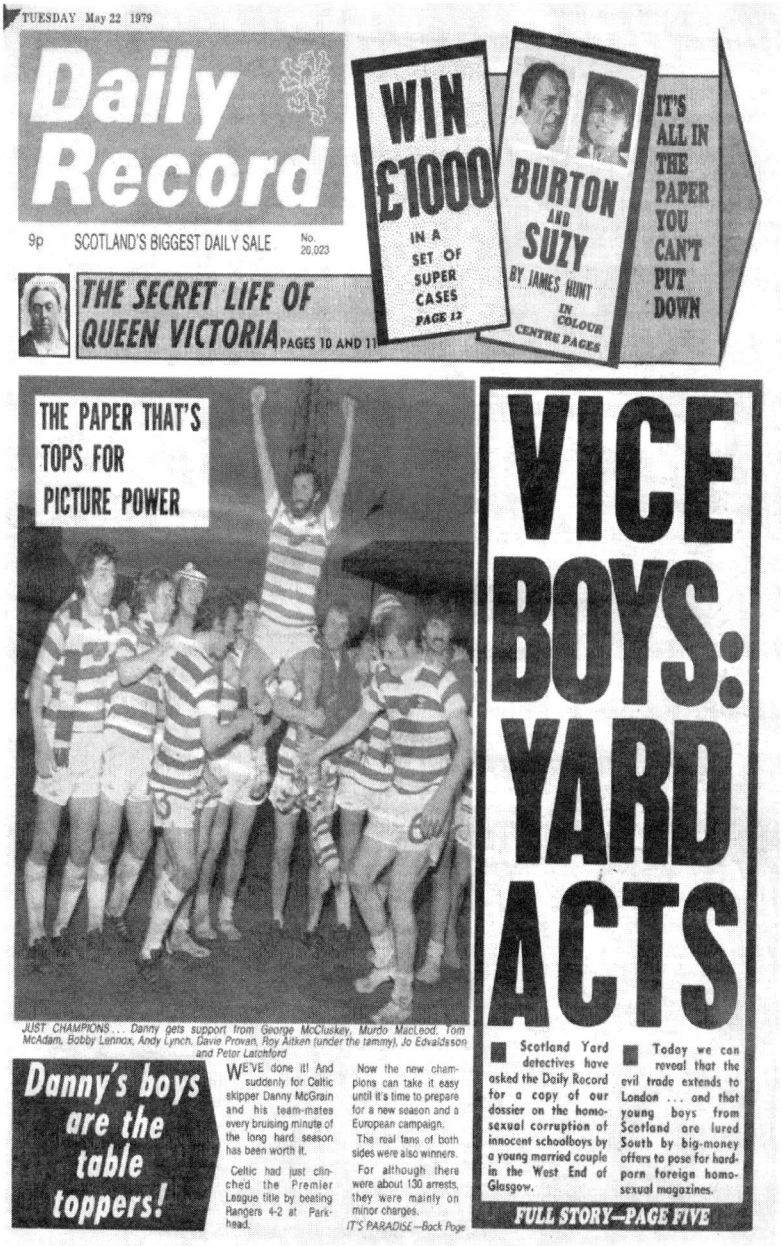

The heroic Celtic team are front page news in May 1979.

There had been concerns about crowd disorder following the match after Celtic won such an important game in dramatic circumstances. However, the following day a police spokesman was satisfied overall by the behaviour of both sets of fans. He stated that there had been one hundred and thirty arrests, mostly for minor charges, and there had been no serious incidents of note.

As Celtic revelled in their glory, John Greig was required to pick up his Rangers team, with three games left to play. The two remaining league games were academic. For the record, Rangers beat Partick Thistle 1-0 at Ibrox, but lost 2-1 to Hibs at Easter Road. The Ibrox game recorded one of the smallest attendances to ever witness a game in the stadium, a paltry 2,000 fans turning up for what had become a meaningless fixture. These results ensured that Celtic won the title by a margin of three points in the end.

The second Scottish Cup replay was a more eventful affair than the two previous games, with Rangers running out winners by 3-2, virtue of an Arthur Duncan own goal. The game needed extra time to settle the tie, with the teams being level at 2-2. Although Rangers won and collected their second domestic cup of the season, there was still a black cloud of despair hanging over Ibrox. Only 30,602 turned up, a fairly sparse crowd inside Hampden's huge bowl. The paying public seemed reluctant to turn out in numbers for a third game, with the further inconvenience of it being played in midweek.

The attendance at this match brought back memories of the 1973 League Cup final between Celtic and Dundee, when 27,924 fans turned out at the national stadium. The absence of fans on this occasion was due to the country experiencing the turmoil of the three day week, atrocious winter weather and bus strikes.

John Greig could argue that his first season be deemed a success, with two trophies and some fine European displays. Nevertheless, surrendering the title at Parkhead would mark the beginning of the end for this Rangers team. Greig would never come as close to winning the league title during the rest of his reign. Aberdeen and Dundee United were about to gate crash the Scottish football scene to tremendous effect, and would push Rangers to the sidelines. It was ironic that the one man John Greig couldn't replace was John Greig himself, as without his drive and leadership on the field of play, Rangers at times seemed rudderless. In many ways the fine Rangers team which was created by Jock Wallace, and enjoyed tremendous success during the mid to late 1970's, died that night at Celtic Park. Greig had retired as a player less than twelve months previously, and it was difficult to imagine Rangers capitulating as they had done at Celtic Park, had he been team captain.

There was much sympathy for the unfortunate Colin Jackson whose own goal had given Celtic that vital third goal. Jackson was to rue his unintentional contribution on the night. *'Peter McCloy came out for a McCluskey cross and just got to it. But I was moving towards goal and I couldn't get out of the way of the ball. It hit me on the shoulder and went straight into the net. They said afterwards that I headed it in but it was more inelegant than that and I think that won the game for them. I went off on my own after the game and stopped at a pub I'd never been in before. I just sat glumly and met another couple of Rangers supporters who looked as stunned as me. We went back to their house and had a good drink. We've been friends ever since. It's surprising what adversity brings you.'*

Jackson's fellow team mate Alex Miller would later remark, *'I am not a drinker so I couldn't even have the consolation of getting drunk but it was without doubt the worst night I ever spent in my life.'*

Billy McNeill could feel satisfied that he had been vindicated in releasing a number of experienced players during his short reign as manager, building the nucleus of a new team with the young players he had at the club. Considering that Roy Aitken was twenty, Tommy Burns twenty two, George McCluskey twenty one, Mike Conroy twenty one, Murdo MacLeod twenty and Davie Provan twenty three, the progress made was remarkable, and these players would form the backbone of the Celtic team for many years to come.

In later years McNeill looked back on that initial first season when he was in control of what was very much a transitional period. *'I remember a newspaper report which said I had taken a ruthless approach, something I never thought of until I read that. But it was ruthless as I had decided that I had to get new blood in and I was lucky that Provan and MacLeod were available. Funnily enough when I looked at Murdo at Dumbarton they had Graeme Sharp up front. I fancied him as well but I thought no, there's no way Dumbarton could have two quality youngsters in their side, but I was wrong as Graeme proved when he went down to Everton where he was such a great success. I've often thought what would have happened if I had taken both of them.'* And so on this occasion Celtic's loss was to be Everton's gain.

McNeill had rightly taken most of the plaudits for his team's success, but Andy Lynch believes that another member of the back room team was deserving of great credit also. *'John Clark was a tremendous number two for Billy. He was a bit calmer and he would come up and have wee chat about things like one on one's on the pitch and he would put you right. He had a calming influence on the players and there were times when we needed that. Billy and John worked great together but like his football career maybe John didn't get the credit perhaps that he should have.'*

It is reckoned that Celtic's biggest advantage on the night was that they knew they had to win, and this helped to give them more impetus, whilst Rangers knew they had the benefit of two remaining league games. The Ibrox men played a huge total of sixty three games during their 1978-79 campaign. Their success in the cup competitions had ultimately been their undoing, as fatigue surely set in. In comparison, Celtic had only played fifty five matches, so there is little doubt that the number of games each side played had been a contributing factor.

Celtic's dramatic triumph against Rangers is headline news in May 1979.

Another notable piece of football history was created by the victorious Celtic players on the evening of 21st May. This was the first time Celtic had won a Scottish League title by virtue of winning a game at Parkhead since 14th April 1926, when they defeated Morton 3-1, with goals from legendary Celts Jimmy McGrory, Paddy Connolly and Tommy McInally. This remains a fascinating statistic, and it's extremely doubtful if anyone who was in attendance at the 4-2 match could actually recall this event, fifty three years before. It should be noted that Celtic did clinch a league title at a home game against Ayr United in 1971, but this game was moved to Hampden Park, due to construction of the new main stand at Celtic Park.

In terms of statistics, the Celts won the league title with forty eight points. This was lowest points total amassed by any winning side since Jimmy McGrory's Celtic team won the title in 1953-54, with a total of 43 points. Between 28th March and 21st May, Celtic played a remarkable total of sixteen games. This meant that during a period of almost eight weeks, Billy McNeill's side averaged a game every 3.5 days. They had won twelve, drawn one and lost three in that period, and it's noticeable that neither the manager nor the players commented about tiredness or fatigue, which is in sharp contrast to the pampered individuals of the 21st Century. Teams nowadays have the luxury of huge playing squads and modern rotation systems, where players very rarely play twice in a week over long periods.

These sixteen matches had been stamina sapping events for the Celtic players, with McNeill only having a small squad at his disposal. They dredged the depths of their energy levels to the full to ensure that their club triumphed in the end. In the late 1970's footballers were becoming more mercenary, and older Celtic fans in particular fretted that the days of the 'jersey' player may be over. However, this group of players delighted the fans by dispelling this notion, and proving that this was not an outdated concept. Sheer determination, love of the jersey and a need to repay a faithful support were enough to see them through. Bertie Auld once claimed that Celtic players should not have the energy to run off the field after an Old Firm game, and there can be no doubt that this team had given their all for the Celtic cause.

Astonishingly, this Celtic side won the league title with Tom McAdam and Andy Lynch as joint top scorers with a meagre seven league goals apiece, and it is difficult to recall any Scottish side winning a championship when their top scorers had netted on so few occasions. Celtic's strength had been their ability to score from all areas of the park, and seventeen different players added to the goals column during the season. McAdam was top scorer in all competitions with fifteen goals, although it is interesting to note that he did not score again after the 3-2 League cup defeat to Rangers on 13th December.

Lynch netted on thirteen occasions, which was a terrific contribution from a full-back, although ten of these came from the penalty spot. Lynch's contribution from penalties proved to be highly significant, particularly the vital winner against Dundee United on 28th April, the day when many believed for the first time that Billy McNeill's young side were actually championship material.

Bobby Lennox had always been a huge favourite with the Celtic support and they were delighted with his performances and goals in the league run in. The wee man's experience had been hugely influential in the deciding game against Rangers. On that night, the last of the Lisbon Lions had roared loudly, and there would be no free transfer now for the evergreen Lennox. McNeill remarked that after Bobby's contribution in the title decider, he could play on now for as long as he liked - *'He knows what it means to wear a Celtic jersey and he is a great influence on the younger players.'* The Lisbon veteran would play for another successful season, before retiring through injury in late 1980.

It's interesting to note that no formal presentation of the League trophy was ever made to Celtic. It is understandable that the football authorities would have been reluctant to hand out silverware after the heat of an Old Firm game. However, when the league flag was unfurled at Parkhead on 11th August 1979, before the first game against Morton, the league trophy was nowhere to be seen.

Celtic were similarly low key when presenting the League winners medals to their own players. Joe Filippi played twenty games during that victorious League campaign, and was due a winner's medal. He still laments the fact that he didn't received one. *'A lot of people don't know this but I never got a medal although I never asked for one either but to this day I don't know why I never got one. It was a sore point. I don't know how they gave out the medals in the end.'* Mike Conroy helps to clarify matters. *'I got my medal the following season when they were handed out very informally on the bus en route to an away game.'* So it appears that Celtic didn't have a formal presentation ceremony or a function to celebrate one of the greatest achievements in their entire history, resorting to handing the medals out on a bus, which must have been something of an anticlimax for the players.

For Danny McGrain the league title success represented a major landmark in his career, because it was the first trophy he won as Celtic captain. Since his injury on 1st October 1977, until his return to the side, Celtic played forty seven games, with a disappointing record of twenty wins, ten draws and seventeen defeats. Since McGrain's return to the side on 3rd March 1979, Celtic's record improved dramatically. He played in eighteen games, of which the team won fourteen, drew one and lost three. These statistics don't lie. There can be no doubt that the League Championship of 1979 would not have been possible without his influential presence on the park.

There were still a number of fixtures for the Scottish national team to fulfil before the season could end. Just twenty four hours after Celtic's memorable league triumph, Scotland beat Northern Ireland 1-0 at Hampden, courtesy of an Arthur Graham goal, and on 26th May, Jock Stein's men travelled south for the bi-annual pilgrimage to Wembley. The Scotland manager had the misfortune of having a high number of call offs. He was also deprived of players from the big Glasgow clubs and lost the influential Nottingham Forest trio of Archie Gemmill, Kenny Burns and John Robertson, who were preparing for their European Cup final clash, with the Swedes of Malmo, in Munich.

The nation was desperate for the players to restore some much needed pride, following the debacle in Argentina the previous summer. There is little that the Scots' fan enjoys more than a win on the hallowed turf of the Auld Enemy. Scotland had such great advantage in terms of the number of fans, (it's estimated that Scotland had 70,000 fans in the 98,000 crowd), that it was remarked that only the band seemed to be supporting England. The fans were delighted by their team's first half performance as Scotland dominated, and they had a 1-0 lead through a John Wark goal after forty five minutes.

England then stunned the Scots when they equalised in first half injury time, when Manchester City winger, Peter Barnes, scored with a soft goal. The frustration for Scotland was that the Portuguese referee, Antonio Garrido, only added time on at the end of the half due to a drunken, flag waving Scotland fan who ran on to the park. It then took the police two minutes to catch him and march him unceremoniously from the field. Scotland collapsed in the second half and went down tamely in the end, by 3-1. Their Anglo-Scot goalkeeper, Everton's George Wood, bore the brunt of media criticism for being at fault for England's first two goals. Wembley was once again described as a graveyard for Scottish goalkeepers.

On Saturday 2nd June the Glasgow footballing public were given a rare treat, when World Champions Argentina arrived to play a glamour friendly at Hampden. On a sunny day the Argentinians showed their class, during a fine game where Scotland competed well, eventually going down by 3-1. The main talking point afterwards, was the performance of the precocious eighteen year old forward, Diego Maradona. He gave a virtuoso performance, where he exhibited his talents to the full, and gave a glimpse of what football fans everywhere were to enjoy in the years to come.

On 7th June Scotland travelled to Oslo to play Norway in a European Championship qualifying game. The squad was bolstered by the addition of Nottingham Forest's Scots trio of Burns, Gemmill and Robertson, who had returned victorious from their European Cup triumph over Malmo. Scotland ran out worthy winners in a comprehensive 4-0 win. Finally, at last, this longest of long seasons was over.

CHAPTER 14 • RECOLLECTIONS

Celtic players and fans recall their own memories of the events of 21st May 1979, on and off the field of play.

THE PLAYERS

Mike Conroy was a twenty one year old Celtic midfielder on the night of the 4-2 game in 1979. He vividly recalls the events before, during and after that great night.

I had a routine for night games where I would drive in the morning to the little back road between Port Glasgow and Kilmacolm, where there is a little bridge with a gate where you can park your car and go for a walk. I would get a bit of fresh air and go for a short walk, it was quiet and I would get my mind into what my role was going to be and what my responsibilities were going to be during the game. My mum and Dad both worked, my Mum was a nurse and Dad was an electrician, so I would then go to my Gran's and she would make me steak and potatoes. I would go back home and go to bed for an hour and a half or so then get back up and have poached eggs on toast and a vitamin C tablet. and then I would go to the game. That was the exact routine I kept all my time at Celtic for midweek matches.

Davie Provan then picked me up as was usual as he was coming from Gourock about quarter past five. As we passed through Port Glasgow, we saw the red ash pitches we had played on as young boys, Davie played for Port Glasgow Rovers and I had played for Holy Family, Port Glasgow Hibs and Port Glasgow youth club. We both recalled playing on those pitches and I remember we talked about how when we were boys we had long dreamed of being involved in a game of this magnitude.
As we got closer to Glasgow the nerves began to kick in and Davie said that he had played in three Old Firm games and

hadn't won one yet. But me and Davie convinced each other that we were going to win, and I don't think we had any fear of any opponent and we felt if we played well we would win.

We weren't aware of the cameras being on strike. We started well but Cooper ran down the right and I caught wee Alex MacDonald over my shoulder. As the ball went past me I thought that's behind the two of us and then I heard the net rippling and knew he had scored.

Rangers almost scored a second when Danny managed to clear one off the line, but there was no sense of panic in the dressing room. Billy was calm and said we were playing well and the chances would come, and not to panic. Then Doylie got sent off and there was real panic. For fifteen minutes after that it was like the OK Corral, there were people turning up in positions you wouldn't believe, everything went out the window. Big Roy got the equaliser and then Billy took me off to put Bobby Lennox on. He said as I came off, 'we need to win', and I said 'no problem at all, if anyone is going to win it, its wee Bobby.'

Frank Connor and Neilly Mochan were on the bench and they were convinced we would see it through when George scored to make it 2-1. Then Bobby Russell equalised and big Billy kept saying to Frank, 'The Big Man up there is making it hard for us', and Frank kept reassuring him that we'd be fine, and just after that we took the lead through a Colin Jackson own goal.

I remember with four or five minutes left Davie Provan was in the left-back position and swept up an attack back to Peter Latchford. It was that type of game. People were popping up everywhere and doing things you wouldn't normally expect. Murdo MacLeod went striding forward and on the bench we're shouting, 'Keep it, just keep it', and then he let one go right into the postage stamp corner. I was so excited I cracked my head off the dugout which was quite low back then.

Johnny Doyle was distraught in the dressing room afterwards and at the time we thought, when he was sent off, there was nothing in it, but the film later showed he had a dig at Alex MacDonald right enough. He was gutted. The dressing room afterwards was awash with ex players, Mums and Dads and us, running about half naked. It was a great feeling and at twenty years of age I thought if this all ends tomorrow I've had a great ride.

My Mum and Dad were there and they had friends over from America and they had no idea about football, and they wanted to go to the 'ball game' that was on that night, so I managed to scrape up some more tickets again at short notice. They couldn't believe what they were seeing with all this madness going on all around them. The dressing room afterwards was chaos, just chaos. My Mum and Dad ended up where the pies and sandwiches were and George McCluskey's Dad was in the dressing room singing like mad, some of the Lisbon Lions were in there and it was just mayhem.

Afterwards Davie Provan, Andy Lynch and I went into town to a Casino to celebrate, nothing heavy just a couple of shandies and Davie drove me home to Port Glasgow. I couldn't sleep after what had happened and was up early to go for the papers. I stopped the car at the newsagents and there were men going to their work in Kingston's shipyards across the road. A lot of them were shouting in the street, 'Well done', although a couple shouted that I was a Fenian so and so!

We then went on a week's break to Majorca as a reward for the season. I didn't really drink at all back then, maybe a shandy in the close season. Sitting in the sun we all enjoyed some bottles of San Miguel which I found pretty strong and although I can't recall that much, there was one night in a night club, we ended up on top of the tables singing. It was an unforgettable time.

Celtic players receive the league flag in May 1979.

Davie Provan became Celtic's record signing in September 1978, when he signed from Kilmarnock for £125,000. He was Celtic's number seven on the right wing on the night of the 4-2 game.

I had played against Rangers three times that season, two league games - one loss, one draw - and in between that we lost the League Cup semi-final at Hampden. That was three Old Firm games and I hadn't won one yet and I remember driving to the game with Mick Conroy, and I said we have just got to win this, we've got to win, and no one is going to hand it to us, we will have to play out of our skin.

Billy did the right thing by not taking us to Seamill on the night before the Rangers game. He said it would be better for the boys to be in their own homes, in their own beds. It was a league game and not a cup final and we never went to Seamill for league games. Billy was very calm beforehand and was very good at hiding his feelings because he must have been under great pressure at the time.

In the first half I hit a free-kick into the box and Roy Aitken hit it flush with his head and it came off the underside of the bar and at half-time we were a goal down but Billy just said to keep playing the way we were and we would be okay.

We were a reasonably young team but the energy we showed after Doylie was sent off was tremendous and was a tribute to the fitness of the team, and our fitness levels were colossal that night. I never remember feeling tired in that game at all, the adrenalin was going through the roof.

At 3-2 I was on Murdo's left and was screaming to him to give me the ball for me to go to the corner flag and kill time and I'm thinking Murdo, don't shoot, it will only go into Peter McCloy's arms and he will launch it upfield and we only have ten men. The wee man just stuck it in the top corner and that was the first time I allowed myself to think we had won it.

I practically jumped into the Jungle at the final whistle. I took my boots off and threw them into the Jungle and I was trying to get my strip off, and big Johannes Edvaldsson jumped on me and said, 'Haw, calm down, calm down.' I was going to throw my jersey in but I'm glad now I didn't, because I still have it now. I've played in better Celtic teams than that one but I've never played in a team or been in a dressing room that had that spirit about it

I remember Desmond White coming into the dressing room after the game, you couldn't move in it, there was Jinky Johnstone, Bobby Murdoch, it was just mayhem. Desmond asked for silence, and said that this was the club's finest hour since Lisbon which was a phenomenal compliment. We could have won the European Cup after that and the euphoria wouldn't have matched the feeling of that night when we won that title.

Doylie said afterwards if we hadn't won then he would have just got dressed and headed down London Road because big Billy would have had him. He was a bit sheepish but all the boys were brilliant with him.

I remember looking up at the director's box after the game trying to spot my parents who were in the stand, and there was a wooden ledge in front of the director's box and there was Tam Burns standing on top of it, next to the Celtic directors proudly holding aloft a Celtic scarf which wasn't exactly the done thing in that area. I came across my mum in the tunnel and the dressing room was terrific, I always remember Jinky and Bobby being in and everyone hugging and singing.

The trip to Majorca afterwards was brilliant with Vic Davidson holding court and him, Tom McAdam and Bobby Lennox were always the first ones at the pool each next morning for the San Miguel. I always remember Tam Burns getting really bad sun burn because there was not the same level of information back in those days about skin care.

Andy Lynch was Celtic's vice captain on the night, and was one of the more experienced players in a young Celtic team.

I was reasonably optimistic we would win but the fact was Rangers only needed a draw, and they had a strong side back then although we had a feeling that we could create a bit of history if we could win the league at home.

Early on I tried to keep Davie Cooper on his right foot but his cross gave Rangers their first goal, and I was annoyed at that, as I should have cut it out but Alex MacDonald was great at those late runs into the box and it was 1-0 for them. I didn't feel good when John Doyle got sent off and I thought, 'Oh, here we go.' There was no hiding place after that and it was a case of sleeves rolled up, and just do your job and hope we get a break. The tension that night was unbelievable, and Doylie was always ready to snap at any given time.

proud to say that stood us in good stead on the night, when we were required to dig deep.

Andy Lynch celebrates Celtic's league success with Billy McNeill and John Clark.

Bobby Lennox was a thirty five year old veteran, who was already regarded as a Celtic legend, even before his contribution on the night of the 4-2 game. He recalls how his second spell as a Celt came about.

I was due back from America in September 1978 and Jock Stein called me to alert me to the fact that Billy was short of players, and asked if I was willing to help out for six months. I was delighted, and even although other teams were interested, I jumped at the chance to help Celtic and Billy out.

It was difficult for me at first because I kept calling Billy 'Caesar', and it took me a long while to get used to calling him 'Boss'.

Billy just asked me to use my experience to good effect and to do what I could, especially with the younger guys.

I noticed a big difference in the team since I'd left. I used to phone Roy Aitken from America and one week we lost 4-1 at Easter Road, and I asked who scored. Roy said it was Michael Conroy, and I said, 'who?', as I'd never heard of him, although he was to become a good friend. Davie Provan and Murdo MacLeod also arrived and this gave the team a huge lift.

I well remember the trip to Estoril in the winter when I think we won 4-0, especially the night after the game when we ended up in this wee lounge bar which was empty except for a solo pianist. We had a great sing song and it was a great bonding session which brought us all together. Tom McAdam was a good singer and we all had a great time, nothing too boozy just really good fun.

There's a quiz question that says 'When did George McCluskey and Bobby Lennox both score with headers in a game at Ibrox?'. George and I were so great in the air - not ! This was a game against St Mirren, when we had to play at Ibrox, and I'm proud to say I was the last Celtic player to score in front of the Celtic fans at the old Ibrox, before it was made all seated.

In the 4-2 game I came on for Mick Conroy, and Billy just asked me to run the channels and trouble the Rangers defence. The thing I remember most is Rangers' second goal, when the ball flew past a number of us, and I still can't believe it went in. We were gutted at the time but fought back well to win.

After the final whistle I was delighted to see my old pals Jimmy Johnstone and Bobby Murdoch in the dressing room and they were overjoyed for me getting another medal at this late stage in my career.

That game is easily one of the highlights of my career and I had only signed to the end of the season, but after the St Mirren game at Ibrox in early May, Billy had confided with me that he was keeping me on. This made the success of the 4-2 game all the better, as I knew I was now staying on. That team had great camaraderie, and there was a great spirit amongst all the boys.

Hugely popular Celtic goalkeeper Peter Latchford recounts how this was actually one of his quieter Old Firm games.

We had a lot of games to play in the last couple of months of the season and I thought this was brilliant, because it meant no training. All we did was play games and rest. I enjoyed that, although the midfield players who were running round may not have enjoyed it so much. Footballers just like to play football and training can be the hard bit.

We did go on a good run towards the end of the season, and Jock Stein used to tell us that winning is a good habit to have, and to get used to it, and keep it up. I was confident going into the game as we were doing well, and Billy's team talk was basically, 'If you win tonight lads you win the league. If you don't, you've lost it. What do you want to do?'

Incredible as it seems, that game was one of the quietest I ever had as a goalkeeper. I didn't have a lot to do, although I was annoyed at the two goals we lost. Tom McAdam was very new to playing the centre-half role, and I tried to help him out by shouting at him where he should go. Tom played really well that night, and he was a player who didn't get the credit he should have in his career.

It was actually quite a mediocre game until John Doyle was sent off, you can't print what I was thinking about him at that point because in those days you had to do something pretty bad to be ordered off. Nobody said much when he ran up the tunnel, but I remember we all looked at each other, and collectively rolled our sleeves up. That sending off was the catalyst we needed, and it galvanised the players to play for each other.

At the end of the match it was bonkers. The directors all came in, which was very unusual in those days, and there was *champagne corks popping. We went back out for a wee lap of honour, and if you notice we had no boots, we were all in socks or bare feet.*

That Rangers game was the night you dream about. Some players play their whole career and never get a chance to play in a game of that magnitude. It was definitely the highlight of my career. The atmosphere that night was unbelievable and only the Real Madrid game in March 1980 can compare to it.

We went to Majorca afterwards as a reward for winning the title, and these were the days well before mobile phones and texts, and I recall Danny McGrain sent Rangers' Sandy Jardine an old fashioned telegram wishing him all the best and 'we are the champions.' All good natured stuff.

Danny McGrain was Celtic's captain and the team's talisman in the 1978-79 season. He recalls his long struggle to return to the side after injury.

Two days after a game against Hibs in October 1977 I awoke and couldn't stand up for the pain in the ball of my foot. It was really sore, and this lasted for weeks, before the pain moved to my ankle and then to my big toe. The pain moved around and was never confined to one area.

For eight months this went on and no one could diagnose it, and it kept me from playing. I went to a specialist in Oswestry in Wales, and they couldn't help, and then I missed the 1978 World Cup finals in Argentina. Jimmy Steel, the Celtic masseur, was very keen on health foods and modern medicines which was quite unusual back then, and he recommended a guy called Jan De Vries, who was an acupuncturist and was based in Troon. I went to see him, and he said he knew how to treat me, so I went there every Thursday night for three months with 'Steely'.

I think my foot was improving slowly anyway, but there's no doubt that acupuncture speeded up the process, and in the end the problem disappeared as quickly as it came. I know there were rumours at the time about my retiring from football through injury, but never at any time did it cross my mind that I wouldn't make it back into the Celtic first team. It was hard to get back to full fitness, but there was a guy called Jackie Connor, who was a big Celtic fan, and was a great friend of Jock Stein's. He would take me out cycling, which I discovered was a great way of getting fit without putting any pressure on the injured foot. It was hard work, but well worth it in the end, and Jackie became a good friend of mine.

I was disappointed when Jock Stein left in the summer of 1978, as he was the only manager I had until then. He didn't say any sentimental goodbyes or anything like that, and the next thing we knew Billy McNeil had took over. I found it hard in the beginning to call him boss, as he was always 'Billy' or 'big man' to me, and I did make a few' faux pas' to begin with.

When I returned to first team action we were chasing the title, and I remember the goal I scored against Hibs in May, when I scored from far out. I didn't score many, so that was a great moment for me, they tell me Jim McArthur didn't even move for it.

I was delighted to play in the deciding game against Rangers. When Doylie was sent off I thought, 'What have you done?' The stakes were very high in a game like that and now we had just ten men. In saying that, he helped to make that game more famous. We knew we were up against it, and I still can't believe that the team coped so well playing all that time with a man short.

I have to say I was relieved afterwards that we won, as I should have prevented Bobby Russell's goal going in to make it 2-2, when I was on the post. To this day, I still think it's going by, and I was hoping that it would waste a bit of time in doing so. When it crept in I thought, 'Aw naw', and I couldn't believe I made such a stupid mistake.

I can still remember looking up and seeing Murdo letting rip for the fourth goal. I know he'll claim he meant it, but I wonder if he meant it the way it went in, because it was so spectacular. I was fortunate enough to play in a lot of great games, but there's no doubt that the night of the 4-2 game is right up there with the best of them, and I am tremendously proud of that game because that was my first success as a Celtic captain.

Billy McNeill enjoyed his first success as a manager on the night of the 4-2 game and he looks back on a night of wild celebration. (Courtesy of The Celtic View).

During the winter period, there was basically no football at all because of the freezing weather and I always thought that really assisted us because it condensed the end part of the season. We went on a period where we were winning games like nobody's business. But then, all of a sudden, along came the Rangers game. It was the last game of the season for us and what an event for us into the bargain. The players were absolutely brilliant because they were so prepared for that game. It was absolutely incredible. There were so many things about it that were tremendous. The crowd and the amount of former players that were at the game, giving their support and joining in the celebrations at the end of the game was absolutely incredible. It was quite brilliant but it just epitomised the feeling that Celtic can generate.

My instruction to the players in the dressing was not to allow Rangers to have any spaces on the pitch that would allow them to control that game. I was determined to get my team ready for us keeping a hold of the ball and keeping control of it. And that's exactly what the players did, they were absolutely brilliant.

The first thing that comes to mind when I think about the action on the park was wee Doyley. When he got sent off I thought that was it. We were already a goal down and now we were down to ten men as well. When he walked up that tunnel I think we all thought that was the end of our season. But it didn't seem to matter as the boys just took on all the added responsibility and I don't think we even noticed that we had only ten men on the pitch.

The game just seemed to fly in and it was as quick as anything. I always remember thinking that. And then Murdo got that ball and I was shouting to him, 'Shoot, shoot'. It wasn't as if I was necessarily wanting him to hit the target, but Celtic Park in those days was the huge bowl-shaped stadium with the running track behind both goals and the supporters quite a bit back from the goal-line. So it always took a wee bit of time for the ball to get back to the field of play and I thought if Murdo blasted it then we might gain a few valuable seconds. He did hit it and the ball screamed into the back of the net – that was brilliant and we knew then that the game, not to mention the championship was tied up – the whole thing.

A draw would have suited Rangers on the night but we had to win and the very fact that we had to go out there and win, I'm sure suited us in that game. We had a great shower of boys who gave their all, they gave everything that they had to give and it certainly got Doyley off the hook.

The pressure that night was incessant, it was incredible. Murdo's goal just epitomised the many goals he scored during that season. Big Roy Aitken was absolutely out of this world but it's difficult to just pinpoint individual players because everybody contributed.

When the final whistle went it was absolutely amazing. The number of former players at the game was incredible and they were all in the dressing room at the end of the game, it was astonishing. The crowd's reaction was absolutely fantastic and I remember Tommy Burns, who was out injured, dancing about in his shirt and tie in front of the supporters. That also just showed you what a great team effort it was and their attitude was perfect.

There was a whole load of us stayed behind that night. I don't know if the players took it upon themselves to go out and celebrate but we also had to take care of all these former players who wanted to go and congratulate the team – the place was packed. We ended up having a celebration that night in the old snooker room at Celtic Park. It was an absolutely brilliant night. None of us were running home to watch it on the TV even though it was one of the biggest games in our history, and as it turned out it wasn't even on the telly that night.

It was one big party and all the groundsmen at the park joined in that night as well and, as the night went on, they asked me if they could just sleep in the dressing room. At first I was a wee bit wary about that but at the end of the night I just turned the key and locked the door with them still inside and away we went. I came in the next morning nice and early because I knew that the press would be looking for a reaction to the game and winning the title. When I got to the park I heard this banging on the door and I suddenly remembered that they were in there. They had spent the entire night in the dressing room.

Seventeen year old Celtic player Danny Crainie was on the ground staff at the time, and recalls how he and his fellow team mates tricked Celtic kit man Neilly Mochan on the night.

At that time there were five of us on the ground staff - myself, Charlie Nicholas, Willie McStay, Gerry Crawley and Hugh Ferry. We were working hard all day, cleaning the players' boots, scrubbing the dressing rooms and making sure the carbolic soap was put out, and we were looking forward to going to the match that night.

Neilly Mochan was the kit man, and when he went for his lunch I knew where he kept the sets of strips for the team, so I grabbed five jerseys for us to wear to the game I put them in a bag and then later on, we all went to my house in Kilsyth for a bit of dinner. We got the local supporters' bus to Parkhead, but kept the jerseys in the bag until we got to the turnstiles, and then we put them on. We were getting funny looks from the fans as these were real Celtic jerseys, with the embroidered badge, and the fashion of adults wearing replica strips hadn't really taken off yet. We walked through the Celtic end to the corner of the Jungle and kept getting admiring looks for our jerseys.

The thing I remember most during the game is when Bobby Russell played a one-two at the edge of the box, and went through and placed it, and the Rangers fans all jumped up, I thought he had scored but it slid past the post. I remember thinking, 'That was it'. At time up, we all went mad with delight. After the game we couldn't celebrate too much as we were working the next day, and I had to get the jerseys back before Neilly found out, but to my knowledge he never did. Had he caught us he would probably have told us off, but knowing him, deep down he would have thought, 'Good on you wee man.'

The next day we managed to smuggle a ball on to the pitch after we had completed clearing up from the night before, and had a good kick about, and we all dreamed that one day we would get to play on that same pitch in a game of that importance.

Gordon Smith was in his second full season as a Rangers player on the night of 21st May 1979. He was in a successful team that were heading for their second consecutive Scottish treble.

It was a huge shock to me when Jock Wallace left Rangers, and it was like a death in the family for the players, and we didn't know who was going to be the new manager. There was a lot of talk about Jim McLean getting the job, and even Alex Ferguson. In the end up John Greig got it, although I didn't have a great relationship with John, even as a team mate, so I was unsure what would happen.

I have to admit John was unlucky as a manager, because after beating Juventus and PSV we had injuries when we lost to Cologne. That was a huge blow as we would have fancied our chances against Nottingham Forest in the semis, and that year Malmo actually got to the final.

When the season started we couldn't quite find the same form we had the previous year, but as the season wore on we got better. That was the season when there was a huge fixture backlog, and we had to play fourteen games in something like fifty days near the end of the campaign. We were challenging for four tournaments after the New Year and the games were coming thick and fast.

In early May we beat Celtic 1-0 to go top, and we were the better team and should have won by three or four. We were confident of winning another treble going in to the last few games, and we were aware the Parkhead game was a decider.

On 21st May we were confident that we could tie up the title by winning, but also aware that we could get a draw, and then win the league in our last two fixtures. I can barely remember anything about the Parkhead game other than afterwards when we were sitting dejected in the dressing room, and we could hear the Celtic players in their dressing room celebrating, and the fans singing outside. We were dazed and just sat there feeling numb.

After the 4-2 game we still had the Scottish Cup final replay against Hibs to contend with, and I have to say we were still on a downer, and we came in for a lot of criticism for losing to ten men. I was dropped for that game and came on as a sub at 2-2. Davie Cooper sent in a cross which I was about to head in for the winner, when Arthur Duncan barged me out of the way and headed it into his own net. Referee Brian McGinlay actually said that he would have given a penalty had the ball not gone in. But I was just gutted that I had been deprived the honour of scoring the winning goal in a cup final.

It's ironic to think that I tried to talk John Greig into signing Davie Provan at the start of the season, when he was in dispute with Kilmarnock, as I thought he'd be a great signing for

Rangers. John wasn't convinced though, and he thought Davie was a bit soft, as he had played directly against him when he was a player. Davie signed for Celtic not long after and he became a great Celtic player, and he played a huge part on that night they won the league.

THE FANS

A Celtic fan who was a serving police officer on duty during the 4-2 game describes his contrasting emotions on the night. He wishes to remain anonymous. (From the book, *Jungle Tales,* by John Quinn)

'One of the perks of being a 'Polis' in Glasgow is getting the chance of working overtime at football matches and, with a bit of luck, you might find yourself getting paid to watch your favourite team. That happened to me on many occasions but the most memorable was the Old Firm match in May 1979 when Celtic needed two points to win the league.

At that time I worked in the north side of the City and a few days before the big decider my sergeant, who was a big bluenose, told me - 'You've won a watch, wee-man, you're working at the game. Now do you want the bad news? So am I and I'm going to enjoy your team getting stuffed.' The cop I worked with was also a Celtic fan and he was told that he was also working at the match but the chance of us working together was remote to say the least, if not impossible.

On the evening of the match the atmosphere in the city was electric, much more so than I ever experienced. There had been a build up of tension for several days as the season hinged on this one result for both teams. When I arrived at Celtic Park I was told right away where I was working that night and I couldn't believe it. Me and my pal were paired together and were working in the Jungle. This night, we hoped, would be one to remember.'

As we stood there, keeping an eye on the crowds arriving and listening to the songs and patter of the fans, the excitement was growing by the minute. Suddenly I was aware of a presence behind me and was our sergeant. He resembled the 'Honey Monster' in the TV adverts wearing a police uniform - all six foot six inches of him. 'Right you two, nae jumpin' up and doon when the Gers score' he joked. If it was a joke it was his first. He was a huge man and his face fitted in with his size but he wore a permanent frown like an undertaker and only his lower chin moved up and down - he reminded me of a character in the kids' TV show Captain Pugwash.

It wasn't long before the street wise characters in the Jungle realised me and my pal were Celtic fans. Maybe it was because we were joining in the singing - miming of course! Tomorrow we might give them the jail but for tonight an amnesty was in place.

The first half was a disaster and is better off left at that but soon the second half was underway and Rangers were a goal ahead and that that great, evergreen Celt Johnny Doyle was sent off. But ten-man Celtic buckled down and fought back quickly, stepping up a gear. Roy Aitken equalised and shortly after that George McCluskey score to put us 2-1 ahead. The excitement was fantastic, one of the best atmospheres I ever experienced at a football match.

I suppose that's when we were noticed, my mate and I. Let's face it, the punters in the Jungle don't often get the chance to throw the polis up in the air. Once we managed to get our hats back from a wee wummin' - who said they would keep the neds away if she hung them in her hallway - we were told by a fan that our sergeant was trying to get our attention.

There he was, out on the track, pointed to us like Kitchener on the war posters. We were beckoned over to see him and the Jungle fans began to shout, 'Sergeant, sergeant, leave them alone!' This just made him even worse, he was seething. We were given a lecture about letting the force down and then he made his judgement. 'Make your way to the corner of

Springfield Road and London Rod - points duty.' We were shattered, right in the middle of the most important game match for years. As we walked away he shouted, ' I'll see you both in the morning.' It sounded ominous.

As we walked round the track we approached the dug outs and glanced at the Celtic back room staff. Huge smiles were on every face although you could still feel the tension.

Then it all changed in a flash. In the few short strides it took us to pass the dug outs Bobby Russell scored to make it 2-2. It was going to be one of these nights. We walked out of the park and into the car park. It was like night and day, all quiet on the outside and bedlam inside the ground. I groaned to my mate about points duty at London Road and Springfield Road. London Road was like Aberdeen on a flag day - dead. As we stood there having a post mortem on the night's events and wondering what awaited us in the morning, an almighty roar descended from the night sky above the park. It meant only one thing; someone had scored, but who? Even the songs that filled the night air failed to determine the answer. Just then a Rangers fan came along Springfield Road from the ground.

'Who scored?' I enquired, trying to keep my voice as impartial as possible which was not easy given the circumstances.

'Jackson', he replied. 'Colin Jackson.'

Me and my mate just looked at each other. I swear we could see each other's blood just draining away. But the Rangers punter hadn't finished. Still running, obviously trying to get as far away from Celtic Park in the shortest space of time, he shouted over his shoulder, 'Aye, f****** Jackson, own goal, big stupid b******.'

Me and my mate went daft. Like wee boys we celebrated jumping up and down and hugging each other in the middle of the road - empty, thank God but at that time we weren't caring.

If the sergeant has seen us it wouldn't have been points duty it would have been the Siberian salt mines.

It was still not over however and minutes later another roar blasted the night air - but this time we knew what had happened as a tidal wave of Rangers fans flooded out of the stadium. The streets were flooded with blue and white scarves and the tears of their fans. They were inconsolable. A point would have done them and made them champions but the unthinkable had happened and they had lost. This time it took us a bit longer to find out who the late goal hero was as no one in blue would volunteer the information.

It was another hour before we were told we could go home and as we stood in the Gallowgate waiting for a bus, a supporters bus pulled up and a happy Celtic fan leaned out and said, 'Where to, boys ?' Incredible as it may seem from that crowd of 52,000 it was one of the lads from the Jungle who we had celebrated with earlier in the evening. The bus sang its way through the east end before dropping us off, hurrying home to see the highlights on television. Unfortunately there was a strike and we never saw the goals until much later courtesy of Celtic films.

Maybe that was a blessing in disguise as you would have seen more than the goals. The Chief Constable and my Mother - and I don't know who I fear most - would have seen me and my pal being thrown in the air and then shown the polis equivalent of the red card.

What a night!

Seamus Murphy was based in England and recalls the agony of not being at the big game through his employment. (From the book, *Voices of the Old Firm*, by Stephen Walsh)

I was working in Vauxhall's in Luton and couldn't get time off. I was working night shift - 8pm to 7am - working on the line spot, welding car bodies. My mate Bill Muldoon, who was in quality control at the end of the line, about fifty - sixty feet away, gave me sign language that Rangers were one up and that Celtic were down to ten men, then a Celtic equaliser, then Celtic ahead, then Rangers' equaliser.

Then nothing....my head was in total spin. I had four weld guns on each car and you had about one and a half minutes on each car; how I managed to keep the welds perfect I'll never know. I kept looking up to Bill - no signs. My stomach was churning and to top it all, our foreman, big Bill McPherson was a Hun and was watching me. After an eternity Bill stuck his hands up and gestured '4-2'. I assumed Rangers had won.....then a huge grin slowly spread on his face from ear to ear, leaving McPherson in a foul mood for the rest of the night.

Charles Murray looks back on the memorable return journey on a Celtic supporters' bus and the following day at school:

My Dad took me to the 4-2 game on the Govan South West Celtic bus, which left from Donnelly's pub on the Govan Road (now the Old Govan Arms). After the game had finished and the bus arrived in Govan, the bus convenor decided we would take a tour of Govan to celebrate. We drove through the dark streets, and everyone on the bus was going absolutely mental, singing like mad and roaring with delight.

One of the members decided we should stop the bus on the Govan Road and shout up at the window of his pal who was a big blue nose. They had a discussion, and decided that he wouldn't answer if he knew it was them, so this one guy said he knew a way to get him to open his window. He got off the bus and shouted, 'Haw Jimmy, somebody's screwing your motor!' This made the guy open his window up in alarm, and the whole bus started cheering and shouting, 'We are the Champions!' at the top of their voices in the street, in full view of him. The window was slammed shut and the bus continued on its merry way.

I was in St Gerard's secondary school at the time of the 4-2 game. I will never forget the next day, when we went to school there was hardly a male teacher in the building. It seems that all of them had taken a day on the sick after the merriment of the night before. We had a Maths teacher who was a big Rangers fan, and an intimidating man. When he came into the class we all spontaneously burst into song and were stamping our feet - 'Ten men won the league tra-la-la-la!' He went mental and started shouting for us to be quiet, and then he shook his head and burst out laughing, and we burst out laughing as well. He took it in good stead. Matt Lynch, the ex-Celtic player, was also a Maths teacher, and he made a point of dropping in which started us up again, and our teacher just sat there with his head in his hands.

Joe McLaughlin reminisces about the difficult return journey from Parkhead to Govan, without the aid of public transport.

There was a bus strike that night and me and my mate walked it to the game, and back again, from Govan. Getting there was okay, but it was a bit hairy on the way back. It was okay walking back through the Gorbals but when we approached Tradeston and Plantation, there were Rangers fans about looking for trouble, so we kept our scarves 'up our jooks'. We were like something out of the film 'The Warriors', trying to get back home safely in one piece, only this was for real in Glasgow and not a film in New York. We were a bit deflated after a great victory until we got to Summerton Road, behind the old Govan town hall, when we saw guys running about with Irish tricolours on the road side. We knew we were home safe then and there was some celebrating after that.

John O'Malley, a Celtic fan of sixty years standing, was another who was a distance away from home but whose heart was at Celtic Park on the night.

I was a trade union official in NUPE (National Union of Public Employees) and our annual conference was arranged in

London from 19th May until 22nd May. I had already made arrangements well in advance to go before the date of the Celtic v Rangers game was confirmed for 21st May. I had no way of getting out and I was absolutely mad that I would miss it.

We were in the hotel lounge with other union delegates, and all evening all I could think about was the game. In those days there was no internet, no mobile phones or even teletext to find the result, and it was when I phoned home there was no answer. Back then if you phoned the Daily Record sports' desk, they would man the desk and tell you the score, so when it got to half past ten I decided to phone them as I couldn't wait any longer.

I got through quickly and when I heard the voice at the other end I realised it was Allan Herron of the Sunday Mail, as he was on television as a pundit sometimes. I asked him what the score was, and he said he wasn't sure. I told him he must know the score, as the game was over, and that I was a long way away in London and just needed to know the score.

I asked him again and he said, '4-2', in a terse voice. I excitedly asked him, 'Who for?', and he yells, 'Bloody Celtic that's who for!', and slammed the phone down. He didn't sound best pleased but I was ecstatic, and the union expenses got hammered well into the night I can tell you.

A current resident of Geneva, Jim O'Donnell was living in East Kilbride in 1979 and remembers the 4-2 game for a variety of personal reasons.

I was 16 at the time and in the middle of my exams. I also had the flu! I pleaded with my mum to let me go to the game even though I really wasn't well, and finally she relented. At that age I went everywhere on the supporters' bus, (Culbryde CSC, East Kilbride), with my dad, who was the club president. For some reason however, Parks of Hamilton didn't hire buses that night, and my dad drove to the game.

We used to stand with my dad's mates in the Celtic End, near the floodlight closest to the main stand. As the first half went on I was feeling really sick, and feeling very dizzy. I can remember the half-time whistle, next thing I remember, some ambulance men standing over me - I had fainted! After convincing them I was alright, they left....next thing I know I'm on a stretcher getting wheeled along the front of the main stand. I had blacked out again!

I can remember being in the first aid room under the main stand at the Rangers end, with my dad threatening me that if I had to go to hospital he'd make sure it was worth my while going to casualty!

Just as we got the all clear to return, there was a huge roar and we both thought, 'Aw naw, they've scored again', and we both ran out to the track to see Johnny Doyle walking off the pitch.

Amazingly, we walked back along the track in front of the main stand without anyone, police or stewards, saying anything to us, and went back to our place on the terrace. Shortly after that Roy Aitken scored, and the rest is history (and I got through the rest of the game without any further mishap!!)

I vividly remember the pandemonium after the third and fourth goals.....then being sneaked into a pub somewhere near Bridgeton Cross whilst my dad and his mates had a few to celebrate (it was a pub near the old bus garage).

I was in bed the whole of the next day, and sat my Economics higher the day after...which I just scraped through.

EPILOGUE

In the following season Billy McNeill's energetic young Celtic side would prove that winning the league with ten men had been no fluke. Over the course of the 1979-80 campaign Celtic found themselves in the position of being a man short on four occasions. Yet again, drawing on great reserves of strength and energy, the ten Celts went on to draw one and win three of those games, to the great delight of their support and the utter frustration of their opponents. Two of these games are worthy of recalling in greater detail.

18 August 1979 Premier Division

Rangers	**2-2**	**Celtic**
MacDonald 49		Sneddon 84
Russell 54		McAdam 87

Attendance: 36,000

Work had finally been completed on Rangers' new Copland Road stand. The old west terracing, the traditional Celtic end of the ground, had been demolished and another new stand, the Broomloan stand, was in the process of being built.

During the previous season, Rangers chose to move their home games against Celtic, in order to utilise Hampden's large capacity, whilst the Copland Road stand was in the process of being built. Controversially, the Ibrox club had decided that Hampden would not be needed for Old Firm matches for the new season, meaning Celtic's allocation of tickets would be slashed to a mere 6,000, in a reduced capacity of 36,000 within the stadium.

In the week leading up to the game Rangers got themselves into some bother, as the authorities were not convinced that the new Copland Road stand was worthy of a safety certificate. Strathclyde Regional Council and Glasgow District Council both refused to give the new stand the required documentation. An inspection by the relevant officials was required, as late as Thursday 16th August, before the stand was given the necessary certification for the game to go ahead.

As it was, the official opening of the Copland Road stand took place before the match at 2.45pm, with the veteran Rangers director, George Brown, doing the honours, as the Rangers fans in the ground looked on in admiration. Celtic fans had only been allocated a small number of main stand tickets and were also given the entire west enclosure below the stand. Some Rangers fans were perched in the main stand above the enclosure, and there were many complaints afterwards from the Celtic Supporters Association, of missiles and objects raining down on the Celtic fans in the enclosure.

Although vastly outnumbered, the Celtic support made their presence felt, and as the opening ceremony was underway the Celtic fans taunted their opposite numbers with the following song, to the tune of Boney M's huge chart hit, 'Brown girl in the ring.'

Ten men won the league tra-la-la-lah
Ten men won the league TR-LA-LA-LA-LA-LAH!

Both teams named attacking formations, and there was a lively start, with decent efforts at either end. The players got used to the feel of the lighter Adidas Tango World Cup ball, which was rarely used in Scottish domestic matches. Rangers had the early edge, but Celtic were unruffled and had looked dangerous when attacking. MacLeod was their most dominant player with his forceful runs from midfield.

Disaster then struck in the 35th minute, when Roy Aitken was sent off for a recklessly high, mistimed challenge on Ally Dawson. On another day, Aitken may have been more fortunate and perhaps merited only a yellow card, but on this occasion, referee Ian Foote, had no hesitation in sending off the young

Celt, and thus reduced Celtic to ten men for the duration of the match.

Rangers, remembering their painful experience against Celtic's ten men in May, went for the jugular. In forty eight minutes Alex MacDonald sent a cross in from the left side, for his namesake John to score, with a spectacular diving header past Latchford. The highly rated MacDonald was only eighteen years old, and playing in his first league game against Celtic. This had been a brilliant opportunist goal.

Rangers maintained their forward momentum, and in fifty four minutes they doubled their lead when Bobby Russell scored, with a powerful right foot shot from the edge of the area. The Rangers fans were jubilant and the noise from their new stand raged all around Ibrox. It now looked like there was to be no way back for Celtic. As Rangers continued to buzz around the Celtic goal, the Celtic manager Billy McNeill made a bold move, replacing George McCluskey and Johannes Edvaldsson with the faster, more mobile, duo of Johnny Doyle and Bobby Lennox.

This had the desired effect and Celtic forced themselves into the game. Rangers still looked comfortable in defending their lead, with time fast running out, as Celtic's small band of fans continued to roar them on. In the 84th minute Danny McGrain, always an inspiration and playing in the left-back position, held the ball cleverly on the left flank, waiting for the right moment to cross the ball. His full-back partner, Alan Sneddon, made a great run forward and when McGrain's perfectly timed cross came over, Sneddon bravely launched himself forward to score, with an impressive flying header.

Rangers became nervy after this goal and Celtic smelled blood. Now all drive and aggression, they threw players forward and forced Rangers back. With only three minutes remaining, the Rangers defence hesitated when a cross was launched deep into their penalty box. Tom McAdam then took full advantage of

Rangers' dithering, by lashing a close range shot past Peter McCloy.

The Rangers players looked distraught and several of them threw themselves to the ground, punching the turf in frustration, as they realised that they had blown yet another tremendous opportunity against their greatest rivals, whilst holding a man advantage for a long period of the match. The Celtic players celebrated ecstatically at full-time, as if they had gained a victory, and in a way this result felt as good as a victory. The Celtic fans noisily marched along Edmiston Drive to their supporters' buses parked in the traditional area of Helen Street, and yet again they celebrated a fine result against the odds.

Mike Conroy, a fine player on the day, typified the spirit of this Celtic team by playing a great part of the game with a broken nose. He was taken to hospital for urgent medical treatment immediately after the final whistle. McNeill's young team had shown that they were deserving champions, and that no game would be lost without a real struggle. Conroy recalls his part in the events.

'I remember it well. Ten men again and 2-0 down. Kenny Watson caught me with an elbow, accidental I think, but I knew it was broken as I heard the crack and felt it out of shape. Brian Scott came on and said 'You won't be going out any where tonight looking like that.' We got back in to it when Alan Sneddon scored then Tom McAdam equalised and believe or not I think John Doyle had a chance to win it in injury time. I remember thinking if he cuts this back I have a chance from the edge of the box but he tried a shot and it hit the side netting. There was not a big Celtic support because work was going on at Ibrox but they made themselves heard when we got it level. We got a great reception from the support as we went off. I was shifted straight to hospital without even a drink of water. I had the operation by 7pm and was sitting up in bed later watching the game on Sportscene. There were a couple of blue noses in the ward - but the banter was good. One of them said, 'You got

lucky today'. I said, 'It's tough with ten, that's twice now in a few months - we might try you with nine next time!'

Rangers - McCloy Miller Dawson Jardine Jackson Watson Cooper Russell (Smith) Johnstone A MacDonald J MacDonald Sub: McLean

Celtic - Latchford Sneddon McGrain Aitken MacDonald Edvaldsson (Lennox) Provan Conroy McCluskey (Doyle) MacLeod McAdam

20 February 1980: Scottish Cup fourth round replay

St Mirren	**2-3**	**Celtic (after extra time)**
Bone 11		Doyle 30, 91
Somner 59		Lennox pen 72

Attendance: 27,166

At approximately 4.45pm, on Saturday 16th February 1980, Celtic were well on their way to exiting from the Scottish Cup. There were only two minutes remaining and St Mirren were due a deserved victory, as they had been the better side on the day, although Celtic were making their expected late charge to find an equaliser. The best Celt on the day had been Davie Provan, and it was he who procured the equaliser, when he created space on the left, and chipped over a fine cross for Murdo MacLeod to score, with a downward header. This goal ensured a replay would be required.

A fine crowd had attended the first cup tie, and the replay at Love Street four days later really caught the imagination of the paying public. Both teams had a fine reputation for attacking football, with Celtic on top of the Premier Division and St Mirren close behind, in third place.

A huge crowd of 27,166 crammed into the tight Love Street ground, creating a wonderful cup tie atmosphere. The kick off was held up for fifteen minutes as fans struggled to gain entrance, with thousands outside impatiently seeking entry. Inside the ground spectators climbed perilously on to floodlight pylons to gain a better view of the proceedings. The fans were not to know it but they would be treated to two hours of frantic football. The lucky ones gained entry, for there were thousands of fans locked outside when the police insisted on closing the turnstiles for safety reasons, shortly after the kick off.

St Mirren started brightly, and could have scored before Bone got the opener in eleven minutes, when his looping header from a Richardson free-kick found the net, with Latchford badly at fault. McCluskey carried Celtic's biggest threat, and had a couple of fine runs, which deserved greater reward, before Celtic were dealt a huge blow in eighteen minutes.

Celtic defender Tom McAdam, and St Mirren striker Frank McDougall, clashed off the ball, after McAdam cleared the ball upfield. Most people in the ground missed the incident, including referee Ian Foote, but after consulting the far side linesman, he elected to book McDougall and chose to send off McAdam. This seemed a harsh decision, and a hail of cans and missiles rained down on the linesman, from incensed Celtic fans. Officials and players took refuge on the field of play, away from the trouble, as police sought to restore order. Alcohol was still allowed in football grounds in early 1980, and the majority of Celtic fans within the covered enclosure were heavily intoxicated, which was still no excuse for such behaviour.

He may not have realised it at the time, but Foote inadvertently did Celtic a favour. The Celtic fans, angered by a sense of injustice, roared out their usual battle cry, in what was now an increasingly familiar situation to them.

We only need ten men
We only need ten men
We only need...
We only need ten men!

Celtic players now showed an increased sense of urgency, and they pulled themselves level on the half hour. McCluskey cleverly beat an opponent, and his through ball sent Doyle clear on goal. The Celtic forward cleverly feinted to shoot, allowing keeper Thomson to make his move before calmly placing the ball past him into the net. It was a wonderful finish, and Doyle milked the adulation of the fans behind the Love Street end goal.

Just before half-time, McDougall went down after a heavy tackle from McGrain, and after he had been treated by the Saints' physio, was stretchered from the field. He was replaced by Brian Docherty. As he left the pitch, McDougall was barracked loudly by the Celtic support, who saw him as the instigator of McAdam's dismissal, and took great delight that McGrain's tackle had been a sufficient reprisal. Regrettably for McDougall, it was later announced that he had suffered a broken leg, and would miss the rest of the season.

The relentless pace carried on after the interval, and McDonald became a huge threat to St Mirren in the air. Twice he came close to giving Celts the lead from towering headers, with Saints keeper Thomson again proving he reserved his best form for games against Celtic, as the ten men Celts took the game to their opponents.

Controversy reigned again in the 59th minute, when Weir appeared to stumble after a Provan challenge in the area. Ian Foote had no hesitation in giving a penalty, despite the protests of the aggrieved Celtic players. Latchford was almost the hero after he saved Somner's initial attempt from the spot, but the Saints man kept his composure and slotted the rebound past the Celtic goalkeeper, putting his team in front.

Celtic's sense of injustice burned deep inside them, and the players now increased their efforts to get back on level terms. McCluskey was inches past with a shot, when Celtic were awarded a penalty of their own. Provan and Doyle worked a short corner, and as Doyle raced into the penalty box, Weir sent him crashing to the ground with a clumsy tackle. The veteran Lennox showed commendable coolness, placing his penalty calmly past the gallant Thomson at the Caledonia Street end, to force the game into extra time.

The additional period had barely started, when Doyle again took a hold of proceedings. He raced clear from the half way line, knocking the ball one way past a defender, running round the other side of him. McCluskey was in an offside position, and had he moved towards the ball he would have been flagged, but he stopped to allow Doyle the chance to chase after his own pass. As Thomson came out from his goal, Doyle went past him, but knocked the ball too far ahead. He then managed to retrieve the ball on the bye line, just before the ball went out of play, with Thomson back on his line and the Saints' players racing back. Showing great quickness of thought, Doyle looked over as if to cross, only to turn and hammer the ball at Thomson, at his near post. The Saints' keeper was taken totally by surprise, and the ball rebounded off him and into the net.

Doyle raced away in delight, and the roar of appreciation from the Celtic fans was deafening. For the remainder of extra time, Doyle, Provan, MacLeod and the other Celts continued to run as strongly at the end of a two hour stint, as they had at the beginning, in an impressive show of fitness. Manager McNeill was left with the luxury of not having to using either of his substitutes, Sullivan and Casey, so satisfied was he with the performance and fitness of his players.

Some observers commented that Celtic had played as if they actually had twelve men, rather than a reduced ten, and St Mirren now looked a broken team, with little spirit to fight back. At the end of the game there was much celebrating from Celtic players and fans, and this time the highlights were actually shown on television, later that night. By now the supporters were becoming accustomed to their team's ten men heroics, and they sang a familiar tune in praise.

*Ten men done it again
Tra-la-la-la-la
Ten men done it again
Tra-la-la-la-la-la!*

'They should have filmed this Scottish Cup replay in glorious Cinemascope for it was another mighty epic of searing endeavour, raw courage, a tremendous fight against the odds and heart stopping action. Celtic took all the Oscars in sight and their 3-2 victory at a Love Street which seethed and shook like an earthquake for one hundred and twenty pulsating minutes will go down in history as a supreme example of what makes a club great. Evening Times, 21 February 1980.

'There were no bad players in this Celtic side, only a few supermen and a bionic player or two. Saints, who left the field with the look of men who had climbed Everest only to find it had grown overnight, did everything possible to stem the energy from this Parkhead machine. It was not enough in the end but they did give it one heck of a try. Glasgow Herald, 21 February 1980.

St Mirren: Thomson Young Munro Richardson Fulton Copland Bone Stark Somner McDougall (Docherty) Weir Sub: Beckett

Celtic: Latchford Sneddon McGrain Aitken MacDonald McAdam Provan McCluskey Lennox MacLeod Doyle Subs: Sullivan Casey

One man could rightly feel a great deal of satisfaction and a sense of achievement as he sat in the sanctuary of the St Mirren dressing room. The Celtic forward, a two goal hero who was his team's inspiration on the night. He ran himself into the ground for two hours, all for the honour of wearing a Celtic jersey. He would have been burning with pride to hear the sound of the fans singing his name in praise, long and loud, as they exited into the cold Paisley night air. He knew that he had repaid in full the debt he owed to both team mates and fans.

John Doyle, the villain of the piece in the 4-2 game in May 1979, had found redemption at last.

John Doyle scores a dramatic extra time winner against St Mirren, at Love Street, in February 1980

THE LAST WORD

The boy's parents took him on holiday to Blackpool, during the Glasgow Fair fortnight of 1978. There were shops in Blackpool selling tee shirts, on which you could print your own name or slogan, which was a very new concept at that time.

One morning his family were sitting at the breakfast table when a man walked into the dining room wearing a new tee shirt with the phrase, 'BIG TAM EATS TIMS FOR BREAKFAST', emblazoned on the front in huge letters. This was a reference to Rangers powerful and popular defender, Tom Forsyth, who was nicknamed 'Jaws', and was one of their best players at that time. The boy's Dad was livid, but as it turned out, he got talking to the man in the bar later that night. He discovered that the tee shirt wearing bluenose was actually a miner from Fife. The boy's Dad worked in the Clyde shipyards, so whilst they may have been poles apart in football terms, the two men found that they got on famously, when talking about Trades Unions, politics and life in general.

The big Rangers fan was a decent sort, but he ribbed the boy mercilessly for an entire week about Rangers winning the treble, and about how poor Celtic had been the previous season, not even qualifying for Europe. He waxed lyrical about Derek Johnstone's forty goals, and told the boy Rangers would do it all over again in the new season.

Exactly a year later, and the boy's parents took him back to Blackpool. They were in the same street, next to the Winter Gardens, but stayed in a different hotel this time around. One evening, the boy decided to set out for a walk after dinner. He passed by the hotel he had stayed in a year previously, and found his eyes drawn towards the bay windows of the hotel lounge, which faced out on to the street. There, sitting at the window looking out, was the same big Fife Rangers supporter, from a year earlier. He hadn't changed a bit. The boy stared at him and couldn't believe his luck. He shouted excitedly to get his attention, 'Hey big man, big man!'

The Rangers fan turned round and looked out in curiosity, and saw the boy standing in the street, only yards away. The boy, beaming with pride, then held aloft four fingers on his right hand and two fingers on his left hand, and at the top of his voice, bellowed:

'4-2 big man, 4-2!'....'Ten men won the league..! Ye-e-e-e-e-s!'

The Rangers fan realised immediately what the boy meant but took it all good naturedly, hiding his head in his hands in mock horror.

Celtic celebrations were lasting long into the summer.

APPENDIX

Celtic results 1978/79

Premier Division

12 Aug	Morton	a	2-1	Glavin, MacDonald
19 Aug	Hearts	h	4-0	Conn 2, McAdam, Burns
26 Aug	Motherwell	a	5-1	Conn 2, Aitken 2, McAdam
09 Sep	Rangers	h	3-1	McAdam 2, McCluskey
16 Sep	Hibernian	h	0-1	
23 Sep	Partick Thistle	a	3-2	Aitken, Lynch pen, MacDonald
30 Sep	St Mirren	h	2-1	Lynch pen, Conn
07 Oct	Aberdeen	a	1-4	McAdam
14 Oct	Dundee U	a	0-1	
21 Oct	Morton	h	0-0	
28 Oct	Hearts	a	0-2	
04 Nov	Motherwell	h	1-2	McAdam
11 Nov	Rangers	a	1-1	Lynch
18 Nov	Hibernian	a	2-2	Provan, MacLeod
25 Nov	Partick Thistle	h	1-0	McAdam
09 Dec	Aberdeen	h	0-0	
16 Dec	Dundee U	h	1-1	Lynch pen
23 Dec	Morton	a	0-1	
03 Mar	Aberdeen	h	1-0	Conn
17 Mar	Motherwell	h	2-1	Lennox 2
28 Mar	Morton	h	3-0	Provan, Burns, Glavin
31 Mar	Hibernian	a	1-2	Glavin pen
04 Apr	Motherwell	a	4-3	McGrain, Doyle, Davidson, Lennox pen
07 Apr	Partick Thistle	h	2-0	Conroy, Lynch

288

14 Apr	St Mirren	a	1-0	McCluskey
18 Apr	Hearts	a	3-0	MacLeod, Conroy, Burns
21 Apr	Aberdeen	a	1-1	Lynch pen
25 Apr	St Mirren	h	2-1	Edvaldsson, Aitken
28 Apr	Dundee U	h	2-1	Doyle, Lynch pen
02 May	Hibs	h	3-1	Conroy, Provan, McGrain
05 May	Rangers	a	0-1	
07 May	Partick Thistle	a	2-1	Provan, McCluskey
11 May	St Mirren	a	2-0	McCluskey, Lennox
14 May	Hearts	h	1-0	Conroy
21 May	Rangers	h	4-2	Aitken, McCluskey, Jackson og, MacLeod

Scottish Cup

31 Jan	Montrose	A	4-2	McCluskey 3, Lynch pen
26 Feb	Berwick R	H	3-0	Lynch pen, Burns, McDowell OG
10 Mar	Aberdeen	A	1-1	Doyle
14 Mar	Aberdeen	H	1-2	Lennox

League Cup

16 Aug	Dundee	H	3-1	McAdam 2, Glavin
23 Aug	Dundee	A	3-0	Doyle 2, Conn
30 Aug	Dundee U	A	3-2	Lynch, MacDonald, Conroy
02 Sep	Dundee U	H	1-0	Glavin pen
04 Oct	Motherwell	H	0-1	
11 Oct	Motherwell	A	4-1	McAdam 2, Lennox, Aitken
08 Nov	Montrose	A	1-1	Lynch pen
15 Nov	Montrose	H	3-1	McAdam, Lynch pen, Edvaldsson
13 Dec	Rangers	N	2-3	Doyle, McAdam

Anglo-Scottish Cup

03 Aug	Clyde	h	2-1	Conn, Burns
05 Aug	Clyde	a	6-1	Conn 2, McAdam 2, Glavin 2
12 Sep	Burnley	a	0-1	
27 Sep	Burnley	h	1-2	Lynch pen

Appearances (sub appearances in brackets)

	L	SC	LC	A/SC
Peter Latchford	27	4	6	4
Roy Baines	7	-	3	-
Pat Bonner	2	-	-	-
Danny McGrain	18	4	1	1
Andy Lynch	27 (1)	4	7	3
Alan Sneddon	4	-	1	2
Joe Filippi	19 (1)	1	8	1
Roddy MacDonald	18	4	9	2
Roy Aitken	36	3	9	4
Jim Casey	1 (4)	-	1 (3)	-
Ronnie Glavin	9 (1)	-	4 (2)	3
John Doyle	23 (4)	4	6 (1)	1
Johannes Edvaldsson	34	4	9	4
Paul Wilson	0 (1)	-	1 (1)	0 (1)
Davie Provan	30	4	5	1
Tommy Burns	28 (1)	3	8	4
Alfie Conn	12 (1)	2	5	3
Tom McAdam	24 (4)	0 (1)	9	4
Mike Conroy	20 (1)	-	5	2
George McCluskey	16 (5)	2	1 (3)	3
Bobby Lennox	6 (8)	1	1 (1)	1 (1)
Peter Mackie	0 (2)	-	-	-
Joe Craig	0 (1)	-	-	-
Murdo MacLeod	23	4	-	-
Vic Davidson	12	-	-	-
Jim Lumsden	-	-	-	1

Goals

	L	SC	LC	A/SC	**Total**
Tom McAdam	7	0	6	2	**15**
Andy Lynch	7	2	3	1	**13**
Alfie Conn	6	0	1	3	**10**
George McCluskey	5	3	0	0	**8**
Ronnie Glavin	3	0	2	2	**7**
Roy Aitken	5	0	1	0	**6**
Bobby Lennox	4	1	1	0	**6**
Johnny Doyle	2	1	3	0	**6**
Mike Conroy	4	0	1	0	**5**
Tommy Burns	3	1	0	1	**5**
Davie Provan	4	0	0	0	**4**
Murdo MacLeod	3	0	0	0	**3**
Roddy MacDonald	2	0	1	0	**3**
Danny McGrain	2	0	0	0	**2**
Vic Davidson	2	0	0	0	**2**
Jo Edvaldsson	1	0	1	0	**2**
Own Goals	1	1	0	0	**2**

ACKNOWLEDGEMENTS

The idea of this book first came to mind around 2009. It had long been my opinion that there was a story to be told of the legend of the 4-2 game, and I thought it surprising that no one had written in detail about the subject before.

I had a few ideas, but my hopes were initially dashed at John Doyle's graveside in Kilmarnock, on the 30th anniversary of his death, in October 2011. There was a commemoration for John, and Celtic fans, who were conveniently en route to the afternoon game at Rugby Park, took the chance to pay tribute to John's memory. A chance meeting afterwards, with Celtic author Tom Campbell, led to him informing me that he was working on a book about the 4-2 game. Tom is an author of some renown, so feeling rather crestfallen, I forgot all about my own project and left him to it.

By 2012 there was no further news on Tom's project, and my wife urged me to write something, even if only for my own pleasure. And so began a wonderful journey, which led to this book being published. Initially the idea was to tell the story of the 4-2 game itself. I then decided it was best to tell the story of the entire season, to put that game into context.

It has been my great privilege to speak to some of the squad from the 1978-79 season, and they were all a pleasure to meet. My thanks go to Davie Provan for providing the foreword, and for kindly giving his time to help me. A meeting with Dom Sullivan led to contact with Mike Conroy, who is based in Cork these days. It was an absolute thrill to hear his vivid recollections of the period, and he gave me tremendous support.

I was also honoured to meet the great Danny McGrain, and was taken aback by his humility and modesty. Although Danny won't like to hear me say it, the 1979 title win would never have been possible without his presence in the side.

Peter Latchford was also great to talk to, and as he says, apart from anything else, playing football back then was tremendous fun and hugely enjoyable. Some of the modern day stars would do well to remember this.

The great Lisbon Lion, Bobby Lennox, was a joy to speak with, and when I explained I was just a fan his reply was, *'That's alright son, I'm just a fan as well.'*

My thanks also go to Andy Lynch, Danny Crainie and Joe Filippi for sharing their memories and giving up their time to speak to me. They say you should never meet your heroes in case they disappoint. I can categorically confirm that this is not true and it was an absolute honour to meet them.

And, there is one more ex-player I would like to thank. I thought it only right that this book should have some Rangers input, for reasons of objectivity. When I called Gordon Smith, he would have had every right to chase me and tell me where to go. He did muse that he had been trying to forget the 4-2 game for thirty five years and now I wanted him to talk about it! Gordon was great company, and it is a measure of the man that he gave his time willingly to discuss a subject I know is still painful for him to speak of.

Robert Grieve, Paul Cuddihy and John McLauchlan helped put me in touch with the players I interviewed, for which I extend my gratitude. Many others helped along the way, providing me with support and encouragement. Special thanks must go to David Warnock, Stephen Colligan, Brian Gilmour, Derek Proudfoot, Jason Henderson and Qasim Siddiquie, who helped me greatly with their ideas and suggestions.

Further thanks go to Celtic badge collector David Hood, for trusting a complete stranger with some of his precious items from the late 1970's which were used in the designing of the book covers.

My gratitude also goes to Claire Quigley, for the cover photography, and for showing an interest in this book even though, in her own admission, she has no interest in football whatsoever.

Part of the pleasure of producing this book was selecting the photographs from the period. Brian Gallagher from the Daily Record, and Julie Campbell from the Herald were of great assistance, as was Kevin Smith at the Mitchell Library. Photos are printed with permission from The Herald, Daily Record, The Celtic View and courtesy of Andy Lynch and Mike Conroy.

On the subject of photographs, my grateful thanks go to Celtic fans, Kenny Donnelly, Stuart Cassidy, Brendan Devanney, Michael Dempsie and Jim Leck for their hugely generous gesture, in sponsoring some of the photos used.

The ever reliable Celtic Wiki, (*www.thecelticwiki.com*), was a great source of inspiration and statistics as always.

A big thank you goes to Andrew Reilly, for his patience in helping a technophobe like me through the process of self publishing, and to the hugely talented, *Cartuja*, for his terrific design of the front and back covers.

Finally, this book would not have been possible without the painstaking editing, which was carried out by Susanne.

Writing this book has been a tremendous experience for me from beginning to end. The wee boy who watched his heroes win in 1979 was rekindled, and I got to experience it all over again, which was truly wonderful. I could never have imagined then that I would write a book and talk to my Celtic heroes from that era.

Lastly, thank you to the Celtic players, and the Celtic supporters, for creating history on 21st May 1979. Your tremendous efforts that night deserve to be remembered, and it is my dearest hope that this book does justice to your efforts on that night.

Stephen Murray
November 2014

Printed in Great Britain
by Amazon.co.uk, Ltd.,
Marston Gate.